The Tears of Llorona

A Californian Odyssey of Place, Myth, and Homecoming

Craig Chalquist, PhD

Book One of the *Animate California Trilogy*

World Soul Books
654 Center Street
Walnut Creek, CA 94595

Printed in the United States of America
ISBN 9780615291475

Front cover graphic by Carlos Encinas.

Back cover photograph by Craig Chalquist.

Table of Contents

The Animate California Trilogy

The capacity to exploit and destroy entire landscapes has loomed in step with the loss of the sense of the world as alive and ensouled. We will not appreciate or protect what we do not love, have not gotten to know in depth, and cannot perceive apart from our industrially amplified cravings to conquer or consume.

The Animate California Trilogy offers heartfelt and reflectively researched studies, sketches, and experiential snapshots that behold the land of California not as an object to be marked off, measured out, or used up, but as a living subject worthy of understanding, safeguarding, and care. To that end the focus lingers with stories, images, and recurring motifs that join this fabled and edgy land, in sickness and in health, to the "inner" life of its inhabitants.

World Soul Books hopes that by introducing and illustrating the "personhood" of the Golden State, the Animate California Trilogy will invite the reader into richer contact with the subjectivity of the land, its creatures, its sea, its sky, and even the matter composing them. In the end, perhaps we are only as humane as we choose to cherish and feel at home in the places that nurture us.

ACKNOWLEDGMENTS

To Mary Watkins, Elizabeth Nelson, and Chellis Glendinning, the three Graces of my grad school days;

To Daniel Graham and Sandra Adamson, for love and support and a roof over my head in a difficult time;

To Linda Buzzell-Saltzman, friend, colleague, and comrade-in-arms;

To Terry Vitorelo and Kathryn Quick, who read and critiqued the first draft of this book;

To every historical society from San Diego to Sonoma, inclusive;

And to the spirits of my ancestors watching over me:

I thank you with more gratitude than words can express.

DEDICATION

To Llorona, who taught me to see in the dark.

INTRODUCTION:
In the Shadow of Cross and Sword

California can only be understood by those for whom the symbols, if they come at all, follow the land itself in the order of apprehension: it can only be known in all its dimensions by the native, or by those like him, from within and never from without.

— Wilson Carey McWilliams

It is my experience that the myths we enter most deeply are not ones that we choose out of some book of myths. Rather, in some profound way, these myths choose us.

— Christine Downing

Sing in me, O Muse, and through me tell the tale...

On May Day of 2000, having returned to San Diego County after being gone for eighteen years, I was shelving some books when one of them decided to strike my crown on its way to the carpet. I bent to pick up the travel-worn tome and inspected its creased gold cover: Homer's *Odyssey*.

1

I shook my head and put it away without recognizing this as the first of several signposts inviting me into a deeper relationship with my battered, exploited homeland. I had lived all my life in California without ever really learning her story.

The second signpost arrived in the shape of a gray, melancholic mood accompanied by a puzzling free-floating defensiveness building up at work and in my new relationship. At work my friendly former boss, having gone out on a stress disability, was replaced by a micromanaging ex-Navy supervisor so controlling that he complained if we kept coffee cups on our desks. He refused to work with me on my school schedule, making it plain that my choice was to keep my job or stay in school. So I quit, not realizing that this would mean five frightening years of hardship. Others quit too, but for me it marked the leading edge of a long but ultimately life-changing descent.

As the relationship began to sag beneath the weight of a mutual caginess as mystifying as the falling gloom, I was doing my best to attend to the San Diegan activists and welfare parents my psychological fieldwork required I get to know. Meanwhile I tried to ignore the city itself. The passing years had not been kind to the place, what with the massive sprawl from overdevelopment, the ubiquitous flying, marching, and maneuvering military, the fearful demands to strengthen the border, the noisy crowded beaches, the ritualistic flagolatry preening itself as patriotism... As jets on patrol tore the air over an ecologically tarnished bay plowed by long gray warships, maneuvering tanks and troop carriers churned up cloudbanks of dust at scrub-covered Camp Pendleton. Had San Diego been a therapy client, I would have considered her both paranoid and depressed.

The third signpost awakened me abruptly to the fact that something new had entered my life just as my relationship departed. In a dream I held out my arms to a feminine figure I took for my former partner. She shook her head angrily when I uttered what I thought was her name. *That is not my name*, said her frown.

Then who are you? I asked as I felt myself beginning to wake up.

San Diego, she told me sternly as the dream—and my life—came apart all around me. *My name is San Diego.*

I will never forget the consuming astonishment as my still-glis-tening eyes sprang open, or the chilling certainty that the defen-siveness of the militarized city of my birth had fallen down into my personal and professional relationships—yes, even into my suppos-edly inner world. The very act of turning away from seeing and feel-ing what had been done to defended San Diego had twisted the iron key that wound up the terrible pendulum until its swings had knocked me flat. Later I would bless that astonishment for barring easy, reductive explanations for what had happened to me in that animate place.

I was not projecting or fooling myself. Somehow the presence of this place had not only *pressed* on me, it had actively called out to me, finally personifying itself into a dream figure far grimmer and more warlike than the woman I had loved had ever been. But how?

> A particular place in the land is never, for an oral culture, just a passive or inert setting for the human events that occur there. It is an active participant in those occurrences. Indeed, by virtue of its underly-ing and enveloping presence, the place may even be felt to be the source, the primary power that expresses itself through the various events that unfold there. It is for precisely this reason that sto-ries are not told without identifying the earthly sites where the events in those stories occur.
>
> — David Abram

Now, I thought, the real research begins.

Although it seemed crazy at first, at least to my inner critic, I decided to experiment by thinking about my city as a person: a non-human, unconscious, and far-flung person injured by three hundred years of conquest and urban overdevelopment but ancient beyond knowing. What would happen if I studied the "soul" of guarded San Diego with assessment tools like those I had employed with psychotherapy clients? If the city were my client, what would I do first?

Take a case history, or rather a place history. I needed information. I needed to know my client.

So I began going back through the history of San Diego, and then of California, land of my many wanderings over the years. I read about that brutal butcher Cortés, responsible for the deaths of millions of indigenous people; about Cabrillo and Vizcaíno, those transient seafaring explorers who came, saw, claimed territory, and left; and about Father Junípero Serra, who opened a mission in San Diego before moving on to bless eight more (nine if we count Santa Barbara) before he died. It was he who led the first European colonization of California. Statues of the chamber of commerce version of him—hooded robe, sandals, shepherd's staff in one hand, faraway look in the eyes—stand here and there along the coast.

Responding to a subvocal restlessness, I got up from my studies one evening, made my way around piles of books, and went for a walk through the Escondido Hills. Ten miles to the south stood the Elfin Forest, among whose green boughs and quiet dirt paths a ghostly woman in white was said to search in the night for her lost children. A familiar hawk circled high above my right shoulder.

The history wouldn't let go of me. In my mind's eye I saw a map of California with twenty-one crosses near the coast, each indicating a mission: an enclosed adobe complex in which padres who sailed over from Spain and walked north from Mexico in 1769 had sought to convert the native peoples of California into laboring Christians and God-fearing soldiers. Back in Spain crowned heads were afraid that the Russians were coming to the West Coast. Perhaps they were, if only to pull otters from the cold currents of the northern coast.

That jagged pattern of crosses...it seemed familiar, struck a hidden chord, refused to go away. I halted for a moment, puzzled. Distantly my ears caught the cry of the hawk. And then, abruptly, I had it as another signpost swung into view. Those crosses marked the path of my wanderings throughout California. Every town I'd ever lived in, felt compelled to get acquainted with, or visited for more than a few days was a mission town along El Camino Real, the "royal road" that linked them all. Serra had compared the chain to a rosary.

For most of my life, then, I had unknowingly pursued him up and down what had once been an actual paradise, the verdant, game-rich home of responsible and sophisticated earth-based people made out to be childlike savages by colonizing consciences eager to be soothed. Having witnessed what a place had become, I had moved on—was moved on—up the old King's Highway to the next stop on my Californian odyssey. But why? What was it all for?

My doctoral studies were initiating me into depth psychology, the tradition of inquiry, therapy, and deep research raised for more than a century now on the strong foundation laid by Pierre Janet, William James, Sigmund Freud, and C. G. Jung. Basic to depth psychology is the premise that we always move within some storied situation, some psychic framework of fantasy, fable, or myth. Janet discovered unrecognized symbols and silenced stories in the psychological symptoms of his hospital patients. Biographers of James, the first psychologist to take spirituality seriously enough to study it, have rightly called his creative life "Promethean." "I am Oedipus," Freud confessed in a letter to his one-time friend Wilhelm Fleiss decades before following his daughter Anna out of Nazi-occupied Vienna, as the limping king had followed his Antigone out of plague-stricken Thebes. As for Jung, he started his autobiographical *Memories, Dreams, Reflections* by telling the beginnings of his "personal myth." In old age he believed myth to be an instrument of higher precision than science in describing and doing justice to the meaning of a life. He would have agreed with cognitive linguist George Lakoff that image precedes thought, and with Nietzsche's pithy description of truth as a mobile army of metaphors.

It was through depth psychology's attention to myth that I realized I was not alone, for another figure haunted me just as I had shadowed Serra.

Not long after the Aztec Empire fell to the bloody ministrations of Hernando Cortés, a ghostly woman was said to shimmer into being in the streets of destroyed Tenochtitlán (now Mexico City), roaming and weeping and wailing. Stories about her proliferated, but in most versions a young, pretty mother gave birth to the son of an unfaithful lover, a heartless and powerful man who threatened to abandon her and take the newborn with him. To prevent this, she drowned the child (in some versions two children) under the full moon, and then she lost her mind. When she finally died, she was condemned to wander near bodies of water, a sad ghost wailing for her lost children, whose souls she must find in order to attain redemption. To this day some Mexican mothers still warn their own children not to stay out late or La Llorona ("lah-yoh-ROH-nah," the Weeping Woman) might snatch them away, mistaking them for her own.

The Llorona sightings which occurred locally—and, as I would soon learn, in every mission county—did not interest me much until I reflected on her presence in my own story.

I had been born in San Diego below a full moon, the double-Cancer son of a dark-eyed mother who had lived on boats and bays and beaches. A self-styled gypsy, she did not want to raise children. but her family felt otherwise. To solve this dilemma, my mother arranged a secret adoption, then told the entire family—including my father, according to him—that I had died of heart failure at birth. I passed briefly into foster care and landed in the home of my adoptive parents, where I grew up without knowing much about my past.

When I finally learned my mother's name after a long quest after my roots, it eerily echoed that of the Weeping Woman—for it was Lorna, dark of hair, olive of skin, and born with eyes biologically devoid of night vision.

> No matter how estranged we may consider our-
> selves from the tangled, improbable—indeed mon-
> strous—world of myth, in various ways and under
> certain circumstances unwilling tributes to its
> signs, fictions, and symbols are wrung from us.
>
> — Frederick Turner

Defensive lows, familiar routes, revelatory dreams, and now regionally active myths: beyond their obvious personal dimensions I was learning to understand these as threads of the story that bound me to California. Although not raised in the animistic traditions that regarded Earth as responsive and places as alive, it was dawning on me against my Western will that if my conquered homeland was capable of a kind of dreaming, then events that made up my life were included in that dream. What I had thought of as my separate self had been transmuted in a few intense weeks into one small branch or *qvist* in the dense imaginal and ecological network of California's past and presence.

These coastal places with their life linked to mine: their stories were my stories, their history mine, their outer geographies a match for inner landscapes I had believed to be autonomous. To my daylight self my homeland was a montage of mountains and strip malls, sunsets and smog alerts, timber and traffic, but at a deeper level California had been seething like some vast, troubled cauldron. I had bent to study her as something external taken oddly into myself, only to realize at last that I was part of her, and that my life course was not "on the path" in some story of supposedly free ascension up a ladder made of spirit, but a perpetual setting out on an earthy El Camino Real rich with history, paved with dreams, and watered with many tears.

A series of post-colonial coastal pilgrimages, a wandering, weeping specter, and cities of ambition and asphalt sprung up from the former missions: doubled images seen but through a glass darkly. What did they all have in common? The old Mission Trail itself.

I still did not know what this story, San Diego, or California wanted from me. I resolved to follow El Camino Real all the way north to listen more consciously than before into unburied pasts and underground themes still pulsing in the shadow of what we like to call development (from words that mean both "enclose" and "expose"), a contemporary legacy of the relentless march of Cross and Sword six hundred miles up what are now routes 5, 72, 101, 1, 82, 280, 37, 121, and 12 (west fork), and 87, 92, 238, 185, and 123 (east fork), before angling once again toward 101. Only thus could I begin to fathom what I now think of as "deep California": our land as a neglected source of interiority, a strange, polycentric attractor of legends, myths, dramas, dreams, griffins of the mind, and ecologies of the troubled heart.

> It is not accidental that "home" and "haunt" share deep roots in Old English, that we speak of the home of an animal as its haunt, or that "haunt" can mean both a place of regular habitation and a place marked by the presence of spirits. Like scars, the spirits are reminders—traces by which the past remains present.
>
> — Jack Turner

I went forth to study the history, environment, architecture, politics, and lore of the mission cities and counties of California, stopping in each to allow its presence and mood and pain to inhabit my body, my thoughts, my fantasies, and my dreams as I sought for a gnosis of place. I had lived in some of these locations and visited others; this time I would engage them as knowingly and sensitively as I could. And as I retraced the trail of Serra northward I often encountered Llorona's sorrowful shade still pacing in lore, artwork, and nightmare the path of the Cross and Sword like a persistent wound seeking healing from what it could not find alone.

Along the way I found I needed tools other than those offered by psychology or ecology or any single discipline familiar to me. From this need came my book *Terrapsychology*, which introduced the deep study of the presence of the places we inhabit and that inhabit us, usually without our knowing it. It has long been surmised that the spirit or soul of place exerts an unrecorded and perhaps unrecordable but important influence on the human psyche, blowing through it like wind raising ripples on a lake. Terrapsychology offers a conceptual framework for understanding this influence and techniques for tracing and demonstrating it more convincingly than appeals to "energy" or "vibes" could ever do.

What I found upon the trail of Serra and Llorona and ultimately myself was that if we resist the greed for quantifiable proof of our deep connection to place and instead open ourselves to patterns of story and resonance, we can discern recurrent motifs and unfinished plotlines strung across many domains of experience, whether earthly, cultural, personal, and spiritual. These *ecological complexes* operate at the level of shared metaphor and correspondence—the natural language of the unconscious—rather than limiting themselves to the literal causal chains they contain. Their multidimensional radiations illuminate the character or spirit or soul of a place; for in the final reckoning, the aliveness of a place transcends the sum of the parts that flesh out its ongoing story. (You will find recurrent syndromes of the mission counties described in my book *Deep California*.) That is why this aliveness must be understood from the inside, on its own animated terms.

Each chapter in this book, a biography of coastal California's geopsychic personhood, emerged from within a complex of motifs active in a particular locale. Each illustrates how what happens somewhere takes on and resonates with that somewhere's particular character, color, spirit, and mood. What effect the resonance exerts, whether it explodes, hammers, soars, or sings, depends on whether it goes ignored or receives the invitation to express itself benignly.

The book as a whole unfolds the tale of a native's journey up the King's Highway to its terminus and further revelations awaiting him there. Events from my Californian life have been included, if with a certain reticence, to show how thoroughly a life can be permeated by the human and nonhuman dynamics of place.

As these sketches of the seaside psyche of California should make clear, the depth-psychological discoveries of the compulsion to repeat and of the return of the repressed operate for places much as they do for people. Perhaps there was a time when the slumbering citizens of a conquering power could remain undisturbed by the consequences of conquest, but if so, that time has vanished like dew in a desert dawn. What was done to the oppressed and their lands ricochets back into the lives of the occupiers for generations unless very deep healing and earnest witnessing bring back home what was exiled and deprived of voice.

Doing this will also require a careful tending of the symbols and images that connect people to place and that comprise the verbs and nouns of the language of geographically framed experience. Understanding the intricacies of how this language emanates from the land and the elements encourages efforts to protect the places we love, and our innermost selves, from being damaged any further.

As for Llorona, to describe her as a mythic figure is not to declare her unreal (those who so regard her do it at their peril), nor does it reduce her to a byproduct of human culture. She sweeps through mission towns as a wailing psychic body, a tortured tissue of dream-stuff looking in on maulings by malls and damnings by dams, and transgressing at will our customary notions of propriety, landscape, gender, and power. Hers is the voice that will not be silenced and only grows louder with attempts at repression.

The fictional Ramona of Helen Hunt Jackson's sappy novel of that name remains California's most well-known weeping woman, but she is in no danger of being our most vocal. Shunned everywhere else, Llorona comes forth from the shadows of the mission communities to haunt this work here and there, contemplate its stops along El Camino Real, and moisten it with a few of her copious tears.

This is as it should be because our excursion into the mystery of how the world is deeply with us moves not just through bright Californian daylight, but into the shadows too, where sightseeing must surrender pride of place to another mode of vision, namely: soulseeing.

Part One: Departure

The Cry of the Weeping Woman

Five hundred years ago, in the Aztec capital city of Tenochtitlán, the terrified priests of the People of the Sun heard a sorrowing goddess crying out in pain.

She was Cihuacoatl, called Serpent Woman, shapeshifting co-creator of humanity, patron of twins, deity of life and death and Earth. A mother of mothers, she watched over women who died giving birth, and these women became the honored Cihuateteo, dangerous crossroad wraiths that guided the respectful and hounded the arrogant.

Two horns of her hair crossed her forehead; the obsidian knife (*tecpatl*) she left in place of infants who died hung from her back like a swaddled child. Eagle feathers embraced her white-clad shape. Her cries always heralded the advent of war.

"Oh, my children!" she wailed into the deepening night, "your destruction has arrived. Where am I to take you? We are lost!"

By 1492, imperial Spain, riven by war and Inquisition, stood poised to expand into the strongest international power the world had ever seen.

A mere four decades earlier the gilded idea of worldwide conquest seemed all but dead. In 1453, Muslim Turks under Mehmed II

13

had smashed down the walls of Constantinople and by doing so ended the Middle Ages, the Byzantine Empire built on the ruins of the Roman, and the antiquated drive to Crusade. At the Battle of Castillon, the French King Charles VII finished off the Hundred Years War between England and France by capturing Bordeaux. In two more years the Gutenberg printing press was uniting the literate world and the Aztecs were raising a new temple to their god Huitzilopochtli in the heart of their lake-encircled capital city. But in Spain, something shadowy was stirring, at once ancient and new, daringly novel and yet old as centralized power.

Spain had been invaded many times in its long history. When the Moors sailed in from northern Africa in 711, Spain's ruling set of previous conquerors—descendants of Christian Visigoths who had arrived unconverted but ambitious in 415—withdrew to the northern mountains. From there they watched Islamic scholarship, agriculture, learning, and trade flourish throughout the Iberian Peninsula. They dreamed of capturing it, and they drew their martial plans....and waited.

Differences of opinion among the ruling Moors finally emboldened these envious Christian states to launch a series of attacks. By the 13th century Córdoba and Seville had fallen to the religiously charged forces of the "Reconquista" (Reconquest). To hold and defend captured territory, soldiers and priests set up compounds to convert and rearm former Muslims taken in battle. In California these conversion centers would reappear as missions along El Camino Real.

Ferdinand II of Aragon's marriage to Isabella I of Castile in 1469, the year Niccolo Machiavelli was born, dissolved the ongoing rivalry between their two kingdoms. In 1474 the royal couple succeeded Henry IV of Castile, and in 1476, partly in response to an attack by Portugal, Ferdinand organized the Santa Hermandad (Holy Brotherhood), a theocratic military police force chartered to impose religious conformity. In another four years Ferdinand and Isabella bullied Pope Sixtus V into issuing an order authorizing kings and queens to appoint inquisitors to deal with offenders against church doctrine. Those suspected of heresy or of being otherwise dangerous to state security were tortured to elicit a confession, usually by waterboarding or joint dislocation, and then judged and sentenced in secret trials. Some were let go, others jailed or sent into slavery, still others garroted and burned at the stake.

By 1492, then, with once-proud Spain divided, gutted, and depleted by religious warfare, the Crown took the last Muslim stronghold at Granada, issued the Alhambra Decree to expel the Jews from Spain, and, one day later, ordered Christopher Columbus to pilot three ships named after prostitutes to find a westward route to the Indies. He would become the first European to reach North America since Leif Ericson landed there in 1003.

In only four decades, the most culturally advanced and diverse nation in the world had thrown over centuries of achievement to institutionalize racism, terror, theocratic oppression, religiously sanctioned patriarchy, and genocidal warfare. Its toppling of two ancient New World powers—the Aztecs and the Incas—and its merciless annihilation of millions of New World natives would send the gold and silver gleam of pillaged bullion into stock markets for fashioning an Industrial Revolution as feudalism gave way to capitalistic nationalism and globalization. These brutal acts would also write a master plan for the coming campaigns of global displacement and cultural destruction of a ferocity and scope never before witnessed.

In the end, what surprised the victims as much as diseases and guns, steel swords and concentration camps was the cold and utter heartlessness of the victors and their hypocritical appeals to Jesus, Civilization, Patriotism, and Progress.

The word "California" was not yet marked on any map, was not yet even a dream. Nevertheless, the fallout from these sanguinary explosions of colonial ambition would settle heavily over the future Golden State and change the course of its history forever.

...Where am I to take you?
The next apparition of 1502 startled the Aztecs by falling from the skies above them:

> It was like a flaming ear of corn, or a fiery signal, or
> the blaze of daybreak; it seemed to bleed fire, drop
> by drop, like a wound in the sky. It was wide at the
> base and narrow at the peak, and it shone in the
> very heart of the heavens.

— Miguel León-Portilla

Another omen arrived when the temple of the war god
Huitzilopochtli erupted into flame, and another when a bright claw
of lightning struck the fire god's temple. With the sizzling flash fell
a gentle rain, like tears wept from on high.

He was coming, an armored conquistador from over the ruddy
horizon. In 1502, the year Cihuacoatl cried out in pain, plans were
finalized for Hernando Cortés to sail to the Americas.

Although the ideological lockdown of Spain prevented the
Renaissance from achieving full flower there, the authorities did
allow literature that bolstered the Crown's colonial designs. One of
the permitted genres was the chivalric adventure novel, a form
inspired by the growing popularity of the Arthurian cycle of stories
and brought to ironic fruition by Cervantes in *Don Quixote*.

It is tempting at first to think of Garci Rodriguez de Montalvo
as the Sir Thomas Malory of Spain. Little is known of either man
apart from the literature they left. Knighted in 1482, Montalvo settled down to arrange the fantastic knight-errant tales about brave
Amadís of Gaul into four books. Unlike Malory, who kept to his role
as a reteller of tales, Montalvo added a sequel: *The Exploits of
Esplandian*.

> Now I wish you to know about the strangest thing
> ever found anywhere in written texts or in human
> memory.... I tell you that on the right-hand side of
> the Indies there was an island called California,
> which was very close to the region of the Terrestrial
> Paradise. This island was inhabited by black

> women, and there were no males among them at all,
> for their life style was similar to that of the
> Amazons. The island was made up of the wildest
> cliffs and the sharpest precipices found anywhere
> in the world. These women had energetic bodies
> and courageous, ardent hearts, and they were very
> strong.

He could not have known, of course, that a distant, cliff-guarded land at a continent's edge had in fact been built out of colliding island arcs over many millions of years.

So persistent was this exotic image that cartographers represented California as an island on maps centuries after explorers had identified it as a peninsula. Combining with rumors of cities of silver and gold, "California Isle" lured Cortés and many others into believing it contained some basis in geographic reality. Smashing the Aztec Empire was not enough: the wandering warriors yearned to invade the Terrestrial Paradise itself.

Where Montalvo got the word "California" is unclear. "Califerne" appears without explanation in the heroic eleventh-century "Song of Roland," a literary inspirer of the Crusades. The word might point back to Arabic terms for "large province" or "female caliph" (ruler) or even farther back to an ancient Persian paradise guarded by magical griffins of the kind on patrol over Montalvo's imagined isle, buzzing about looking for conquistadors to eat.

Nor is it known who first applied the word to the place Cortés began trying to reach, hidden somewhere north of New Spain (Mexico). Sent to check up on Cortés in 1540, explorer Hernando de Alarcón, the first European to sail up the Colorado River, might have applied the name to the colonization-resistant "isle" in either mockery or irony.

Whatever persistent presence shimmered behind "California" apparently spellbound Montalvo as well.

The *Exploits* introduced not only the wandering Esplandian, son of Amadís, but a sorcerer named Urganda the Unknown who lived in a place called Unfound Island. So much power did she gather as the tale unfolded that in Chapter 99 Urganda warned Montalvo in a dream that she would slay him if he continued to write his novel. Being threatened by an imaginary character he had thought under his control frightened him enough that he laid the book aside for a time. As well he might: Urganda had learned some of her magic from Medea, the mythic Greek mother who had slain her own children and wept.

Eventually, however, he came back to finish telling of how wild and pagan California Isle was conquered by brave Crusade knights, after which he died.

As Montalvo lay in his grave, Cortés approached the New World determined to claim it on behalf of the Old. Once printed, the novel served the conquistador and his men as an inspiration for the conquests to come.

Before planting his battle standards at Vera Cruz in 1519, Cortés had joined in the highly profitable conquests of Hispaniola and Cuba. He had learned how to use local conditions to advantage. By the time his men and guns confronted the Aztecs, his allies included disaffected locals willing to take up arms, a hovering halo of invisible European diseases, and one young slave woman whom the conquistador took as his translator and mistress. The Spaniards renamed her Doña Marina; today she is called La Malinche, possibly from words that mean "captain's woman" or "royal captive." She had been ejected from her family in favor of a male heir and declared dead by them.

The Aztecs were fierce with their opponents but generous to honored guests. Upon entering the Aztec capital Tenochtitlán, a city larger than any in Europe, the Spaniards had been feted like kings. Cortés responded by taking their leader Motecuhzoma prisoner, offering rudeness in return for gifts of gold and polished gemstones, and breaking and defacing their sacred icons. Asked why he showed such passion for the metal known to the Aztecs as the excrement of the gods, Cortés replied that the Spaniards suffered from a disease of the heart which only gold could cure.

When the soldier he left temporarily in command murdered

hundreds of Aztec officials during a ceremonial dance, the ensuing war ended with most of the Aztecs not felled by disease lying massacred in once-clean roadways lit by flaming buildings. As the troopers and missionaries of the newly promoted Governor of New Spain marched outward from the fallen city, 80% of the population of Central America faced death by sword, salvation, and smallpox. The luckier victims died quickly.

Upon the ruins of the burning capital, its poetry, drama, and art all but extinguished, the victors built what is now Mexico City once the inconvenient lake had been drained away.

Looking deeply into the troubled human psyche, psychoanalysis observes that rampant paranoia signifies hostility projected outward. The paranoiac fears from others exactly what he would do in their place. He, therefore, must strike before they do.

The insecure mentality of conquest is especially vulnerable to this distorted logic. With every piece of New World gobbled up by the Spanish government, crowned heads grew more and more uneasy that Spain's rivals would do likewise. Columbus had been financed in part because the Crown feared that the Portuguese would get to Asia first. To a psychological eye, the Inquisition unfurled one vast and bloody testament to the power of paranoia and its ever-lengthening shadow. Every empire eventually turns on its own people, and Spain's was the greatest the world had ever known.

Squinting fearfully around, the Crown had seen how quickly French trade had been dismantled in North America by the French and Indian War. Soon the fearful cyclopean eye spotted Russian attempts to trap otters swimming along the western coast of that largely unexplored virgin continent. Technically this had been Spain's territory since Captain Cabrillo claimed it in 1542 and Captain Vizcaino named it in 1601, but what if the Russians decided to colonize it? Cortés had suffered professional shipwreck by sending ships there that never returned, but other ambitious men awaited their chance to seek out fabled cities of gold said to sparkle and beckon in the distance.

During the Reconquista the forces of the Crown had succeeded in converting captive Muslims into armed defenders of newly acquired territory. Based on the Roman Empire model of presidial occupation, the idea was simple: Isolate the captives in concentrated encampments, force them to work, brutalize them into renouncing culture, religion, and identity, teach them Christianity, reward them for assuming a new identity loyal to Christ and Spain, arm them, train them, and move the army on to the next occupation while they provided a rearguard. Spanish forces that would have been depleted holding down captured lands were augmented instead. Why not do the same in the Californias by turning their heathenish populations into converts and soldiery?

It took until 1697 for Spain to plant a firm foothold in the resistant sands of Baja California. That year the Jesuits arrived to construct a chain of missions and convert the natives, in effect doing unto them what Rome had done to Spain. Here, however, penetration cut far deeper. By 1767, the year the Jesuits were replaced by Franciscans, more than five-sixths of the original seventy thousand inhabitants of Baja were dead, most of them of European diseases. As a priest reported in 1786, nine missions were going extinct because raging syphilis aborted fetuses when it did not kill mother and child outright. Serums then available were not always given to sufferers, many of whom were infants dying of diarrhea-induced dehydration. The keening rising over Baja joined that of Cihuacoatl and Marina.

Nevertheless, the mission project rolled on, a juggernaut hungry for sacrifices, for there were souls to be saved and territories to protect. When King Charles III of Spain ordered the Viceroy of New Spain to build missions next in Alta (Upper) California, attorney and Viceroy-General José de Gálvez was selected to lead the search northward for fabled Monterey.

As it turned out, Gálvez was as mad as Columbus, who, having wrecked the Santa Maria, devastated the native population of Hispaniola, lied to its settlers, and been dragged back to Spain in chains, wrote manically during his last New World voyage of finding heaven itself on an earth he now claimed was shaped like a woman's breast. Gálvez believed himself Motecuhzoma returned from the afterlife. Claiming long-dead St. Francis as his still-living personal spiritual counselor, the Viceroy-General also believed he was followed around New Spain by a shadowy presence he called Prince Incognito.

The plan involved a two-hundred-man thrust into Alta by land and by sea. It would never have succeeded had not more competent leaders carried it out. Gaspar de Portolá, now Governor of the Californias, was a well-organized Catalonian with considerable military seasoning. As the vessels *San Carlos* and *San Antonio* sailed for the rendezvous site in what would become San Diego, Captain Fernando Rivera led one land detachment northward and Portolá the other.

With him walked expedition diarist Father Juan Crespí and Father Junípero Serra, newly appointed Padre Presidente of all the missions of the Californias. Serra had been born on the island of Majorca in 1716. While still a teen he entered the Franciscan Order and took the name Junípero, "juniper," from admiration of Father Juniper, a companion of St. Francis. After earning a doctorate in philosophy Serra became an Inquisitor and conducted missionary work in Mexico, both of which positioned him to take over the missions when the Jesuits were ordered home. At the age of 56 the thin-haired padre stood just over five feet tall and walked with a limp from an imperfectly healed insect bite. He believed in the value of self-scourging—the violence shocked the faithful who witnessed it—and thought of New World natives as children in need of redemption.

Although thousands of indigenous people lay dead in and around the decaying missions behind them, the Cross and Sword marched onward toward San Diego, the first missionary stop in Alta California. California: one day the fabled land of builders, dreamers, reformers, and seekers going about their business without suspecting themselves still haunted by the Prince Incognito ghost of a red colonial past.

With New Spain hemmed in by steel and smoke and most of the Aztecs dead, Cortés married off Marina to an officer and, charmed by Montalvo's novel and possibly by wandering Cabeza de Vaca's accounts of cities of silver and gold, decided to send ships northward to chart and explore the Californias. He could not predict their opposition to colonization, from Baja's mirages and mission-melting storms to Alta's eastern deserts and fierce coastal cliffs. One day fifty galleons would lie moldering offshore at the bottom of the strangely named Pacific. Cortés returned to Spain and to the fate of Columbus, dying out of favor before his life could be rewritten into one of pride and glory. The resistant Californias had ruined him.

The shadow of tragedy hung over what remained of his New World family. It is said that Martín, Marina's child with Cortés, was the first mestizo of Mexico. One day he would be executed for treason, and her daughter Maria Jaramillo would grow up to be robbed of her inheritance.

However, it is also said that Marina murdered her children one night to keep the conquistador from sailing away with them and to punish Cortés for spurning her for his Spanish wife. It was as though dividing the land from its people had opened a split not only within self-divided Marina, but within archetypal images of the sacred feminine as once-whole Cihuacoatl receded before alternating goddesses bright and dark, motherly and terrifying, nurturing and nightmarishly dangerous. This unhealed split would eventually dominate the inner and outer history of California.

A year or two before the bronze-skinned Virgin of Guadalupe appeared singing atop the Hill of Tepeyac in conquered Mexico, a story began to circulate through the lingering fumes of cultural and ecological destruction of how a beautiful mother named Maria or Laura had drowned her child after being cast aside for a rival by her wealthy and powerful lover. For this the lethal woman garbed in white or black was condemned to search watery places for the lost little soul, weeping and wailing into the night as she followed the Cross and Sword northward.

With the full moon blazing overhead and centuries of ghostly wandering ahead of her in Alta California, despairing La Llorona called out into the dark as Marina, Cihuacoatl, Calafía, Medea, native mothers in Baja, and the Lady of Sorrows had all done before her in the aftermath of murderous occupations displacing dwellers from homelands and souls from conquered bodies: "Oh, my child!"

San Diego's Frown

If you were to study San Diego from the air, and if you were to loosen the constraints of imagination a little from the puritanical habit of narrow literality, a habit designed to estrange us forever from this world, you just might see a westward-gazing face, with La Jolla ("Place of Holes" in Kumeyaay) for a forehead, Mission Bay for eyes, Point Loma for a nose, Shelter Island and Harbor Island for squarish teeth, and the Coronado peninsula for a lower lip. A face like that of fierce Hekate, perhaps, mythic guardian of borders and gateways and patron of mother Medea.

Upon reflection you might also notice that the mouth, San Diego Bay, is frowning.

The frown appeared in 1944, when the Army Corps of Engineers connected Navy-owned North Island to Coronado by filling in the Spanish Bight. The eye, clogged by sewage and drainage overflow since the late 1800s, widened and welled up a year later when the Corps diverted the San Diego River into Mission Bay. Dredging of that Bay proceeded from 1959 until 1962. Sand bars continue to obscure the local vision like the deposits left by some oceanic sand-man.

Perhaps San Diego was frowning and weeping because to those who had invaded her since 1542, she meant nothing except as the first of a chain of outposts bent on conquest.

25

The place now called San Diego had been scouted by two Europeans before Junípero Serra set sandal there in 1769. The first, Juan Cabrillo, had served with Cortés during the conquest of Mexico. In 1542 he arrived in three ships to find "a very good enclosed port," stayed long enough to claim everything in sight for Spain, named the port "San Miguel" after the archangelic commander of the armies of God, and weighed anchor, headed northward along the coast. He died after a skirmish with Channel Island natives, and his body has been missing ever since. A tall monument to Cabrillo stares imperiously across the arc of bay shimmering under Point Loma.

Sebastian Vizcaino landed with three ships and a longboat in 1602. He named the future home of submarines and battleships and aircraft carriers "San Diego" after his armed flagship as well as in commemoration of his arrival date: November 10, two days before the feast of San Diego de Alcalá. St. Diego was also known as St. Didacus, a lay Franciscan healer placed as an infant into the care of a foster parent. Sustaining a huge scurvy casualty rate, Vizcaino went on up the coast renaming what are now cities after saints— San Juan Capistrano, Santa Barbara, and so on—before turning around with his decimated crew and leaving California over the watery horizon.

So matters stood until Serra and Portolá arrived to open their mission and fort. On July 16th, 1769, plants ceremonially torn from the ground on Presidio Hill flew into air peppered with celebratory gunsmoke.

The invaders held July 16th as sacred for another reason: Five centuries earlier, the Spanish forces of the Christian Reconquista had defended the borders of Castile by repulsing the oncoming Muslims at Las Navas de Tolosa. Although the international boundary would not be drawn for another eighty years, San Diego was already split thematically by the social and internal divisions for which fortified borders always stand.

When the first mission opened, the first fence guarded the first military installation in California from attacks by unhappy natives.

Hunting and gathering for time out of mind in a land heavy with fruit and running with game, they were stunned and appalled to see their lands encroached upon, their spirituality looked down upon, their customs derided, their shamans outlawed, their women abused, and their children turned against their ancient traditions. Blind to indigenous horticultural methods similar to those now called permacultural, the Spaniards turned their cattle loose to consume and trample, yet to this day the Catholic Church still takes credit for teaching the hungry savages how to farm.

Children and neophytes who received baptism were forced to surrender their names, their clothes, and their way of life. One Indian child about to be baptized was snatched away at the last minute by his father. The majority of converts would die of sexual and other diseases and end in the ground from which they had been estranged by robe-clad outlanders.

How different it could have been. And it could have been, because not all explorers are invaders or "men of their time." Picture the Spaniards removing their armor to sit down in council with the Kumeyaay elders: *Forgive us for coming here unannounced. We wish to know more about you, and for you to know more about us. We would be glad to stay as long as we are welcome or to leave immediately if we are not. For us this is an opportunity for emissaries from two cultures to meet in equal exchange.* No armies or conversion centers, no enslavement and genocide of California's native people, no beatings, hangings, or syphilis-spreading rapes. When the Americans arrived in the early 1800s, they would have found a model and lesson in how different peoples meet in peace, one land-loving and of ancient heritage and ecological knowledge, the other carrying new languages and technologies under storm-worn sails from far across the sea.

Perhaps just one soldier or priest standing up against the chain of command and, having been moved by all the deaths in Baja, refusing to obey unjust orders would have worked to change the invaders' minds. Events after all are not determinisms so much as dynamisms of interacting forces—historical and political, ecological and psychological, cultural and spiritual—facing off on the stage of human consciousness. In the end a legacy, even a colonial legacy forged in hierarchical authority, is what its perpetuators choose to make of it.

When Kumeyaay war parties attacked the mission, they were repelled with casualties after killing a conversion-pushing padre. Always quick to congratulate itself, the church lost no time in elevating him to martyrdom.

As in Baja, as in every place enshadowed by the conquering Cross and Sword, shrieks and wails of mourning echoed out into the night. Llorona had arrived in San Diego County.

Reports of his death having been greatly exaggerated, Lorna's son resurfaced, nameless and without memory, in a temporary San Diegan foster placement before arriving in the home of his adoptive parents. He would grow up knowing he had arrived from elsewhere. ...*Where am I to take you?*

I never knew my birth mother, but I was told that she had musical talent and was allergic to oranges. As for my father, he had been some kind of military man. Although I visualized him tall, he was not there to snatch me away before my watery introduction to the wonders of organized Christendom. In my birth father's heart (so he told me later) I had carried his full name, but after my death it went to my brother, born years later to a different mother on my birthday: the day that Cabrillo first spotted the Californias.

What's in a name? Gibson, Lynn, Lorna, Legg, Murdoch, and finally Craig, the outcropping of stone, Steven, "crowned," and Chalquist, one small branch of a larger calling, or one Americanized thread in a wide-flung "shawl." Gibson, the name of my mother's first husband: son of a Gib, an order-founding saint as well as a "bright pledge" or "hostage" left over in England from the storming Normans. Lynn: "of the lake," its lady, Lorna Doone, a successful if fictional La Llorona. The speedy arrows of Clan Murdoch of Galloway helped Robert the Bruce liberate Scotland. The Celtic and Germanic branches of my ancestry first intertwined, I now know, in the medieval ferment of Anglo-Saxon England at the time of Artorius Castus. To be named is to be located in history and ancestry and place, the conscious crest of an ancient wave. To be renamed

by a conqueror is to have one's history erased in an uprooting baptism of cultural foreclosing.

From my foster placement I was transferred to my adoptive parents, and we all lived in a box.

"The Box" is what El Cajon means. Situated inland of San Diego
about fifteen miles as the seagull flies, the city squats in a square valley that keeps summers hot and winters mild and cattle from wandering too far, that last being why ranchers settled there to begin
with. Later, other settlers followed, drawn by easy access to gold
mines in Julian and to fertile soils in which raisins, citrus, grapes,
avocadoes, olive trees, and just about anything else would sprout
and flourish.

Mythologist Joseph Campbell suggested that to know the character of a city, consider the nature of its highest building. The highest building in El Cajon was the jail, another kind of box. UFO worshipers and Ku Klux Klansmen have been known to roam the
enclosing hills, both in search of aliens. Where Spanish soldiers
once raped Indian women, teenage mothers of marginal education
push shabby strollers down sidewalks littered with broken glass.
By the mid-1990s they would have much unhappy company as
California led the world in rates of teen pregnancy.

I grew up in Olive Hills, an ageless-feeling former orchard overseen by an abandoned olive factory and a tall white haunted house.
Even in childhood I understood instinctively that within the Big
Box Valley hides a time warp. Many places where I played, fought,
and dreamed look just as they did in my youth. The peacock farm I
was chased from by an ex-colonel sporting a safari hat is gone, true,
and a Highway Patrol station sits on the kite field; but the concrete
street corners haven't altered their inlaid scratchings, the schools I
once attended still crank out relieved graduates, the climbable pines
still shed pungent needles, and the willow trees still weep.

In second grade I was selected to be on local television for a few
moments to explain how the Californian Indians had used tules to
construct baskets and seacraft. The usual psychological logic would
smugly conclude that this event somehow developed into my later
fascination with Californian history. To me, however, it felt like

being handed one more perplexing piece to a puzzle not yet assembled or even discerned. I had not wanted to explain anything to anyone and had to be forced to. Just what, I wondered afterward, did the colonization of this place and its aboriginal people have to do with me?

To construct a mission, a blocky conversion complex for training the natives, you need to gather a work force you can coerce into performing the necessary hard manual labor. Yes, they are actually made to do it themselves, like captured soldiers forced to erect an armed tower to keep watch over them.

First, you take advantage of the locals' tolerant polytheism by giving them another god to worship, in this case Jesus. Then you invite them in, give them new clothes to wear and rituals to perform, teach them a new vocabulary, accustom them to the idea of your cultural and religious superiority, and then, at the proper moment, introduce the gold-plated edict that only one god exists and it happens to be yours. How lucky for them, your arriving just in time to save their souls (if not their bodies) from perdition by bringing them this stern new god whose authority is everywhere but whose accountability is nowhere.

Because older people steeped in their traditions tend to resist colonization, you must take over the education of their children as soon as possible. The children need time to get accustomed to being flogged, caned, whipped, and beaten because their elders do not inflict corporal punishment on the young. As you teach them to idealize your culture and despise their own, you show them building and farming techniques that will come in handy for trade once your cattle have devastated the local food supplies.

Aside from hides and agriculture, the chief product manufactured by this elaborate machinery as it operated in California was the neophyte: the young convert taught to love his oppressors and hate himself. His new name helped blot out who he was and where he came from. His orders were to go and do likewise, monocropping the minds of his people as mechanically as landscapes once tended by shamans and horticulturalists.

As for the mission complex, its ultimately Roman military origin imprinted its straight lines like a defect inherited: square rooms, walls, and pillars hunched protectively around a central quadrangle. Roof beams tied with rawhide, and adobe bricks washed with lime plaster and cut with windows filled with metal rods, completed the carceral atmosphere relieved only by earth-tone designs painted by the inhabitants. Arrow-resistant *tejas*—curved red tiles—eventually covered the roofs to discourage resistant Indians from shooting flaming arrows. A bell tower (sometimes two) gonged regularly to lock mission life away from the sounds and cycles of nature even after the neophytes began to sicken and die.

The name all this went by was "civilization."

This imperial program has proved so malignant that centuries later, California still finds herself in the grip of a mission complex. The original barred-window missions resembled prisons; prisons are now built to resemble missions. So are elementary schools, fast food joints, Jiffy Lubes, churches, banks, strip malls, and other such temples of concentrated alchemical darkening where a living thing enters and a substance is disgorged. Mission parades celebrate the enlightenment of the Indians, most of whom are dead; mission floats waddle down traffic-clogged roadways first trudged by padres and soldiers; mission architecture sells California to tourists and incoming buyers—for the missions, as booster Charles Lummis put it so revealingly, are actually a state of mind.

So is paranoia, that persisting legacy of colonization and product of the long age of empires stretching back to Sargon I's capture of Sumeria. Paranoia: the fear that someone will do to you what you plan to do to them first.

It was paranoia that armed the ships that brought Cortés, that primed the cannon with which he frightened Aztec ambassadors, that garrisoned the naval port of San Diego against Russian attacks that never came; and paranoia that Pacific Ocean-going novelist Herman Wouk made painfully evident to startled young Willie Keith aboard the U.S.S. *Caine*. Both the destroyers Wouk served aboard had visited San Diego, with one, the *Southard*, decommissioned there.

It was paranoia that dipped the teacher's fist to show me the outlines of the USS *Willard Keith*, the destroyer on which my dad had served as quartermaster out of San Diego and around the globe, before she crumpled my sketch under my nose. I had finished her assignment and drawn the ship out of boredom with the routine. At year's end she was fired for hurling a chair at a classmate. Although her name was McQuaid rather than Queeg, she never did turn up any strawberries, there within gray shadows cast by square rooms, neat rows, straight walls, hard chairs, and a buzzing bell to order us to our lessons while at home we were beaten like disobedient neophytes.

In San Diego the movements of water often seem (at least to a place-based sensibility) like earthly reactions to human infringements there: forcible if unwelcome reminders that the sustainable empire has never been built.

In 1820, residents moved out from behind the crumbling walls of the presidio and spread out, Commandant Francisco Maria Ruiz among them. He built the first residential home in California on a site to be covered one day by a golf course. A year later, the San Diego River, which had once forced the mission to move, rose to a crop-leveling flood, decisively changed course, and entered the bay, into which it dumped enough silt to threaten the shipping multiplying rapidly there.

It was Alonzo Horton who ushered in the first major building boom, one of many to be followed by a major bust. A conservative Republican from Connecticut, Horton had survived a riot in Panama when a mob attacked the hotel where he lodged with his pistol and his bags of gold dust. Forsaking the gold, Horton and a group of fellow guests retreated up a gangplank to their cruise ship while the future founder of the American remake of San Diego covered their retreat with his blazing gun, killing eight. What made this incident odd was how it paralleled the frantic retreat of a small band of Spaniards from Tenochtitlán, gold forsaken, their leader covering their stumbling run up a city gangway. Odder still was the name of the ship to which Horton's party withdrew: the *Cortez*.

Like Hernando, Alonzo had been charmed by tales of a distant place reachable by water; and like Hernando, Alonzo had resolved to hammer up a modern city there. If a lesson hid in the thematic Panama repeat, he missed it, for like Hernando, Alonzo would descend to the grave financially broken.

He arrived in San Diego in 1867. Disembarking from the steamer Pacific, he saw dirt roads and rickety storefronts and little else, bought up eight hundred bare acres for $265, and declared "New Town" open for business. In two years land sales allowed him and his Republican workforce (he would only hire Republicans) to construct the city's first wharf. As former Confederate soldiers Drew and James Bailey and their cousins Webb and Mike Julian founded Julian to the east (Oceanside to the north would be founded by ex-Confederate Andrew Jackson Myers), a new paper, the *Union*, was in time to print triumphant black headlines about the local land boom one hundred years after the Cross and Sword had marched into San Diego. Soon the county records were quietly smuggled out of largely Democratic Old Town, and a mysterious fire forced residents to load up and relocate nearer the harbor—and inside Horton's freshly whitewashed New Town.

In a few years the boom went bust. With the lonely city abandoned by half its residents, local businessmen in black coats and white shirts made deals to bring the Santa Fe Railroad and its customers to town. Storms dug watery fingers into the unwisely laid tracks, but by 1885 the line went through despite a downpour. Another boom was on again as the city's population rose and rose in swells until 1888, when the mood and money plopped again. An air bubble doing double duty as obstacle and metaphor blocked the 1889 opening of the San Diego Flume at Fifty and Ivy, and in 1891 the railroad tracks were washed out again.

If bordered San Diego were a human, it would suffer, one might argue, from Borderline Personality Disorder: unstable mood extremes, fear of abandonment, black-and-white thinking, defensiveness alternating with flimsy boundaries, impulsivity, explosive temper, anorexia or bulimia, a poorly organized sense of identity, dramatic floods of emotion, euphoria one moment and depression the next, and sometimes both together. As the entry of Junípero Serra and his triumphant band was idolized yet again on July 16, 1911, the county suicide rate soared. A storm that cried down sixteen inches in two days canceled a pretentiously exuberant Exposition, broke through two dams, and washed out bridges all over San Diego.

Some of the local terrain is etched with this borderline motif. San Diego is cut by deep canyons that separate—or "split" in psychiatric terms—its many craggy mesas from each other. Wide chasms dissociate and compartmentalize entire neighborhoods into semi-autonomous pockets of culture. A hundred and forty million years of geological turbulence have sunk former heights and raised ancient river bottoms a thousand feet above sea level.

Current psychiatric thinking says that the storms and crevasses of Borderline Personality Disorder break forth from a possible genetic predisposition for reactivity to stress amplified by early emotional and sometimes sexual abuse. San Diego has been subjected to an unceasing toxic diet of fencing, blasting, sprawl, pollution, military occupation, massive overbuilding, construction tunneling, and even geological deformation (witness the frown) since the Sacred Expedition landed here in 1769. Can a place become neurotic? Is it possible for its human occupants to be fully sane or healthy after so much sustained abuse, exploitation, and sheer lack of love? What would Llorona say about this?

If San Diego is neurotic, then the border constitutes a defense against feared transgressions and projected chaos. Defenses are what keep the madness going even as they try to contain it. They build literal walls as an expression of internal ones. Politically, walls shut off international dialog, prevent infiltration of ideas and values and even people branded as Other, force the poor into poverty and death, and monumentalize a hysterical overreaction to having a sore spot prodded or one's sanity questioned. They are also good business for companies like Caterpillar, builder of the bulldozers that knock down homes in Palestine.

Since construction started on this wall going up between San Diego and Mexico, thousands of displaced people desperate to make a living have died trying to cross the sun-blasted deserts of Arizona. Others have suffocated in the backs of closed vans or drowned in the All-American Canal. Those who make it work for next to nothing; those who stay behind in Mexico are forced to make even less in industrial plants owned by multinational companies who call this sort of thing "free trade."

> Our United States' "Berlin Wall" has affinity with other such walls. Standing on the parched earth looking south toward Tijuana across the wall, for a moment you might think you are in Israel or the Palestinian-occupied territories. The same kind of bright yellow equipment constructed the Israeli separation wall that is strangling the Palestinian settlements and refugee camps.
>
> – Mary Watkins

Raised on built-up Coronado, the Hotel Del fronts a striped band of shoreline that low tide leaves wide and gleaming with a thin sheet of seawater. A number of women had died or been murdered at the hotel, some wailing, but the placards advertising their infamous rooms had long since been taken down. All that remained was a small sign pointing out where Marilyn Monroe had shot a brief movie scene.

With my bare feet sunk into stippled sand I thought about the transformation of money over the centuries, from exchangeable goods to bags and bars of metal, from mineral dusts and printed paper to glowing numbers on computer monitors, a sublimatory trajectory which philosopher Georg Lukacs described as one of spiritualization, or at any rate etherealization. The very word "money" emanated like an afterthought from the Latin *menta*. Bullion to billing and currency to current, the history of money is a history of the accomplishment of concrete projects through increasingly abstract and mentalistic means until today, when the value of money no longer leans on supplies of gold or other vaulted metals but almost solely on faith. It works because we believe it works, a global financial faith-based initiative. The floor of the New York Stock Exchange resembles nothing so much as a techno-temple, with kiosks for altars and investors staring up at luminous monitors with rapt expressions of reverence, their bare-knuckle "realism" the most entrenched superstition imaginable. Unlike a conscious spiritual system, however, the "invisible hand" bestows no redemption. It takes much and gives little and that unpredictably, a moody, jealous, and bloody god hungry for sacrificial victims.

In Gold we trust—until it fails us. At the height of Pete Wilson's drive to renovate San Diego, a project that was supposed to pay for itself, an edition of *San Diego Magazine* bore a cover with a lone tree drawn by La Jollan resident Ted "Dr. Seuss" Geisel. The tree was dwarfed by oncoming houses, and the caption pleaded, "Leave Something Green."

Where will the progression end? Will we spiritualize the entire world to the point of electronic ethereality while the walls go ever higher? Will we retreat into clean cyberneticism, guts and all, and cease to exist as *Homo sapiens*? Or will we recognize that walls both inner and outer await transmutation into places of meeting and exchange where hybrid possibilities can freely mingle?

Thank the gods I could still walk with bare feet on a dripping beach gleaming suddenly with sand dollars.

San Diego's first European visitors found a welcoming port and welcoming Indians and responded by unsheathing swords, pointing guns, pointing crucifixes, and raising borders. And so: militarized Miramar, North Island, and Fort Rosecrans, whose guns once commanded the bay. And so: a furtive Point Loma submarine base, its nuclear family of subcritical machineries churning below the waters of awareness. Passing through: armed flotilla, naval excursion, freedom expedition, peacekeeping fleet, battle group, task force. From above: sky-borne threats unbottled as "messages" flung out at "rogue nations" across the sad plastic dump of the heaving Pacific.

La Jolla Top Guns, Carlsbad in the Army now, Coronado Navy SEALs of approval. Dry Camp Pendleton semper fever surrounding a Border Patrol checkpoint. Welcome to America's Finest City. Any armed storm in our port.

Warfare involving organized bodies of professional troops under centralized command is not older than ten millennia, yet we persist in attributing systematized murder to a supposedly fixed human nature. The plain fact is that the handful of centuries since the dawning of the Age of Exploration, an interval that includes the "Enlightenment" era of progress and reason, has resulted in waves of human and environmental destruction absolutely without parallel in all of human history. Not even the ancient Romans, inured as they were to the spectacle of perpetual war (a necessity for keeping their Empire propped up), spread so much death and misery with such outward aplomb. So why do people still believe the lie of war's inevitability?

Because if war is not inevitable, then something is profoundly wrong with our "civil" institutions and perhaps even with civilization itself. And that is a terrifying and humiliating thought. Facing up to it is like finding a design flaw in a ship built to be invincible by our best minds and strongest thinking.

If war is not inevitable, then nothing distinguishes hawkish "patriotism" from bloody-minded authoritarianism, and millions have died and are dying for nothing every day while a small high command of antisocial schemers consolidates still more power and control over everyone else. Rather than wake up to this ugly truth and realize that empires are never satiated, let alone just, citizens prefer to wave little flags or turn up the TV. H. L. Mencken snidely called them "the booboisie," but it's difficult to reject what one has been educated for a lifetime to remain dependent upon.

Upon returning to San Diego after my eighteen-year absence I took a job in crowded Mira Mesa as a technical writer under a kindly manager with a wrinkled cheek and a pointed Point Loma nose whose rounded bridge resembled Ocean Beach. Her thoughtful flexibility was matched only by the rigidity of her second in command, a perfectionistic ex-submariner fond of emitting complaints about procedural deviations. A third writer, a sharp ex-Marine with a ready grin, made a pleasant contrast to his ex-Navy counterpart.

As the months wore on, it became clear that the submariner was working below the surface again, this time on undermining the manager. For this he had some support from the upper tiers of the corporate command structure. The trust we were shown as adults capable of minding our work was suspect to men who banked on work-tracking charts and "raising the bar." The manager's smile gradually faded into a disconcerting frown, circles darkened around her eyes, time-wasting meetings were held to emphasize adherence to procedural details, and finally, able to take no more of the madness, she went out on disability. When she quit the submariner surfaced behind her desk.

Similar outrages are enacted every day in companies around the world, and will continue to be so long as insecure and controlling people are given access to the power they crave. What made this situation surreal was that, without knowing it, I seem to have participated in a reenactment of San Diego's history, including the coming of the Navy and Marines, the westward-facing frown lengthening from fills and fortifications, the "brown study" of the dredged and polluted harbor, the fumbling judgmentalism invading city politics...

As I turned in my plastic badge, loosened my tie, and walked out of the building for good, I chuckled to remember my adoptive mother's recurrent question to my childhood self: "Why don't you ever smile?"

The old burglar-barred neighborhoods of North Park lie cracked and littered just east of Hillcrest between downtown and East San Diego. Even the church I entered by a side door was locked and sternly barred. The defenses ended at the sidewalk, letting me into the spartan headquarters of SPIN, the Supportive Parents Information Network, a sanctuary founded by attorney Joni Halpern on loving concern and a shoestring budget. Here at last was an example of the bright side of San Diego's persistent protectiveness.

Joni Halpern, Director of SPIN, has been described as a "rebellious lawyer." Formerly a journalist and then an American Civil

Liberties Union attorney, she founded SPIN in 1989 to make free legal advice available to the poor. At first the county's Health and Human Services blocked her volunteers from offering free information and legal representation at local courthouses, but the ACLU sued, successfully, and SPIN went back to work for their hungry threadbare clients trembling below the Great Seal of California.

Much of Halpern's time goes toward visiting families—close to four hundred of them—in their homes, again for free, to give them crucial advice and support. Few living below the poverty line know their rights, and when the meager money they receive is cut back, they often feel too ashamed of their poverty to protest or file an appeal. SPIN teaches them how. The goal is for them to learn to be their own advocates: important everywhere but vital in San Diego County, where the hateful fable that the poor like being so has prevailed since Horton, and where the relative amount spent on their support has not budged in two decades.

One result of SPIN's generous hard work is that past welfare recipients now deeply involved in promoting community education sit on its board of directors. At one time two board members stayed in college despite threats to their already inadequate state assistance (the state wanted them out on the assembly line, not getting an education). In 2005, after painstaking negotiation, SPIN succeeded in helping destitute families open newly available bank accounts.

I needed a fieldwork site in order to meet my grad school requirements. Having accepted Joni's invitation to sit and talk with some of the parents she worked with, I called several local psychologists to ask if they would do quick pro bono mental health assessments so my group participants could get child care credit. Finally a member of the American Psychological Association returned my call.

"I've never heard of anything like this being done before," he said, "by a doctoral student of psychology or anybody else."

"It is new, and it's needed. Nobody's giving these people any psychological skills or information. My free groups offer them both."

"Some of us do offer free psychotherapy."

"That's great. Some of our participants need it. But others are looking more for education and encouragement and a place to speak to us and each other. I'm doing my best to provide that."

"Well, I've never heard of such a program, and I'm not sure we can be of any help with it."

The sad thing was that this response did not surprise me, nor was it a case of simple greed or territoriality. Our work didn't fit their paradigm of healing. Suffering came from within the mind, not from outer tragedies like poverty.

Some weeks into running my psychological education groups, I asked several welfare parents, "If you could be on national television long enough to tell the audience something true about not having enough money, what would it be?" We had been discussing communication and assertiveness skills. It was a hot afternoon downtown, and a few of us waved flyers at ourselves as a breeze finally crept into the stuffy room and cooled the souring air.

That we are not lazy, and that being poor is no party, they said, sitting at home all day. *We scramble every hour of every waking day for what money we can get. We are all survivors.*

That wondering how to get by on too little money makes you feel crazy all the time, especially when you have kids to worry about.

That when we are ignored or given bad service or a hard time, we know what that's about. It's about fear. Fear of us, and fear of becoming one of us.

That some of us are people of color, most of us are women, and many victims of domestic violence at the hands of our children's broken-down fathers.

That we are tired of being silent.

This last lead to a discussion of what silences: in academic language, the internalization of the oppressor. People won't stay down, the group had come to understand, unless taught to mistrust and despair of themselves. "The example the poor provide," I had mused at the start, "keeps people at their desks and in factories. Who would work a soulless job without the constant and visible threat of poverty?"

Then:

"A psychologist I know," I told them, "believes that all broke people care about is food, money, shelter. Getting by. How about it?

Is that the fullest reach of your range of interests?"

They were outraged. After a moment of appalled silence, one woman with lines of fatigue on her face breathed in a trembling tone that such ignorance hurt her heart. A weary mother sitting to my right wanted to know how a psychologist could fail to realize that *everything*, even cats and dogs, had an urge to grow, to become a little better today than yesterday. How did he suppose that children could bear to live with parents who thought only about how hard life was? No poor person known to the group could survive one day without holding close the sputtering hope that the future could be brighter than a few more cans of soup or a warmer place to collapse at night.

Poignant to watch, there in the iron-barred heart of America's Finest City: parents on welfare suddenly showing pity toward the ignorant passersby who threw scornful glances at them like drivers pitching burger wrappers out of car windows. In the street-sharpened eyes of the hungry, such careless despoilers stood self-condemned as the poorest of us all.

In San Diego, the homeless who sleep in Presidio Park awaken in the cold near brassy monuments extolling the coming of civilization to once-barbarous California. I stopped in the park for a while, observing its occupants and studying the replicated bell hanging from the crook of a metal pole, then made my way to the mission. According to legend, the saint for which this place was named had served the poor, and without judging them either lazy or uneducatable. According to legend, he had seen them as people like himself.

Finding myself frowning, I allowed my vigilant focus to dissolve into a series of stark impressions:

Walking under an archway of hedge and up a flight of stairs. Excavations on the right, Serra's austere quarters on the left, and the quadrangle in front, with a Moorish fountain and cacti all around. Padre living quarters: the only adobe structures to survive two and a half centuries of reactive local weathering. Bare bed frame of crooked slats of wood. Windows high up and out of reach. My ears twitched. For a moment I thought I had caught the sound of a brief, ghostly wail. I would not fathom it until I finally reached the top of El Camino Real.

In the mission museum, a disturbing photograph of a class of glum Indian students flanked by unsmiling nuns. The students frowned as though staring at a gun barrel instead of into a camera lens. Either way...

I thought about the punishment list for sale as a keepsake at the Mason Street School built in 1865 in Old Town, with misbehaviors listed on the left and the number of lashes on the right: *Boys and Girls Playing Together.....4 Lashes*, etc. Amazing when you think about it. Where and when did we sons and daughters of Christianized Europe first start hitting our children? Was it from some hidden need to go on crucifying our childlikeness? A legacy of unspoken hated of redemptive possibilities orphaned by our haste to conquer and consume?

Chapel built in 1777, with the rough tiled floor imported from Our Lady of Guadalupe Basilica in Mexico. In a brief failure of the long Cross and Sword alliance, Army troops stabling horses here in 1850 had fed lonely campfires with pieces of the cross. Today a golden eagle stared down from the top of the altar. Yes. From the depths of the archaic woodwork gazed back hosts of lidless eyes. Lore said the Indians had painted them, but the paranoia symbolized by this disquieting surveillance had originated elsewhere.

Vestments hung in glass cases; in one, a bleeding heart lay punctured by a cross. In another, Jesus himself was bleeding while staring forlornly at a sheaf of corn he held. *Leave something green....*

A statue of gentle St. Francis out front with raised hands splayed as though warding off something unseen in front of him. Yes...

Back at Presidio Hill I looked out over the I-8 ribboning like a path of congealed ashes through sprawling Mission Valley. Below me, a bronze sculpture of a muscular Indian. Behind me, the giant red-brick cross here at the former Indian village of Cosoy, with a plaque praising Serra, who had "planted civilization in California." Before me, a second plaque commemorating Sylvester Pattie of Kentucky for leading the first Americans into Alta over southern trails before becoming the first American to be buried here. Just beyond, flagstone stairs led up to a concrete-and-rock floor above me. Its red tiles outlined the shape of a ruddy pentagram with a black smudge in the center.

No marker now recalls the beginnings of El Camino Real in Old Town. "Birthplace of California" and "Welcome to California" signs face the traffic on Juan Street, with the Caltrans building serving as the monument. Orange tiled roofs and whitened stucco, from here to Sonoma and beyond. Just up the road squats a Padre Inn Hotel for speedy travelers headed elsewhere.

The Devil's Corner

Before I describe what happened in the Devil's Corner, introductions are in order.

Escondido occupies thirty-six and a half square miles located thirty-four miles north of San Diego. Depending on the neighborhood, the elevation rises to average from eight hundred to a thousand feet above sea level. The Pacific lies in glittering sweeps eighteen miles westward, and the Cleveland National Forest carpets hills and vales twelve miles to the east. Though not boxed in or confined, the city finds itself geographically "cornered," one might say, by these and other features of the land situated at its cardinal points. The cornering has proved historically and thematically important.

The climate is dry and mild, with warm summers, evening sea breezes, and cool, but not cold, winters; the temperature can chill crops but rarely drops to freezing. Most of Escondido occupies the Carlsbad Watershed, 48% of which is urbanized, with the northern tip of the city sitting in the San Luis Rey Watershed and the southern segment near Lake Hodges in the San Dieguito Watershed. All in all, Escondido is a place of the in-between, within San Diego County but not far below the Orange County line.

At one time no freeway ran through; now two of them make a cross at the northern end of town. The congested I-15 crawls south to San Diego and limps north to Los Angeles; 78 runs west to

Oceanside and east to Ramona. The city's primary north-south axis is Centre City Parkway, with Grand Avenue standing off perpendicularly eastward. Grand was the first real road in Escondido. The visitor still finds citrus and avocado groves growing here and there, green leafage scraping musically in the evening breeze, but they are thinning out now, like the remaining ranchlands, in a shrinking landscape increasingly dominated by asphalt, parking lots, and new housing tracts.

Nestled into a valley in the Peninsular Ranges, resting on a fault block raised by subduction of the Farallon Plate now hidden under the North American, Escondido contains a 3,420-acre valley of its own in a narrow east-west crack seven miles inland of the city. Spanish missionaries working in San Diego County probably named the many-hued San Pasqual Valley after the saint who performed Mass outdoors in open fields of wildflowers. Galleria forests of sycamore, cottonwood, and oak live near the canyons along with chaparral, grass, Prickly Pear cactus, various succulents, and elderberry. The alders are gone.

The hills are high (to eighteen hundred feet) and steep (some in excess of a 20% grade) and mostly granitic, with scattered metamorphic quartzites. The most common type of rock is the granodiorite: an igneous stone of solidified magma whose lucency falls between the opacity of granite and the clearness of quartz. A common chemical symbol for this salt-and-pepper-colored intermediary stone resembles a series of uncoupled corners. The Valley floor is six miles long and a mile wide and rises a hundred feet as it reaches eastward toward Cleenger Canyon, where the Santa Ysabel Creek flows forth. A northwest-southeast fault line runs underneath this floor.

Escondido's first inhabitants were two tribes of the aboriginal people of California: Luiseños living to the north of the San Pasqual Valley (which they called Alape, "looking up") and Kumeyaay to the south. How long they lived there is unknown, but mortars, metates (holes ground in stone), and other ancient traces go back at least ten thousand years. By 1835, eighty-five Indians formerly at Mission San

Diego had relocated to a small pueblo in the Valley.

Juan Bautista Alvarado had performed a number of administrative roles for the Mexican government in charge of California, and for this he was granted the Rancho Rincon del Diablo in 1845. The name means "Devil's Corner" because the site of future Escondido lay in geographically and spiritually uncharted territory between Missions San Diego to the south and San Luis Rey just inland from present-day Oceanside: uncharted, that is, to the missionaries. Alvarado cemented together an adobe and ranched cattle nearby, a common occupation in an economy dependent on hide sales in Boston and other faraway ports.

1846 brought the Mexican-American War of President Polk and his manifest destiny ambitions, one of which was to annex mineral-laden California. The takeover would be made easier in coming decades by the flooding and drought that wiped out the Mexican hide industry. The American strategy of buying only hides paid off, brutally: the Californios were thrust into poverty and forced to sell their vast land holdings.

Some had fought back. On December 6th, 1846, a force under General Stephen Kearny collided with the army of Andreas Pico at San Pasqual. The Americans were unprepared and confused in the fog, making them simple targets for the sharp willow lances of the Californios. The men retreated with a few deaths and several casualties, among them General Kearny nursing his lance-punctured seat. After spending a shivering night surrounded atop Mule Hill, so named because the starving troopers ate their baggage carriers, three scouts, one of them, the Indian Ponto, snuck through the enemy lines and made it to San Diego to request reinforcements. The exact location of the battle and subsequent cornering is unknown—as hidden, one might say, as subduction valleys, scouts, underground water, and Californio troopers—but a campy pageant commemorates an Indian woman named Felicita said to have bandaged, and then fallen in love with, one of the wounded Americans. Her graceful name also adorns a busy parkway.

Alvarado died in 1850, the year California entered the Union, and in five years his daughters Guadalupe and Maria Antonia signed over much of the ranch to Oliver S. Witherby.

Judge Witherby of Ohio was a former first lieutenant who worked as quartermaster on the committee charged with drawing the boundary between the US and Mexico. He was also a customs collector, an editor, and San Diego's representative in the state assembly. A fat, genial fellow with a big nose on a balding head, he turned the cattle ranch into a sheep ranch and installed a mill to grind gold-bearing ore for what he named the Escondido Mining Company (1860).

How he came up with the name "Escondido" is unclear; most historians believe it refers to the "hidden" nature of the valley, but "Escondida," the feminine form of the name, was scrawled on a map carried by explorer Juan Bautista de Anza on his trip through California. It described a river thought to run from the mountains to the sea into which the Carlsbad Watershed drains. Anza did not find his Escondida River, perhaps because some of it was hidden underground. Such parallels between cartographic fantasy and geographic discovery crop up often in California, whose coastal cliffs and island-like terrain appeared in a sixteenth-century novel decades before any European explorers set foot here. A sculpture of Queen Calafia, the dark-skinned liege of a fantasy kingdom named California, now crouches watchfully in Escondido's Kit Carson Park.

As settlers arrived, finding by experimentation that Muscat grapes flourished in the well-drained soil, a post office that opened in 1881 called itself by the pointy, looking-upward name of Apex. Helen Hunt Jackson came through a year later to collect material for her novel *Ramona*. In 1886, when the land was deeded to the Escondido Land & Town Company, the subdividing began, along with the planting of other crops, wells drilled for irrigation, the first annexation (8.71 acres east of Ash), and the laying out of streets between Mission and Felicita. The population, some of it Chinese farmers and laborers, reached two hundred fifty by the time the city incorporated in 1888. Soon Mexicans, Japanese, Filipinos, and Jamaicans would arrive as well to labor in the warm fields and the noisy packing warehouses.

It soon became apparent that wells could not supply all the water needed in the burgeoning agricultural community. Bonds issued in 1890 funneled water from the San Luis Rey River into the Escondido Reservoir (now Lake Wohlford) at Bear Valley, and when the bonds were repaid in 1905—at 43% of the amount due in forgiveness of the debt—they were ritualistically burned in front of three thousand celebrants at what is now Grape Day Park in a festival faithfully commemorated for years afterward on September 9th, the day California achieved statehood.

If water remained hard to reach above ground, it was plentiful below back then. The vein of gold- and silver-bearing quartz hidden just southeast of the city near Bear Valley Parkway attracted shovel-toting miners, but the shafts they dug from 1894 on had to be closed because of flooding. The Oro Fino closed in 1903, and the Escondido/Cleveland Pacific in 1911 as the abundant pyrite winked as though in laughter at the retreating miners.

In the town site of the time—a squarish, four-cornered diamond bounded by 5th Avenue to the north, 13th to the south, Grand Avenue to the west, and Chestnut to the east—north/south-running streets bore the names of plants, from Ash to Tulip, and east-west streets the names of states. As citrus and grape production picked up, however, and the mayor began calling Escondido the Sun Kissed Vale, a name that shortened to Sunkist, the street names changed too, most of them into numbers, although Lime became Broadway. Oranges, apples, lemons, cabbages, and avocados turned a profit well into the early 1900s. Black granite quarried nearby glistened on the faces of new buildings in San Diego, and one day revenue from eggs and dairy products would stabilize Escondido's economy during the Depression.

In 1905, the town's first palm trees gazed down at the first car in town, a little red Rambler. The vintage cars parked up and down the street for the Friday evening "Cruisin' Grand" event of today mirror the vehicles of yesterday—first carriages, then automobiles—angled along the same street to allow their drivers to view the Grape Day processions. In another five years electric lights sprang on, the First Baptist Church went up, Indians were forcibly moved from their San Pasqual village to a reservation in Bear Valley (named after the last grizzly shot in Southern California), and the Pickwick Stage Line ran what might have been the first bus service in the U.S. before eventually lengthening into a Greyhound.

In 1914, local high school students snatched each other's class flags and replaced them with their own: an interesting if unintentional comment on the irrationality of world wars. All haste is of the devil, however, if not all red Ramblers, and the flag pole sunk by the Masons at Broadway and Grand in 1927 had to come down after proving a dangerous obstacle to traffic. It now stands in front of City Hall, but its effect on slowing down the rush of overdevelopment remains ineffectual.

Throughout the rest of the century that rush remained typically Southern Californian but sometimes took an Escondido twist. There was nothing unusual about having a country club (1924), or about the city governing board transforming itself into a city council (1930), with Leslie Wharton its first mayor. A city in love with the auto was a logical place for Joor Muffler to open its doors in 1931. Flynn's Candies, though more sugary than what was packaged at the Escondido Lemon Association, preceded the Jon Charles Company, the second-largest U.S. producer of sweets (late 1940s-1960s). The company was said to have made lemons from lemonade by cooking up rock candy to be hidden in secret caves in case of a nuclear war.

The old ditty might have been written with Escondido in mind:

> Oh the buzzin' of the bees
> In the cigarette trees
> Near the soda water fountain
> At the lemonade springs
> Where the bluebird sings
> On the big rock candy mountains....

Then rolled in Highway 395 from San Diego in 1950, and with the traffic, the defense contracts, and the vineyard-eating subdivisions to the east of a city eleven times larger than its original size loomed the malls: Escondido Village on East Valley Pkwy in 1964, the Auto Park in 1970, the North County Fair in 1988. By the new millennium, retail trade accounted for 16% of local industry and construction 14%, followed by technical jobs and health care. Construction is a self-supporting business here if ever there was one, making it difficult ever to drive through Escondido without running across lines of flame-colored safety cones.

To the west, the Elfin Forest/Harmony Grove township success-fully left the City of Escondido's area of influence, but only to fall into the grasping, earth-toned arms of New Urban West and its supposedly rural "village." Tactics employed by this real estate com-pany included circulating an innocuous-sounding "Friends of Escondido" newsletter actually written by company employees and rubbing shoulders with influential locals known to favor the pro-posed construction. The Escondido Creek Conservancy continues to fight such invasions through alliances and land trusts, and the city pursues recycling projects aggressively—as well it might, with a hundred and thirty-four thousand tons of solid trash buried in nine landfills around the state in 2000 alone.

Nevertheless, the sprawl that now hosts Lawrence Welk's Village, the Golden Door Spa, the Wild Animal Park, a sixteen-plex movie theater, a park named after homicidal Kit Carson, forty-six thousand housing units, various golf courses, strip malls, hotels and motels, gas stations, grocery stores, fast food joints, the California Center for the Arts ("bread cast upon the waters become club sand-wiches," boasted the architect with no hint of irony), and a hundred and forty thousand people strives to invite even more business into the area. A new two-hundred-acre industrial park is projected to bring four thousand jobs with it as well as a gas-fired power plant to supplement the expensive electricity doled out by San Diego Gas and Electric.

Such rapid expansion brings grim consequences, which in Escondido include smog, traffic, pollution, crime (especially theft, graffiti, and vandalism), homelessness (Grape Day Park next door to City Hall is a place to sleep in a city where 10% live below the poverty line), teen pregnancy, reckless driving, and overcrowding.

Situated just south of a freeway checkpoint, Escondido is one of the North County cities swept by Border Patrol officers—"*la migra*"—searching for illegal immigrants. The Border Patrol claims that such sweeps are based on "intelligence," not ethnic composition; it is therefore a complete coincidence that Latinos comprise 42% of Escondido's. As a result, even legal citizens are avoiding public markets and ethnic stores for fear of being stopped and questioned. During sweeps sales drop at El Tigre Foods, and Quince goes bare of the usual foot traffic. Hundreds of residents have been arrested, and more arrests are certain to follow as a new wall seals off the border.

The result, however, is predictable. The relative handful of laborers who get captured will be returned to the nation where the Border Patrol buys its uniforms. Many of the returned will head back here again in a desperate search for work once agribusiness barons put out the word. If work is available, the workers will break their backs to keep a respectable portion of the state's economy running. It has been that way since before plantation owners balked by the Civil War emigrated to California to set up shop again; even before the vast rancho estates, in fact: all the way back to missions which amassed enormous wealth and giant land holdings tended and grown by the sweat of the Native Californians.

Some places seem to name or nickname themselves, as with San Diego of the protected bay, named in honor of the defense of a Spanish border—but a border attacked in a previous century, long before the Americans separated Alta California from Mexico. In *The Log from the Sea of Cortez*, John Steinbeck surmised as much:

> ...A name emerges almost automatically from a place as well as from a man and the relationship between name and thing is very close. In the naming of places in the West this has seemed apparent... In geographic naming it seems almost as though the place contributed something to its own

name... "The point draws the waves"—can we say,
"The place draws the name."

As a place's geographical, ecological, historical, mythological, and anthropological dimensions resonate together, expressing an ancient "protostory" that personifies the ruling character or spirit, the resulting concatenations of image and history and trauma gather into local ecological complexes that filter into the language of local events. A motif of *bedevilment*, for example—occasionally dark but often merry—runs with a mind of its own throughout Escondido's history and later expansionism.

A "devil's corner" split by wild canyons, raised from below by subterranean clashings, and roughly boxed in by two missions, two watersheds, and other "cornering" geological features seems a likely haunt for an ancient devilishness, a reactive spirit of place characterized in ancient times by Pan, the goatlike god and Green Man of woodlands, meadows, and pastures. The Middle Ages saw his horns and hooves and prominent erotic fertility transmogrified into the Christian image of the devil as nature itself was demonized.

Can turning over his likeness here like a chunk of igneous stone disclose various facets of his Corner as well? Can we obtain some idea of its character by running through the symbols that recur here across so many dimensions of local experience? Perhaps we can by thinking about Escondido not as a clash of measurable variables, but as a provocative painting, or a poem written on the land, or a dream whose meanings disclose themselves through kaleidoscopic metaphors and images rather than in pale literalities exhumed by scientific analysis.

The number six has long been thought to signify Satan, especially when grouped in threes. Believers like those who ran the local missions, and like those who now lobby to erase the rancho's traditional name, sometimes mutter fearfully about "the number of the beast." Archetypally, however, six points to the Panlike quality of generativity; a honeycomb has six sides, for instance. In some numerology systems twos are feminine and threes masculine, so multiplying them procreates the number whose name in English reaches back to Old Frisian for "sex." Only Pan knows what energy six tripled might contain, but fearing it scorns an invitation to explore.

Significantly, the cattle brand for Rancho Rincon del Diablo resembles an S with its bottom curve closed. In Greek, the language of the four approved Gospels, the letter Sigma (herein mistyped "stigma" the first time), which looks like σ, carries a numeric value of six. Sixes dot the history of Escondido both before and after the December (6 + 6 = 12) 6 (making three sixes) Battle of San Pasqual. Alvarado fathered six children and lived in a six-room adobe on lands once occupied by six Indian villages. After he died in 1850, his daughters Maria Antonia and Guadalupe signed over the ranch five years later to Judge Witherby—for $666.66.

The local syndrome of deviltry wears less numerical aspects too. Mobile Pan can be difficult to spot in the open. He likes to hide—in Hellhole Canyon, among other local haunts—and make the bushes tremble to frighten passersby, something I was reminded of when, out walking at night on Village Drive, some unseen henchman of the place's devilish energy hurled a Big Gulp cup full of water at me from a passing car.

This proved to be one of many startling bids for attention. Out riding a bicycle while thinking about whether places could speak to us (not being separate from us after all), and if so, how, and mentally cursing Escondido for making it so hard to find a job, I felt an unseen bee buzz straight into my mouth. Had I made a big gulp instead of spitting it out reflexively, its venom might have triggered an allergic reaction akin to physiological panic. Was it possible that the world from which all intelligence evolved—a world of vastly greater complexity than any of its creatures—could address me, not with words or lessons or omens, but in the primal language of symbols?

I had in fact first landed in Escondido in a panic about money— on May Day. My ancestors knew the day as Beltane, "Bright Fire," first day of summer and, later, the witch's sabbat, and lit torches and bonfires, if not water bonds, to celebrate it. The style of this place was working its way into me. Its "words" were events, odd parallels, and uncanny happenings unfolding and igniting in my life there. I was not projecting into Escondido, then, so much as it was projecting into me.

Consider a related motif: *hiddenness*, as with Escondido's name and location, of course, and the unfound river on Anza's map: there after all, flowing in the depths, imagined accurately from afar but reluctant to be charted by the greedy eyes of conquest. The vanished gold mines and precious minerals went the way of the unseen river, their chimerical wealth here today and gone the next.

In the upper realm hot-tempered Peter Abel was shot in 1870, but the Cain who pulled the trigger disappeared. The fog-hidden Californio troops, the three concealed scouts, and the unlocated San Pasqual battlefield all echo this thematic joining of attempted conquest met by unexpected concealment, like a hard-sought image retreating into the psychic underworld to escape confinement in the ego world. The Chinese and Japanese laborers of old—where did they go? In the civic realm, the original vanished street names of Old Escondido mirrored the fate of an earthen jar stuffed with newspapers, business cards, coins, drafts, sample checks, and other papers and lowered into a granite cornerstone in 1905 for a new First National Bank, only to disappear during the 1957 remodeling as though fearful of the quickening pace of urban life. Maybe Pan made off with it.

Of the details that stood out for me within the blinding white façade of Mission San Luis Rey to the north of Escondido—the photograph of a weeping Indian woman crouched on a grave; the sign that shouted SACRED GARDEN PLEASE DO NOT ENTER; a bronze cowboy propping a rifle on one shoulder just across the room from a painting of the Last Judgment; a white Jesus in the graveyard holding up his hands as though to say, "Stop!"—the one that haunted me most was the large yellow NO OUTLET sign out in front of the complex where so many neophytes lay buried in the ground.

Many expressions of the local motif of hiding distinguish themselves from mere absences by conveying a somewhat sinister impression, such as Hodgee, the unfindable serpent swimming in

Lake Hodges, where mining equipment (an instrument of ecological penetration) was damaged in 1923 by an unknown vandal who left no footprints. Other examples of uncomfortably present absences include property stolen by local burglars, rock candy hidden like dwarves' treasure under mountains, and, in my case, the astonishing frequency with which I misplaced things while living here, something that happened nowhere else. The spirits themselves like to hide from the border patrol vigilance of daylight consciousness: the unseen ghosts lurking in Harmony Grove, for example, and the White Woman said to haunt the Elfin Forest at night. Are they real? They are real as persisting psychological facts. To the imaginative nose sensitive to symbol, each emits a faint odor of brimstone as frenetic Pan fades away around the next corner.

What about the symbol of penetration? A theme of looking up ("Alape") to an Apex, as the post office named itself, does not necessarily protuberate the phallic presence of colossally randy Pan, but all those deep-sunk mine shafts—an entire underground network flooded out by gushes of fluid from below—thematically belong with long lances leveled at San Pasqual and the pointed cacti now covering Mule Hill. Angry bees in the roof of the First Baptist Church poked at everyone but one calm man with a drone resting on his upward-pointing fingertip: like cures like, as ancient alchemists knew, especially when the little winged pitchforks secreted eucalyptus-tasting honey for cough syrup. In 1903, Henry Putnam, who invented the safety pin and the horseshoe nail, held all the water bonds before they went up in a festive bonfire. In 1912, Rodriquez Mountain was finally pierced for a water bypass tunnel not by blasting, in the end, but by drilling.

Some pokings of the local devil's pitchfork suggest the aspect of sight. The first trains through were nicknamed One-Eyed Monsters, the telescope at Palomar the Giant Eye, and the romance Felicita was penned by an optician. In C. G. Jung's psychological thought, eyes in dreams can indicate an element of consciousness present in the unconscious—in Escondido's case that of the land's phallic dreamings into soaring palms and flagpole wars. After I moved in, the neighbor next door suddenly planted a new flagpole. My roommate bought a telescope and broke a mirror; the camera I bought locally harbored a blurred lens, a match for several bouts of painful conjunctivitis. Random events signifying nothing, or an ecoreactive place shaking hands with its reluctant new investigator?

In many cases the penetration metaphor does evoke reproduction. Even the sterility implicit in the name Mule Hill pairs itself, if only by contrast, with a grim local rise in teen pregnancy and a Nobel Sperm Bank whose transactions would have amused the ever-busy goat god. Its founder bore the same last name as my roommate. In the days of booming avocado sales, pin-pricked cloth stretched over a fertile avocado seed left granodiorite-like watermarks. Such retracings of homegrown geology piercing itself into visibility accrete with other hints that the very minerals hidden in the ground are imagistically fertile, as alchemy believed them to be. Think about the enormous snake sculpture—half in the ground, half out—penetrating the soil in Kit Carson Park, and all those snaky vines of musky Muscats.

Cruising, an activity loaded with erotic implications, was a popular pastime in supposedly bygone days, but in 1916 an unknown and uncaught devotee of Pan scattered tacks in the road, perhaps to slow things down. On my first stay in town I replaced several punctured bicycle tire tubes and three pierced car tires. I eventually returned in another car, only to find a nail stuck in the left rear tire.

Images so redolent with the thrust of fertilization also cast a reproductive shadow. The Wild Animal Park stores six thousand DNA samples for breeding and cloning endangered species before releasing them into what's left of the wilderness. Is this project an interspecies panopticon or genetic pandemonium? Are any of the scientists thinking about Pandora? Perhaps not: after all, she is just a myth, and everyone knows that myths aren't real....until they come back to life.

Tire deflations and coned-off sections of roadway forced me to meander more than I wanted to, downshifting me into a more reflective geographical intercourse. Taking the hint, I applied the brakes and gazed around for a more leisurely cruise, or perambulation, as the old term mandalically expresses it. I spent part of a pleasantly sunny afternoon watching the tallest palm in the neighborhood waving toward me in the wind. After driving around to observe it from several angles, I finally waved back. Speaking of cars and gazing, what has the giant Muffler Man really been holding downtown since 1972? The one-eyed automotive reverse of a fully functional mine shaft? Pan as Muffler Man, his presence become flash and pedestalled among us. Driving by, I thought: Maybe we should introduce him to Calafía.

Ithyphallic proddings greeted my return to Escondido after a stay elsewhere, the first a pointed steak-turner newly hammered by a nearby blacksmith for my roommate. A hidden plant poked upward through cracks in a bedroom floor before opening up for a look around. Such events had not struck me as proddings at first. I had put them down to my own selective and perhaps Freudian attention until I realized that paying heed to what was urgent and thematically repetitious brought a different outer response (a gift of free honey) than ignoring it did (a bee in the mouth). Working with series of dreams had taught me long ago that an emphatic image not tended in one dream often returned in the next with greater intensity. Something similar was afoot here, and perhaps everywhere else, had we but ears to hear it.

Nevertheless, it was strange to find a gift under the back wheel well of my newly purchased used car. Groping around for a tire iron, my fingers touched a small token cavalry sword with To Lenny from Douglas Fairbanks Jr. inscribed on it. Little did I know that when the Kinema Theater opened on Grand in 1920, moving pictures were a new spectacle in Escondido, and the first, starring Douglas Fairbanks Sr., opened below a flashy title my deflated tires would have recognized at once: *The Mark of Zorro*. The mark was a signature left by a masked, sword-wielding Pan who swung in out of nowhere to panic and skewer the tyrants of Spanish California, that what was hidden by them might be revealed.

I felt marked and skewered as well, pierced by these animated arrows and the pasts they pointed to, and fell to wondering at the legacy of swashbuckling carried down from Sr. to Jr. and then from

Jr. to "Lenny," possibly the composer Leonard Bernstein, in whose talented hands the pen drove mightier than any sword. Interpreting all this as a possible wink to keep moving from a Herculean save-the-Earth posture into a more Odyssean tuning in to its underworld voices, I placed the trinket next to my keyboard as a reminder to keep writing things down.

Speaking of marking, graffiti in Escondido often clusters next to angular figures sprayed by utility workers to mark what is buried underground. A glance downward discloses a street corner filigreed with arrows, numbers, letters, and the occasional U shape pronged like a pitchfork. A glance upward lights on gang-style cursives defacing a stop sign. Sigma or stigma? Both, perhaps, but in a reversal of customary notions of propriety, the illicit scrawls often top the official ones.

Escondido's taggers are so persistent that new graffiti often lands within hours of the old's erasure, or even right on top of it. A local company hopes to market a device that triggers an alarm at the sound of a spray can—as though the graffiti itself were not alarm enough. Meanwhile, civic boosters of the type who pitched for replacing the original street names with numbers have started a graffiti erasure program to hide errant markings. No one seems to wonder what drives such a profligate urge to inscribe, let alone the impulse to erase. The same smug deafness ignores the repressed voice of youthful rebellion and the repressed voice of the ancient terrain. Both then shout to make known their demands.

According to a display at the Escondido Historical Society, the first graffiti in town was scrawled on a wall of dark lumber. They know this because they kept the wall. Examining the black markings, I looked up at what may have been the earliest; the considerate writer dated it Feb. 10, 1900 as though he were making a journal entry. A chalkboard next to the wall invited the viewer to leave a mark behind in another local example of like curing like, in effect extracting the sting from the syndrome by giving it a forum. The chalkboard reminded me of the whiteboard on which my roommate and I wrote messages to each other in colored inks even when we were both at home.

All this points back in time to much earlier markings. Intricate, maze-shaped petroglyphs in the rocky hills above Escondido anticipate the squiggles and scrawls and the squarish platting of the city streets. A story goes with one of the designs found at Painted Rock:

One day an Indian named Que-ahl spotted his wife Re-ha-re talking enthusiastically with a male cousin. Filled with jealousy, Que-ahl planned to puncture her with an arrow until husband and wife saw an image of the deed inscribed in advance on a rock. With this stony criticism his jealousy departed, like cured by like, and they lived together in peace for the rest of their days. The rocky image had apparently known what the inhabitants tend to forget: that nature's inscriptions can rebalance troubling moods and relationships, but only when seen and heard as meaningful utterances in an ongoing dialog. Better after all to be marked by the land than to puncture or be punctured by it.

I decided to keep a journal as I continued listening in on Escondido. Until the bee flew into my mouth I would never have guessed how deeply a geographic locale could reach into me. With no suitable framework for guidance, I was slowly having to learn one prodding at a time that what happened around me also happened within me, with neither dynamic reducible to the other:

7/8/04: A day of research in the Pioneer Room at the Escondido Public Library. Went through five books of surface-only stuff: old photos, anecdotes meant to be funny followed by mandatory exclamation points, terms like "y'all" to set the reader apart from those early bumpkin settlers, embarrassed-looking Grape Day Queens, a bit of boosting. Nothing deep, which probably indicates something, because the place itself has remarkable depths. But like the city's name, they are hidden unless you seek them out, such as one of the best collections of Californiana to be found anywhere stacked away in a library guarded by old men mumbling to themselves near an ugly piece of artwork cardinally titled "North by Northwest." How to get one's bearings?

North by northwest; there's something to that. Corner (Rincon) theme? Out walking at sunset, a boy in the park I made my way through ran by shouting, "Triangulate! Triangulate!" as his father aimed a golf club. I find myself unable to believe any longer that these inner-outer pairings are random or projected. This place is somehow responding to my efforts to know it better.

7/9: Went to the Friday Night "Cruisin' Grand" car show on Grand. Most in attendance probably had no idea the event went back to the old Grape Day Parade, when visitors parked their cars on Grand to watch the floats clank by.

7/10: Visited the historical museum. When I asked a man living here since 1951 which changes were the most prominent he had noticed in Escondido, he answered without hesitation: "Subdivisions." Learned that because the Southern Pacific train tracks had gone in wrong in San Marcos, the early buildings were moved closer to them. Reminded me that Saint Mark is sometimes depicted with a halter around his neck (the Octopus vs. the Lion?).

7/13: Finished with the Pioneer Room today. Very hot weather last few days. Work interrupted by extreme dental pain triggered by an attempt to jog (had a tooth pulled before coming here that gave me a dry socket). Could not sleep. Will ask Escondido for dreams tonight. Trying not to let unemployment and dire financial situation impinge unduly on solving this mystery between me and California.

7/15: Woke up two or three times with vague memories of dreaming about a fictional character (male) in an otherwise factual novel about Escondido. (Reading a biography of Upton Sinclair, who in the absence of *The Jungle*, *Oil!*, and *Boston* could safely be considered the Kilgore Trout of American novelists.) Do we have it backwards, thinking ourselves intelligent and nature dumb? What if we are actually the walking dreams of place, continent, Earth?
The final dream of the night was much clearer:

I am out in a dry field sitting in an experimental vehicle of some sort—a truck, perhaps—when a UFO descends next to me. It is square with rounded corners. Fearing its crew will abduct me, yet also thinking this to be my destiny, I drive off into town so I can be around other people. I meet my romantic partner there (in waking life I don't have one anymore), and when she asks if she can share something that's on her mind, I ask, heart still beating hard, if I can talk first. I tell her about the UFO, all the while fearing that it will take me away from her. She hears me out, then asks what time the incident occurred. "Around 3:00," I reply, at which point she smiles and says, "How impressive!" I'm awaiting her explanation—clearly she has seen a parallel with something going on with her at that hour—when I wake up.

The dry, waiting field reminds me of old photos of how Escondido looked before the developers drove in. I had examined such pictures at the historical museum a few days ago. The experimental vehicle, I would guess, is the "terrapsychology" framework I'm assembling for understanding our deep connections to place. Yesterday I had wondered how much longer I would be in town. The alien ship is square (devil's corner), and the girlfriend is clearly connected with its visitation. UFOs tend to represent a nod from the future in my dreams, alerting me that things are about to change just up ahead. I had had trouble getting to sleep last night and did not turn in until 3:00 a.m., when a sudden wave of tiredness sent me to bed.

7/16: A sense of a lot going on last night, but no clear dreams.
Took some pictures downtown around the Civic Center and Old Escondido, including one of a very red house off Juniper. Amazing, all the diamond shapes that jumped out; it was like looking at the

original city map over and over again. Or the tip of the devil's tail....

7/19: Trip due to work opportunity. Not certain when I'll be able to come back.

I never did, to live anyway, and so my departure prevented me from learning exactly what, if anything, the soul of Escondido got out of my study. I think the dream woman would have told me of my imminent departure had I not interrupted her.

My impression before leaving town was that its reactivity had diminished, at least toward me. The cycle of flat tires ended, as did the strange yells of passing drivers whose faces I could not see. I stopped losing things and even found things I had previously lost. Cars and even bees went out of their way to let me pass. A curious but unmistakable sense of lightness told me that the psychic "pull" of Escondido on me had lessened. The feeling of calm after a storm was palpable, so much so that I felt a trifle lonely, although I had no wish to bring back the prior tumult.

After I left, however, news of three significant changes arrived all at once to herald a softening in the place's devilish mythos:

- The east side of Grand Avenue was finally opened up, a clear and long-awaited victory for Latino businesses downtown.
- Money poured in and became available for replacing the invasive Arunda plants choking Escondido Creek with benign native plantings that filtered a more open stream flow.
- Although the Harmony Grove Village development so strenuously fought did go through to completion, gains by long-term residents included a thinning of the planned housing density from 7.3 units per acre to 1.6 and the protection of natural wildlife corridors from artificial conversion into covered aqueducts thrust downward into storm drains.

Somehow, destructive (because unconsciously enacted) states of hiddenness and potential panic and congestion had undergone transformation as the wild energies of Pan made their way at last into the open—out from behind and around the Devil's Corner—for freer, more balanced, and more outward expression.

I wondered, of course, if the place had hinted at this trinity of changes by asking me in a dream, in the shape of a companionable woman coming in off those formerly wide-open fields, the departure-related question whose answer was "around 3:00" (a round three). The changes seemed akin to the slow healing of a core psychic conflict as symptoms evolve into synonyms. What after all is the demonic but daimonic wildness silenced and pathologized? Everything living yearns to make its mark.

The "girlfriend" figure in the dream alerted me to another possibility.

Who was she, and why show up so late in the work? This made no sense until I realized that she had been there all along. She was easy to miss underneath the overbuilt sprawl, and if her name is any indication, she prefers to remain off the heights. The civic hub of the city turns downtown around the City Hall area, but the ecological and spiritual heart of the place beats elsewhere. The story of Re-ha-re personified her, and Anza's map had named her. The girlfriend figure in the dream is Escondida, central image, soul, and *genius loci* flowing with the creek at the bottom of the Valley of San Pasqual. She is the hidden, wildflower-wearing power whose allure draws the energies of Pan out of his groves and into the city streets.

It has been suggested that her remark, "How impressive!" refers to my work, but I departed in confusion and heartbreak without having thought enough about the honey living in the igneous stone. May her fate be as safe as Re-ha-re's from the penetrating arrows of competitive maldevelopment.

As for me, the stories of her place have come home to circulate redly in a heart still pierced open and somewhat enlarged. I left there changed, which is more than I ever asked of her, but enough, I hope, for what she had asked of me.

The Great Indoors

I received the following note from a friend in his early sixties:

> I had a bleak but very interesting experience last week I thought you might be interested in. My job sent me for five days of training in Orange County. I have had nightmares about the place since returning...The area around Santa Anna and Irvine lacks any soul. I felt that any connection to whatever the area had been had been obliterated. There was no past left to connect to. I wouldn't have minded a week in a real city like San Francisco or even New York. But Orange County is some weird suburban hybrid with no redeeming features of a real city and no connection to nature. I have childhood memories of the great citrus groves both in Orange County and the San Fernando Valley. Orange County has succeeded in utterly destroying any remnants of that era let alone the earlier environment of the Native Americans...All I felt was an empty dead hole.

Although my highly intelligent friend has a good life, stays physically active, and is not prone to depression, it took him a week to
feel like himself again after his encounter with this dismembered
landscape.

I can understand that. When the Irvine Company began teaming
up with developers to dig up 1960s Orange County farmland for
housing tracts and malls, most of the county was organically intact.
Meadows and orchards still stood in 1970, when rising property
taxes began to force farmers to sell out. Through the eighties, as
backhoes and bulldozers tore into what was left of the once-rich
soil, local master planning popularized the use of marketing studies
and customer profiling to forecast and lock in real estate sales.
Today, rows of identical stucco frame houses jammed lawn to lawn
cover entire hills and valleys. Welcome to what an Irvine Spectrum
billboard referred to as the Great Indoors: entire hectares of sealed,
monitored, air-conditioned malls and neighborhoods and business
parks so vast they cannot be meaningfully surveyed on foot.

The transformed landscape has been converted into a shiny land
of stationary giants among whose steel and glass legs crowds of
"consumers" scurry to buy away awareness of their smallness. You
feel human standing next to an orange tree; what do you feel like
next to a blockbusting department store? Anything at all? And that
of course is the point: buying not to feel. Buying to remain unconscious of the depression and despair of watching the natural world
go under one handshake and shovelful at a time.

Freud spoke of symptoms, dreams, and nightmares as "compromise formations," meaning that they simultaneously repress and
express a hidden desire. Giant structures in Orange County—the
long history of them includes the Irvine Meadows, the Crystal
Cathedral, UC Irvine, the Irvine Ranch, Disneyland, Knott's, and
the first of all such manmade colossi, a huge chapel that fell at the
mission during an earthquake that rang the bells frantically—
express a persistent local giantism even while enclosing it in hard,
smooth surfaces.

At one time the county was a land of giants, a tale told by whale
skeletons unearthed amid the clanking and hammering of housing

projects going up in San Juan Capistrano and Laguna Hills. Giant pools of oil flow out through rusting black pumps in Long Beach. An enormous arm of the sea once covered most of the county. Tall volcanoes blew their tops here eons ago; unthinkable subterranean slow-motion crashes thrust titanic chunks of granite into the heated air. The effects of all that commotion linger and somehow the human psyche senses them, shrinking back in terror even while building over the larger-than-human landscape in order to silence and control it.

Ancient vulcanism and clashes of the elements have made of this county one vast, seething workshop of the industrious gods. Little wonder autopias and Animatronics do well here. Digs into prehistoric soil have thrown up Indian artifacts that look like stony cogwheels.

Snapshots of the Master Plan of the Great Indoors:

Interiorization:

An exit off 5 at Crown Valley Parkway, a left turn near a mall with a thing on top like a giant radar dish pointing at the heavens, and then up and then down the manicured Street of the Golden Lantern. I see fountained apartment complexes guarded by metal gates and American flag banners secured to street side lamp posts. This is Laguna Niguel, a planned community on fourteen very square miles. "Laguna" from the Spanish word for lagoon. "Niguel" from Nigueli, an extinct Juaneño village near Aliso Creek.

In the year 1874, when Ranchos Lomas de Santiago, San Joaquin, and Niguel owned much of the western Saddleback Valley, Lewis Moulton and Jean Piedra Daguerre bought Rancho Niguel from Don Juan Avila and widened the original grant to twenty-two thousand acres. In 1959 Cabot, Cabot, and Forbes formed the Laguna Niguel Corporation to take over the Moulton Niguel Ranch, clear out the sheep and cattle, and subdivide it into one of the first planned communities in California. Rockwell contributed a giant ziggurat in 1971. Roughly a third of the area remains undeveloped...for now. The population hovers around sixty-two thousand and is predominantly white.

On my very first visit to the white-walled complex where my

mate lived I am tailgated by a Mercedes and cut off by a BMW, in that order. The driveway before me divides in two: guests to the right, residents to the left. The four guest spaces are taken, however, and a wide grillwork gate on wheels blocks entry into the complex until a code is entered on a nearby keypad. I have no code, so I wait until the gate swings open to admit a resident so I can sneak in behind her and park in an unmarked space. My fantasy is of breaking into, rather than out of, a prison. Lines from *The Matrix* echo in my mind as I lock the car door: *Most of these people are not ready to be unplugged....* Around and above me, hundreds of two-story units pre-assembled into a sprawling stucco palace sink level by level and fence by fence into tennis courts and carports flanked by needle-shedding pines.

In the morning my car is gone. Without leaving so much as a courtesy notice, the security staff have ordered it towed away to Lake Forest.

Interiorization:

The heavy wooden doors of cacti-guarded Mission San Juan Capistrano open onto a street of restaurants and tourist shops. I enter and head for the museum-like chapel. It is a bit like touring a closed-down slaughterhouse made over into a museum to celebrate the history of meat packing. In one intriguing painting a skull glowers from beneath a crucified Jesus behind whom lurks a mission-style building. Poinsettias, saints, and gold implements deck out the elaborate altar. A saint at the top hoists a carmine standard.

Just outside but still within the enclosure, a rose garden and a fountain bobbing with lily pads offset the rows of spiky plants along the mission perimeter. Here lie the burned bricks of the oldest metalworking furnaces in Alta California. I make my way through a maze of low walls toward the ruined church—the hulk yet again under construction—and behold an enormous American flag draped over the scaffolded remains and the arched ruins. The stonework bears the names of corporate sponsors engraved in its shiny surface as well as a plaque commemorating the 1969 visit of Richard Nixon. His wife had rung the nearby bell. Most of the bells—they have names: San Vicente, San Juan, San Antonio, San

Rafael—had fallen during the statewide 1812 earthquake and been dented or broken. The bell towers now contain hidden speakers. Below the red, white, and blue canvas as large as a ship's mainsail, a replica of Serra lays one paternal arm on an Indian boy and points a finger at the sky.

Interiorization:

The "Franciscan Plaza" project of 1998 builds up—"renovates"—downtown San Juan Capistrano with new retailers, Mission Style cafes, red-tiled roofs, bistros, an Edwards Theater, and a multi-level parking garage, thereby converting more and more of the outside into a semblance of the inside: the hard straight planes of the dominion mentality running backward to Serra and beyond. We desperately need to devise an anamnesis of what could be called Conquest Disorder.

Interiorization:

California resident Richard Nixon withdraws into the "Western White House" in San Clemente after resigning from office in disgrace. Locals unimpressed with the gravity of his crimes observe by way of justification that he had done pretty well with the Chinese.

Interiorization:

After haunting Trabuco Creek, where a Spanish soldier had lost his rifle, Llorona goes indoors in 1967 and assumes the form of a wet-haired woman in a white nightgown. She appears to a startled Westminster neighbor from the window of a newly built tract home.

Interiorization:

In 1889 Modesta Avila of San Juan Capistrano strings her laundry across the tracks of the oncoming Santa Fe Railroad. For this act of defiance, and for being pregnant and unmarried, she is sentenced to San Quentin, where she dies at age 24.

Interiorization:

On the Feast of the Immaculate Conception, 1817, forty worshipers are killed at Mass as an earthquake brings down the mission church around and on top of them. The bodies are left buried where they knelt. Afterward, a dead girl named Magdalena is said to haunt the mission on nights of a crescent moon. When she comes forth from the shadows the bells ring by themselves.

Interiorization:

Fast forward to the new millennium already rushing into a colonial past down the Pacific Coast Highway near Main in Huntington Beach, where the longest concrete municipal pier on the west coast sticks its rail-lined tongue out at the setting sun. Rebuilt yet again in 1992, it hangs there nine miles south of sealless Seal Beach, where Boeing had sought to pour out a business park: Seal Beach, home of the Seal Beach Naval Weapons Station and of an enclosed "senior citizen" community selling itself as a Leisure World to those who can afford to retire and regress.

Henry Huntington had married his dead uncle's wife to seize a share in the Southern Pacific. In 1904 the rolling red cars of his garish trolley system conquered the town named after him as Fourth of July fireworks exploded overhead. Get out of the car, change tense, look around....

A curious display had been arranged in front of the pier where Navy personnel had scanned the sea for enemy submarines during World War II. A skeleton wearing a hard hat sat strapped with earthquake tape to a red plastic chair atop a small four-wheeled cart. A large red sign next to him suggested NOTHING BUT THE BLOOD OF JESUS. An empty table stood before the helmeted apparition. I wondered where he had left his trolley ticket. The arranger of this tableau was nowhere in sight.

In the distance a fleet of freighters headed for the Port of Los Angeles. I turned my head to see a tiled wall on which beachgoers of various historical periods passed before an oil rig with a Spanish vessel cutting across the water behind it. The mural, the skeleton, the hard hat, the tape, the rig, the dark line of ships going by: none of this jumble stage-lit by the relentless sunshine went together, and yet it did. The very confusion felt like a point of its own.

Up on the pier, local artists had hung their paintings along the metal railing. I stooped to look them over. In one a woman in a white dress held a child on her hip; in the foreground, a coin-operated telescope labeled DISTANT VIEWING swung seaward beyond her. In another a mother and child calmly watched as a cresting wave swept toward them. I shook my head. Had I followed Llorona here, or had she followed me? A bell tower near Mission San Juan Capistrano had begun to peal and clang as soon as I drove up. Was she sitting invisibly in the passenger seat? Who was she, really? And what did she want of me? I shook my head again and hit the road.

Moving inland to Santa Ana, I saw the helmeted skeleton's counterpart: a crusading knight composed of what looked like car parts welded together. Standing at attention in front of the First Presbyterian Church of Santa Ana, he wore a tire rim for a face and a keg for a belly and grasped what looked like a shield and a spear. Maybe he was actually Hephaestos, the conservative blacksmith of the gods, his giant hammers last seen coastward pounding the ground for oil. Behind him a marquee announced the coming Sunday sermon: "Faithfulness Betrayed."

Named indirectly after Christian conqueror William III of Orange, shaped like a tilted brick fringed with ragged edges, Orange County has been home to many famous, and many infamous, citizens whose supposedly "moderate" or "centrist" views lean far over to the right. Nixon was born here, Carl Karcher grilled his first burgers here, Robert Schuller raised his Crystal Cathedral here to preach the gospel of positive thinking. Disney built Disneyland here on top of a former orange grove while ratting out his fellow entertainers during the disgraceful McCarthy witch hunts. A local airport is named after John Wayne, who docked his boat in Newport Harbor and, emulating Disney, told on his fellow actors. The list goes on: Walter Knott and his berry farm, James Utt and his terror of imaginary black paramilitaries saddling up in Cuba, John Bircher John Schmitz, the homophobic Bill Dannemeyer, B-1 Bob Dornan (an occasional Rush Limbaugh stand-in), James Townsend, who coined "CommuNazi" to smear and kill a sex education course that cut teen pregnancies, engineer Ralph Muncaster, the Intelligent Designer who stepped into the shower one day and heard the voice of God, wig-wearing Wally "Combat TV" George of Anaheim, book-banning Wendy Leece of Newport, and of course Bill Butcher and Arnold Forde, the election-swinging "Darth Vaders of Direct Mail." "The delusional," remarked Bill Moyers about the right-wing mentality at the national level, "is no longer marginal." In California it has not been since the Cross and Sword marched in.

I strolled Dana Point, looking at boats at anchor, sniffing the salty air, feeling envious of captains who could just board and go, and thinking about the springs and gears of the reactionary mentality that imprisoned itself and everything it met. My girlfriend had retreated behind stucco and steel; I was alone and becalmed, here where we had walked holding hands, in the harbor named after Richard Henry Dana, the traveler whose *Two Years before the Mast* had popularized California as dreamy and backward. D. H. Lawrence had read the book and remarked, "Let us smash something...."

In 1950, a far-reaching book was published for quite other purposes under the blunt title *The Authoritarian Personality*. Its research findings were compiled by scholars and social scientists seeking to understand how relatively small extremist groups like the Nazis could take over entire nations. The question that drove the research was: What are the psychological roots of anti-Semitism and fascism? With support from the American Jewish Committee and the Institute of Social Research, the team worked patiently for five years, interviewed participants, tabulated results, assembled the data and published it.

The researchers discovered that those most likely to submit to authoritarian leaders and succumb to their irrational propaganda exhibited a consistent personality pattern of "antidemocratic tendencies and fascist potential":

- An entrenched, paranoid obsession with safety, security, and order.
- Rigidly absolutist "black-and-white" thinking (e.g., us against them).
- An overemphasis on "strength," power, and control; a "might makes right" orientation.
- Authoritarian submission: a willingness to blindly

obey the rules of the authorities in power.

- Authoritarian aggression: an aggressive attitude towards individuals or groups disliked by the authorities, often accompanied by bullying individuals or groups perceived to threaten traditional values.
- A belief that negotiation, understanding, empathy, and compromise are weak.
- A belief in the need to punish those who do not follow rules to the letter.
- Scornful rejection of the subjective, imaginative, empathic, and aesthetic dimensions of life.
- Superstition, cliché-mongering, stereotyping, and fatalism.
- A belief in fixed, unalterable, and traditional roles for women.
- Secret insecurity when unable to live up to high standards imposed publicly on others.
- Identification with those in power coupled with an excessive emphasis on posturing toughness.
- Destructiveness, cynicism, general hostility, and a habit of putting down perceived opponents.
- Projection: the tendency to see evil, exploitativeness, and danger in others instead of in oneself.
- An exaggerated concern with other people's sexual activity.

The authors also found a very high correlation between possessing a number of these traits and demonstrating a consistent and malignant prejudice against out-groups.

Although subsequent research has provided support, it has also shown that this contagious syndrome does not confine itself to religious, corporate, or political leaders and is not spawned solely within the dank toxicity of a pathological family. It is found in varying strengths in the populations of entire nations. Predisposing factors include religious traditionalism, rigid moralism, institutionalized paranoia, a history of violence, and a willingness to use aggression to secure power. In other words, authoritarianism is standard empire psychology ratcheted up by fundamentalism and by what psychoanalyst Erich Fromm diagnosed as "group narcissism," the uncritical idolization of one's in-group, whether a sect, a cult, a religion, or a nation.

I drew on a jacket against the chill ocean breeze. Where had this mental contagion sprung from?

Empires are built and financed by men who fear the world and each other so greatly that, feeling aborted from the womb of life, they squander their days and nights setting up artificial worlds where they can finally feel at home.

The thirst for raw power, which always comes down to an obsession with control, rages insatiably in these antisocial people fenced in by their own air-conditioned dread of the natural interconnectedness of things and beings. The thickening delusion of control within parameters always narrower than the horizon only walls its owners away from themselves, other people, and the organic world that offers so generous a natural home. Insisting that it must be customized for their comfort, they blink at it as spectators and tourists, map it and divide it, and even turn their ecocidal blast-furnace fury against it, for they hate and fear it very deeply. So must grim Hephaestos have felt when first cast out of the magical paradise of Olympus. The fall crippled him by twisting his feet to point permanently backwards.

Whether staked out as governments, religions, mass ideologies, or gigantic corporations, empires over matter erect an abstract, procedural Antiworld that feeds off the living one. Nothing wild or surprising can get in until illness, death, or Mother Nature finally pierce the manufactured delusion. Until then, the authoritarians raise and train generations of children to identify with their oppressors and despise their surroundings, especially whatever sectors of it remain uninteriorized, still living outside the box.

The orange sun, dropping fast beyond the bird-decorated statue of Dana, looked faded as though from its long midheavenly journey, eager now to rest behind the wet rim of the world. What found below the solar panorama so far above our heads could heal this belligerent syndrome of hatred, fear, and alienation?

People aren't born with it. They lose heart and soul when sacrificed to a standardized, number-crazed Antiworld education—call it "antication"—that attacks the spirit and dries up their joyful immersion in the earthly sources of human consciousness while forcing them to sit indoors in rows and compete against each other. After graduation they exhibit the kind of pathetic immaturity writ large in the boyish posturing of shock jocks and political candidates whose boasts and insults recall those last heard on the playground. Citizens deprived of public examples of wise, strong, and mature women and men—the kind who look to the needs of future generations, work out problems peacefully, manage their emotions, learn from their mistakes, defend themselves intelligently when necessary, and draw lightly down on planetary resources—stand little chance of growing up emotionally without such guidance. The "adults" best known to stunted imperials are bullies, blowhards, shoppers, workaholics, and sports nuts; but the fact that millions suffer from the same affliction does not turn it into a virtue. (The sitcom *Arrested Development* was set in Orange County.)

That is the regressive trend, here and elsewhere, but it's reversible. Look beyond the blaring surfaces of reactionary giantism and see the numerous experiments blossoming here and elsewhere as people on the edge preserve their ethnic dialects, clothe and house each other, garden luscious foods and spices, tend insects and animals, rebuild communities, restock depleted ponds, and enjoy the sunshine and the ocean breeze. These restorations of sense and soul go on all over the planet now.

By taking our cue from how nature performs its age-old tasks, we learn how ecosystems rebalance and heal themselves through multiple means on multiple levels, growing hardy varieties instead of monocultures so pests don't wipe out entire crops, self-adjusting through intricate feedback loops pumping in new information from outside, relying on redundant local sources of power, water, and daily bread instead of centralizing and totalizing them away, planning die-back for parasites that exceed the proper bounds, and welcoming inputs from all available sources rather than excluding or devaluing any. Much of this ecological horse-, plant- and worm-sense needs translation into culture, politics, and psychology as we relearn how to be about our earthly business and harvest a yield of joy in it too.

Left to its obsessions, the false interiority of the Antiworld collapses one homecoming at a time. Empires burn and economies fail, but tomorrow the sun rises once again. I'm reminded of this by a remark made by writer H.G. Wells toward the end of a long life:

> I am English by origin, but I am Early World Man. And I live in exile from the world community of my desires. I salute that finer, larger world across the generations, and maybe someone down the vista may look back and appreciate an ancestral salutation.

Having foreseen the sexual revolution, aerial warfare, the tank, both World Wars, the German invasion of Poland, the London air blitz, the atom bomb, the League of Nations, the United Nations, space travel, and so much else, I suspect the imaginative believer in human possibility sensed those of us who, down the vista, are busy today imagining and weaving together new kinds of post-empire community and ecological restoration, unafraid to dream toward what we most desire.

Structures built to dominate never last forever. When the giant mission church met its end in the rocky hands of an Orange County earthquake, bells cracked and spirits wailed, but the humbler chapel in the shadow of the wreckage survived.

De/materialization

Gustav Fechner (1801-1887) is mentioned in textbooks of psychology as the man who invented "psychophysics," or what we now call physiological psychology. He balanced weights and stared through lenses and wrote equations for his pioneering work on sensory thresholds, and by doing so helped found experimental psychology. Young Freud attended his Leipzig lectures. To the best of my knowledge Fechner never visited Los Angeles.

What the textbooks do not mention, but what an impressed William James went out of his way to mention, is that after a life-changing period of blindness brought to a close by a pungent meal of raw ham with lemon juice and Rhine wine, Fechner opened fresh and startled eyes to gaze back at an animated world. Existence, he (and James) came to believe, is not held together by an absolute law from above so much as interconnected from inside. Everything possesses an interiority, a "within of things" as Teilhard de Chardin would write it: an urge to be and to unfold. To study the world only from without (empiricism) or from within (subjectivism) was to miss the multidimensional reality of its blessed significance, and of ours as its investigative two-legged inhabitants.

In *Religion of a Scientist* Fechner wrote:

On a certain spring morning I went out to walk. The fields were green, the birds sang, the dew glistened, the smoke was rising, here and there a man appeared; a light as of transfiguration lay on all things. It was only a little bit of earth; it was only one moment of her existence; and yet as my look embraced her more and more it seemed to me not only so beautiful an idea, but so true and clear a fact, that she is an angel, an angel so rich and fresh and flower-like, and yet going her round in the skies so firmly and so at one with herself, turning her whole living face to Heaven, and carrying me along with her into that Heaven, that I asked myself how the opinions of men could ever have so spun themselves away from life so far as to deem the earth only a dry clod, and to seek for angels above it or about it in the emptiness of the sky—only to find them nowhere....

I bring this up because I have come to see Los Angeles as an angel, and not because of its name. Its crackling angelic quality is older than that, older than the stardusty hype of Hollywood, older than its original pre-mission inhabitants.

An angel is a being who materializes and announces something important. Fifteen million years ago, an enormous bubble of magma formed below the sea and burst as uplifting mountains shuffled clockwise around it. From the mountains ran streams that dumped sand, silt, and clay into the miles-wide bowl as more magna pushed it skyward from the depths. Gradually, an enormous stage rotated itself above sea level like a Botticelli clamshell joined at Palos Verdes.

Upon this Venusian stage, now known as the Los Angeles Basin, the ancient Tongva people shared their holy jimsonweed visions. Seeing their fires from afar, Cabrillo named the place "Bay of Smokes," an assessment often shared in our time by the Air Quality Management District. Today radio messages called Sig Alerts warn the driver about which asphalt paths do not to commuting salvation lead.

Angels materialize and so did Los Angeles, inventing itself right there in a vast coastal desert. In his informative *Americans and the California Dream* series, former state librarian Kevin Starr homes in on materialization as a key southland motif. But angels also dematerialize, indulging in what Norman Klein would identify as civic erasure. Only when the buyers, sellers, brigands, and oligarchs rushed to town and erased its human and ecological history did its angel degenerate into a fallen one, its gartered shadow now wearing horns.

Angels are messengers, and in a sense every message erases a previous one. When a camera projects an image, it replaces—dematerializes—the one just before. The town of El Pueblo replaces the Indian village Yang Na, and the Civic Center replaces both. The Army Corps of Engineers replaces the wild Los Angeles River with a long, square tube of concrete. Cecile B. DeMille dies, but an artificial semblance of life replaces the reality of mortality as his house is kept fresh and decorated as though he still lived there. Forest Lawn cheers up death with pleasant music and bright flowers and loved ones not deceased but "out of sight." Plastic surgery is not just a Hollywood treat for those who describe themselves as "— years young" in phobic fear of the word "old," but a dematerialization of the ecological succession of wrinkles and age spots that mark the natural maturation of body and soul. But soul doesn't sell in Hollywood and isn't always pretty.

But it is persistent. Think about Spring Street, moody site of one erased Indian trail, two lynchings, and three noir films. "Spring" is a translation of the original Spanish name *Primavera*, "First View," and the motif of being first, as with the season itself, has repeated itself throughout the street's hundred-and-fifty-year history: first public school in LA, first multi-story building, first four-story hotel housing the first mechanical elevator in Southern California, first brewery and beer garden, first swank café, first nightclub at Buffums Saloon, first café to introduce an orchestra at Rathkeller, which was also the first place where motion picture contracts were signed, first ice skating rink on a stage at Fred Harlow's place, first terminus for transcontinental stage coach lines, first City Hall, first city jail house, first jukebox, first fire station. The street runs from Sunset Boulevard to the Cahuenga Pass where John Fremont marched into the city as its first American conqueror, making it also the first primary artery to the industrializing outside world. It's as though Spring Street itself announces or projects some mysterious quality of Firstness.

In Los Angeles materialization and dematerialization stand so close together on the street corners, in boardrooms, and at pulpits that they interpenetrate. One is seldom found uncontaminated by the other. By the early 1900s, when urban development had pushed its way north and south, a compensatory horizontalism set in when a millionaire socialist (!) paid for the construction of Wilshire Boulevard, the Miracle Mile, on top of another former Indian trail. As a huge cross of asphalt extended over the face of the rising city, symbolic perhaps of the spiritual fads and cults to come, its oily heart disgorged the bones of prehistoric wild animals in an unexpected return of the repressed.

Materialization and dematerialization have always been the business of angels and Angeles alike, but in LA the weight of spreading asphalt garbles the spiritual impulse. The city that saw its first saloon undergo conversion into a church has known wind-blown Joseph Widney of the deep pockets, who arrived in 1868 after encountering God in the deserts of Arizona; the Los Angeles Holiness Band (1881), who sold real estate and claimed not to have sinned for thirty years; the Molokans (1905), who prayed earnestly and gulped lots of milk; William Seymour (1906), who emitted the first fervent cries of Pentecostalism; Albert Powell Warrington (1911), who promoted theosophy in Hollywood; Christine Wetherill Stevenson, an heiress whose pious staging of *The Light of Asia* (1918) led to Buddhist pamphlets and the Hollywood Bowl; Aimee Temple McPherson, who arrived that year to preach in showy pageants; and Fighting Bob Schuller (1920), who rolled in to attack pretty much everyone except Christ and the KKK.

Not surprisingly, local architecture reflected this ongoing collision of the material and the spiritual. In 1922 KJS ("King Jesus
Saves") beamed inspiration skyward as the first religious radio station in Los Angeles. A gaudy electric JESUS SAVES sign soon rose and
shone at the station's headquarters at 6th and Hope as old buildings
fell to the Miracle Mile downtown. In 1923 the Angelus Temple
built and paid for by the followers of Aimee McPherson opened (as
did the Coliseum and the "Hollywoodland" sign), granting Sister
Aimee a stage for dressing up as a football player carrying the ball
for God. In the 1930s, the "I AM" sect thought up by Guy and Edna
Ballard set up shop to claim that Ascended Masters and Saint
Germaine needed "love donations" handed over (materialized) by
eager followers. Ballard claimed to be a reincarnation of George
Washington, but he might have gotten this idea from Sister Aimee,
who liked to dress up like the President when the Spirit moved her.

I AM was followed by the US, the Utopian Society, dreamed up
by Eugene Reed, W. G. Rousseau, and Merritt Kennedy, a stock
salesman for the expired Julian Petroleum Company. US was followed by MU, Mankind United, under Arthur Bell, a plagiarist who
called himself "the Voice" and insisted that the Sponsors, superior
metal beings hiding in the Earth's molten core, were requiring
everyone to surrender to MU all Monetary Units plus liquidatable
worldly goods. Eventually MSIA, the Movement of Spiritual Inner
Awareness, would coagulate around John-Roger, formerly Roger
Hinkins, an English teacher reborn from a coma and charged there-
from with Mystical Traveler Consciousness. This rarefied state of
mind manifested expensive homes and estates in Los Angeles and
Santa Barbara.

Across town, Hubert Eaten reorganized the soothing machinery
of Forest Lawn to go into motion at the behest of one phone call:
drive-through death in scenery so idyllic that the Reagans decided
to marry there.

The Bodhi Tree is the tall fig under which Gautama Buddha
achieved enlightenment. It is also the name of a bookstore off
Melrose Avenue in Hollywood. To reach it I passed the Hollywood

Bowl, turned right off Highland, and fought the traffic past art galleries, gift shops ("Spirituali: Mind Body Sanctuary of the World"), and trendy clothing shops with luminous signs designed to lure teen rebels ("Wasteland"; "Red Balls") until luck smiled and I found a parking space within half a mile of the green, life-sized angel posted outside the used book branch. I was there to nurture my post-Christian interest in spirituality.

Of course, this required buying books on psychology, philosophy, metaphysics, and mysticism, drinking herbal teas while reading, and slowly walking the polished wood floors shining up at photographs of Indian saints and, in one niche, Yoda. It was a relief to find a place mostly free of the cultishness and salesmanship that warped so much spiritual discourse in Los Angeles. None of Shirley MacLean's Chakra Sky Jewelry in here (I hoped), although they did sell books by a winner of the Ig Noble Prize in physics. I bent to examine one. "Spiritual" and "Success" in the same title. Very Los Angeles. Pungent incense turned slowly to ash as bells chimed softly from the speakers above. In a lapse of mental discipline I wondered briefly if it was really true that Krishnamurti had quietly slept for decades with someone else's wife.

The crossroads/intersection that is Los Angeles has been difficult to feel grounded in ever since a Spanish soldier raped an Indian woman and cut her husband's head from his body. The local splits between the flesh and the spirit and the material and the mental are highly polarized here, so polarized that they blend into each other. No conscious unification, that, but an alchemical *massa confuse* ever on the fly. Looking out my car window one day while driving down 405, I nodded to see a lean white sports car splashed all over with quotations from the Gospel of John. In that quintessentially Los Angeles film *Blade Runner*, the watcher is never sure who is manufactured and who is human. Not even Harrison Ford and Ridley Scott could agree afterward on whether Ford's character Deckard was actually a replicant. Deckard's killings in cold blood and the obvious humanity exhibited by his targets blurred the distinction even more. Likewise, the televised reimagination of *Battlestar Galactica* asked: Can souls inhabit machines? And if they can, how do these artifacts stack up against soulless humans?

At first I enjoyed being a seeker living in LA. I liked the exotic reading and the lectures. I enjoyed telling the door-to-door mission-aries who asked if I had read their book, "I have indeed; and also the Bible, the Bhagavad Gita, the Upanishads, the Guru Granth Sahib, the Koran, the Dhammapada, the Tao Te Ching, the Nag Hammadi Library..." until their lifeless eyes began to cross. At times like this all that money spent at the Bodhi Tree came in handy.

Gradually, however, I began to feel an unaccustomed guilt. These spiritual treasures had blossomed in very different climes from mine, and here I was sampling them like salads sold in cafete-rias invented in Los Angeles. *I'll have a little of this, and some of that, and one of these...* When my dreams hinted that I was getting inflated by all the spiritual vapors I inhaled, I began to wonder whether using practices culled from other traditions without having been schooled in the doctrinal preparation they all recommended was really such an enlightened idea. Come to think of it, I scarcely knew a thing about their cultures of origin or the historical soil in which they had grown. How was this kind of uprooting and transplanting any dif-ferent from sending non-native palms shivering sunward like giant stage props rising ludicriously all over the southland?

Because empires thrive on assimilation, their citizens often carry an unconscious sense of entitlement. Yet, "You can't coexist," insists Chickasaw poet Linda Hogan, "with someone when they want what you've got. And now of course people want not only the Indian land base but also the Indian soul. They want the spirituality." Not just American Indian, either.

C. G. Jung, whose work I had started to study, had not been charitable about this imperial habit. In *Archetypes of the Collective Unconscious* he asked bluntly:

> Shall we be able to put on, like a new suit of clothes, ready-made symbols grown on foreign soil, saturat-ed with foreign blood, spoken in a foreign tongue, nourished by a foreign culture, interwoven with foreign history, and so resemble a beggar who wraps himself in kingly raiment, or a king who dis-

guises himself as a beggar? No doubt this is possible. Or is there something in ourselves that commands us to go in for no mummeries, but perhaps even to sew our garments ourselves?

It dawned on me with a sharp knot of discomfort that I knew even less about the history and lore of my own cultural heritage.

As one of thousands, perhaps millions, who had turned away in disgust from the dogmatic stench of Christendom to breathe something more fulfilling and aromatic, I gradually came to understand that I had thrown out the Divine Child with the bath water. Although methods differ widely, states of joy, enlightenment, and sacred consciousness live in every tradition. Those of the Far East, as valid and beautiful and rich as any, have been oversold here as superior, and primarily by ambitious men born in Asia but educated in the West. Yoga in California looks almost nothing like its original forms in its native India, and the "Eastern" primacy of experience over doctrine or scholarship seems to be a modern interpolation, especially in Vedantic, Buddhist, and yogic circles.

On the other hand, we Westerners have evolved our own contemplative methods down the centuries: *meditatio*, gnosis, phenomenology, the *vera imaginatio* ("true imagination") of the alchemists. We too know of karma (called *wyrd* and *örlög*), reincarnation (via the Celts, Plato, Pythagoras, and the Gnostics), the Way of the Warrior (the Code of Chivalry), the mantra (*lectio divini*), and the Tao (Pleroma, Anima Mundi, Music of the Spheres). Our deep seers had given us their own versions of the prayer wheel (May Pole), the chakras (the Sefiroth), *asanas* (prayer postures), feng shui (sacred geometry and ley lines), *prana* and *chi* (*pneuma* and *ruach*), oracular techniques (Tarot, geomancy, runes, tea leaves), energy meridians (humors, animal spirits), and a theory linking health to the balance of the five primal elements. To the Norse, *shaktipat* was *seidr*, taught by loving Freya; the Greeks practiced Tantra as *venia*, the sacred art of the priestesses of Venus. Our gurus were known as bards, druids, shamans, and spiritual directors.

As I dug more deeply into the traditions of the West, I found myself puzzled by another erasure.

While working as a volunteer for the Foundation for Change in San Diego I had met street artists and activists who did not seem to realize that chants and meditation could accomplish all change. They told me tales of shoving newspapers into their sleeves and pantlegs to keep their arms and legs from being broken by police batons during World Trade Organization protests.

In all my book-buying I had seen nothing about this. No books on activism, political transformation, or taking the message out into the streets. Nothing on guerrilla art or gardening, environmental advocacy, social justice, deep ecology, or ecopsychology.

The assumption behind this absence is, of course, that taking it to the streets is unnecessary. Awareness, self-improvement, right-mindedness will suffice for an integral vision of trickle-down idealism, and without messy risks or broken bones. A man alone setting himself in order is felt for a thousand miles, says the I Ching, an ancient oracle printed in a land overrun by secret police. Still the senses and silence the intellect, say the Upanishads, composed on a continent devastated by centuries of poverty, terrorism, and warfare. Let the shorelines darken and the skies weep with acid, journaling and breathing are saving the world; only one never learns how this can be because the vital connection of action with reflection has been neatly dematerialized by formulae for happiness and spiritual success.

So it is that our keenest seekers stay home, reading and chanting and causing no trouble; and the globe and its creatures continue to burn their way into ecological apocalypse.

To view the earliest European example of how the spiritual and the material interpenetrate in Los Angeles, I walked in the Mission District past the cracked campanario of brick and mortar at Grapevine Park and regarded religiously themed sidewalk tiles painted by school children. The slabs of false stonework faced the refurbished mission from the other side of a red-tiled wall. A Pasadena Knights of Columbus plaque commemorated Serra's two hundredth birthday; an El Camino Real sign paid for by the San Gabriel Women's Club advertised to the passing traffic. Tiles in an archway below a crooked lamp praised the heroic friars for bringing "the beginnings of modern civilization" and "the blessing of Christianity to pagan Indians," but to my right the brickwork of the cemetery gate housed a white skull.

In the mission courtyard I took an inventory of the implements of the aforesaid civilization: a cannon, an anvil, a Historic Anchor, a tiled Guadalupe, a stone lion sticking its head out of a Moorish fountain, and a plaque celebrating the "blending together" of two civilizations. The "blessings we enjoy today" part had peeled away. Wine cellar, sacristy, chapel.

A cross raised to salute the Gabrieleño Indians was watched over by a sorrowing Mary. In the sacristy hung a fire-colored painting of the Inferno. The blessings we enjoy today: but who is "we"? On an old wall mural, a family of heavenly beings was cast entirely as Caucasians; the only dark face was that of the Crucified.

On my way out I stooped to examine a final sidewalk tile. It was a child's drawing of a whitewashed restaurant sporting a sign that read MEXICAN FOOD HOTDOG.

Viviana Franco grew up near the 105 freeway in Hawthorne. A hundred feet from her home spread out a third of a grassy acre at 118th and Doty Avenue, and there she played in the 1980s while watching the freeway being paved down. She eventually moved to the greener pastures of Palos Verdes, but she never forgot that vacant lot. Maybe it never forgot her either...

Franco grew up to be an urban planner with a master's degree, an earner of honors from the Cesar Chavez Foundation, and a founder of the nonprofit From Lot to Spot. Her lot, she learned, was owned by Caltrans, who expressed no interest in allowing her to design a park on a piece of property they had not known at first was theirs. The mayor would not agree to the proposal either until Franco came up with the money to buy the land herself—which she could not do without an agreement by the mayor.

Caltrans, it turned out, had auctioned the land to a supporter of the mayor. The supporter did not care for the land either; at last report, according to the FLTS website, it suffered from "large garbage piles, overgrown grass and weeds (which poses a fire threat), car vandalism, prostitution, presence of rodents, raccoons, large cockroaches and opossums." Still, Franco persists in trying to sell the community on the idea of planting a park or garden there. Why?

"That lot is who I am," she told a reporter from the *LA Times*. "You have a shared consciousness in a neighborhood, and that lot stamped us. This was a place of crime and blight, and it shaped our attitudes, our identities. If it was green and had a few trees? Yeah. A whole new world."

This sense of connection to a place is not rare. Here is what "geologian" Thomas Berry wrote about a meadow he came across as a boy growing up in Appalachia:

> The field was covered with lilies rising above the thick grass...This early experience, it seems, has become normative for me throughout the entire range of my thinking. Whatever preserves and enhances this meadow in the natural cycles of its transformation is good, what is opposed to this meadow or negates it is not good. My life orienta-tion is that simple. It is also that pervasive. It applies in economics and political orientation as well as in education and religion....

Most of us can easily think of at least one sacred spot we never forget. One of mine, a kite field where I played as a boy in El Cajon, California, now sits smothered by a CHP parking lot. I still love that field. I will always love it. It is a permanent part of me, and I feel cer-tain that in some ways my boyhood presence there must have become a part of it.

"Look at this," James Hillman tells Los Angeles resident Michael Ventura in the film *Surfing LA*. The two men stare down into a desolate concrete aqueduct as Hillman gestures sadly. "This was a river." It might be one again someday, but only thanks to the unsentimental love and sweaty dedication shown by the Friends of the Los Angeles River and other groups of determined advocates unenchanted by the *maya* of Progress.

How were we ever convinced by those amassing power down here that our only source of spirituality glittered far up in the heavens? In LA I began to overhear seekers who believed—who even hoped—their eternal souls emanated from the distant Pleiades and not from Earth. To all our ancestors it was obvious that spiritual power moved in the ground as well as in the sky, and that the breathing world framed a spacious sacred temple. There's a reason cathedrals resemble grottos and cliff caves. Jesus needed a desert to wake him up, Muhammad Mount Hira, Gautama a fig tree.

Inhabited for millennia as a pilgrimage site for visionaries, Los Angeles the city now covers nearly five hundred square miles. The county extends for more than four thousand. All that pavement to silence her spirit, yet still it inspires from the ground up.

Californian Exodus

A hot, sloping plain of dust, adobe and granite enclosed by an amphitheater of dry hills just northwest of Los Angeles: what a perfect place, this dry Egyptian setting named the San Fernando Valley, for a stage upon which to continually reenact and occasionally rewrite the epic story of Exodus.

Near the top of an imaginary thirteen-mile line joining the valley's north to its south sits what remains of Mission San Fernando in the town of that name. Strip malls warehousing Mission Revival wardens like H & R Block, Wells Fargo, and Western Dental had followed me all the way to the mission across the street from the gang-banging battlefield known here officially as Brand Park. Neighborhoods housing people of means kept well north of the train tracks.

I pulled into the parking lot near the east side of the parish, got out of the car, and tilted my head back to look up at a four-masted altar draped with high-tension lines, wondering whether this metal monster would crouch here had the cross shape never invaded California.

The mission was named after Ferdinand III of the Franciscan Third Order. He inherited León from his father in 1230 and went

Crusading against the Moors. Once the corpses were out of the way his strategy involved turning captured mosques into Christian cathedrals. His victories concluded the Christian retaking of Spain. This, revisioned a "Reconquista," was the bloody outcome of an old campaign that started when Roderick the Visigoth was defeated by General Tariq ibn Ziad. The general sailed in through the strait of Gibraltar bearing seven relatively stable centuries of Islamic rule and culture with him. With the final overthrow of the Moors, Christianity returned to Spain with a vengeance.

At the mission, a Royal Road bell monument manned its post near a gravestone. The cross a few feet away paired well with the electrical tower. From their brickwork base, two wrought-iron rods reached skyward past the wooden arms like antennae protruding from the Van de Graaff generator used to power the first atom-smashers.

Nuclear family. Breeder reactor. Fission, fusion. Ground? Zero. How much we say without hearing ourselves. Critical mass, boiling point, pinch field, strange attractor, control rod, chain reaction, radioactive waste. Angry sermons as *proliferations*. Support groups as *containments*, tantrums as *meltdowns*. One Eve under atom, both now divisible; three quarks for matthew mark. Use the Force, Luke, and don't forget to flush the John. How many angels perch on the head of a neutron?

> The real is produced from miniaturized units, from matrices, memory banks and command models— and with these it can be reproduced an infinite number of times. It no longer has to be rational, since it is no longer measured against some ideal or negative instance. It is nothing more than opera-tional. In fact, since it is no longer enveloped by an imaginary, it is no longer real at all.
>
> — Jean Baudrillard

The next nuclear word that came to mind was "confinement." The grillwork bars over the windows and around the neatly trimmed trees; the hooded mannequin spotlit under glass; a painted padre's arm around a painted Indian; a spiked metal gate guarding the mission workshop; display rooms with entrances entirely covered by cages raised to protect the sacred artifacts. A bust of the sorrowing Jesus thrusting its moaning face from a yellow wall. Neophytes had been humiliated and beaten at all the missions, but here the infamous Father Zalvidea made such frequent use of his whip that Father Lasuén had to defend him in writing on the grounds that the savages had no religion or government. With surprising honesty Father Muñoz noted that the Indians, though "compassionate and generous by nature," suffered a "great change" when born to Christian parents and lost all sense of their roots and traditions.

In this place without laughter, the strains of a wedding commenced in the church below dark rafters before a golden altar. Forest Lawn must have been booked. One day Bob Hope's body would enter the ground here where so many nameless neophytes had been planted and forgotten. Unlike theirs, his would be celebrated. Thanks for the memories.

The sign said OUR LADY of the ARCHIVES. High above, bell-imitating speakers angled outward from within the silent campanario. Even when hope is buried, the ritual must go on.

> City "father" Isaac Lankershim and son-in-law Isaac Newton Van Nuys. Smacks of two Old Testaments and outmoded physics. The original Isaac Newton theorized a universe composed of "building blocks" of matter. Mr. Isaac Newton Van Nuys and father-in-law saw "building blocks" on subdivided land where once was desert wilderness.
>
> — Peace Wilson

As rustling deeds for Mexican land grants shifted into American hands (except for Rancho Ex-Mission, which did not sell at first due to lack of interest), now-familiar names began to arrive in the

Valley: Alexander Bell, Isaac Lankershim, Isaac Newton Van Nuys, the dentist David Burbank. Lankershim and Van Nuys showed particular ambition in the speed with which they snatched North Hollywood, Van Nuys, Canoga Park, and Reseda. Considering former mission neophyte Rogerio Rocha and his family a barrier to progress, the inexorable men of business maneuvered to get the family evicted and donated the resulting moneys to found a theological school.

In 1872 the Southern Pacific Railroad dealt itself into the land game. To the north, George Porter and Charles Maclay sold San Fernando as a new "Garden of Eden" in the midst of a drought. Barely hanging on, the surviving Indian exiles still living at the mission plunged an image of Saint Fernando into water, and within a few days a storm brought moisture down to what had started to feel like an Egyptian desert.

Through it all the elements roared as though in protest. In 1878 a pillar of fire burned eighteen thousand acres of wheat and pasture, and an earthquake rerouted two streams near the mission whose leaky roof would blow off in 1897. A snowstorm that struck in 1882 froze some of the land Maclay divided between his two partners. In 1883 it rained every month, and in 1889, water from the sky pelted recently built houses, railroad tracks, and farmlands, temporarily slowing the building boom. In 1891 a muddy flood flashed destructively through the new Tujunga Wash near North Hollywood Park. After a pause, torrential rain struck settlers in biblically named Zelzah (Northridge), Reseda, and Pacoima in 1910, flooded newly platted Canoga Park in 1912, and provided fishing along Van Nuys Boulevard in Universal City in 1914. As local pharaohs continued to buy up all available land, only the locusts and frogs were missing.

Below the weeping skies, six wealthy men had banded together as The Los Angeles Suburban Homes Company to divide up Sherman Oaks (which went to railroad man M. H. Sherman), Tarzana (to newspaperman Harrison Gray Otis), Canoga Park (to insurance man Otto Brant), Sherman Way and Van Nuys Boulevard (to Harry Chandler of the LA Times and real estate developer H. J. Whitley), and half of Van Nuys (to William Whitset). Engineer

William Mulholland, Fred Eaton (whose family founded Pasadena), Henry Huntington, and others would join this plutocracy to secure land in the Valley and sell it at an astronomical profit once Angelenos had been frightened into paying for an aqueduct to suck water from the Owens Valley, in effect diverting the Red Sea instead of dividing it. The plutarchs of Los Angeles had been trying to absorb the Valley for decades by going after its water supply, but Valley wells nullified their campaign of hydraulic despotism. They finally decided that it was easier just to take territory outright.

For the most part the Valley remained free of their clutches, though not of the lure of the golden calf. In California blatant swindles were relatively common, as when photographers in Ocean Beach stuck oranges onto cacti to create a fantasy orchard, and when boosters distributed flyers showing a nonexistent river flowing through "Simiopolis" to the north. To such swindlers belonged Victor Girard Kleinberger, who created the "dream city" of Girard (1922) by erecting clapboard mosque towers, housing tracts, and even store fronts along Ventura Boulevard. Hoping to stave off bankruptcy, he then attached liens without telling the buyers. His golf course, which was real, still does business as the Woodland Hills Country Club.

Surrounded by false fronts mutated into office dividers, the developer Girard now the executive Gerard, the strait of Gibraltar the strength of the Rock, and Roderick the Spanish survivalist an ambitious coworker named Rod who spoke much and said little, I sat waiting to have my professional head cut off.

The Woodland Hills business park around me had gone up near the Indian village of Tototgna. The village was wiped out long ago by an epidemic, but rock paintings at Sandstone Creek still mark where the sun sets at winter solstice.

The immense cube-shaped pile of stucco where I squinted over convoluted insurance contracts detailing plans that excluded more than they included loomed not far from where rich girls in leggings and lace shopped their way through Reseda making verbal vacuity fashionable. The pile sat on one of two squares of eleven hundred acres once used to breed horses. After a liquidation of real estate holdings, the former Rancho El Escorpion gave way to a master-planned business park renamed the Warner Center.

> Psychologically healthy people have no need to indulge fantasies of absolute power; nor do they need to come to terms with reality by inflicting self-mutilation and prematurely courting death. But the critical weakness of an over-regimented institutional structure—and almost by definition "civilization" was over-regimented from the beginning—is that it does not tend to produce psychologically healthy people. The rigid division of labor and the segregation of castes produce unbalanced characters, while the mechanical routine normalizes—and rewards—those compulsive personalities who are afraid to cope with the embarrassing riches of life.
>
> — Lewis Mumford

I had long given up on earning any more promotions. The Rodericks and Girards had mastered the power lunches, the mission statements, and the cold, coded euphemisms of "team effort" and "utilization of resource management" and ascended correspondingly higher up the shirt-and-tie hierarchy. My concern was with whether my job would exist tomorrow. One of comedian Bobcat Goldthwait's routines repeated itself in my mind as a palliative to rising anxiety: "I lost my job today.....well, I didn't exactly lose my job. I know where it is. It's just that now some other guy is doing it."

The division waited silently for the phones to ring. Each of us sat isolated in a gray cubicle. The first round of layoffs was upon us after several years of money-wasting blunders committed by executives too busy for critical feedback or new ideas. I was wondering why the heads that had formulated those cunningly explained decisions were not on the block with mine when the first ringing bell brought gasps from all over the office. Another silence closed in.

A middle-aged woman with tears in her eyes got up, circled the gray wall, and headed for Human Resources per instructions we'd received should we take the fatal call. It had begun.

One by one, contract consultants under whom we had apprenticed picked up the phone, put it down, and disappeared. Most were just under retirement age. Some had given the company more than three decades. All had been secretly rated on some arbitrary scale of corporate "value" and told on their way out that, well, it was very unfortunate, but somehow they'd been consigned to the "marginal performer" category. You know how it is in business. Thanks for the memories.

When they were gone, more phones began to ring: Phase II of the subdivision of the frightened human resources.

Had I been in my right mind, I would not have waited even that long before getting up and leaving. So stunned was I by the swift, incomprehensible viciousness of the operation being carried out with clinical precision on friends and colleagues I had worked with for years that I found myself unable to move, immobilized more by anger than fear, as rings and hang-up clunks continued on all sides. My phone never rang. Supervisors and managers stayed in their offices waiting to be damned by the bell. An outspoken gay neophyte put his phone down and left. Everyone had guessed he'd be one of the terminated.

The slaughter was shattering to observe. A typesetting specialist lost her mind during the layoffs and left to go be paranoid in the streets. She never recovered. A man (it was whispered) got into his car and drove off a cliff. Muffled sobbing from behind the partitions. Vomit in the men's room sink five mornings in a row. Nightmares of sports stadiums filled with cheerleading corpses dressed in blood-stained suits. The worst was a Willie Loman brand of insurance salesman always ready with a joke and a wink collapsing of a heart attack a week before he was due to be cut loose. Good thing for his family that he carried some of the life insurance we sold. Had he seen the giant Job Fair balloon drifting above the building before his subdivided heart forced him up the heavenly escalator featured in those corny old Prudential commercials?

Even then I didn't quit. Maybe I was waiting for the rest of it to collapse. Only after learning that I was being written up because the quarter of my day spent tracking my own work was insufficient did I look for a less surreal job offering some security and a larger element of trust. I had finally grown tired of writing and rewriting old contracts—broken treaties—for which nobody took responsibility when people got hurt. Mindless bureaucracy, I had learned, was as heartless as the psychopathy that so often authorized it.

After I gave notice I checked my in-tray one last time and found a new memo. I read the thing twice to make sure it was no joke. I had been selected to be on a new committee. Its mission was to determine why there were so many committees.

On my last day I noticed a new row of cubicles assembled just outside Director Gerard's office. We who had struggled with the contract consultant workload, our only extra pay the stress, were getting good news at last, we were told. Money had surfaced for hiring real consultants. And here they were now.

In slow motion my right arm rose to point at the cubes where old faces had turned much older and where new faces beamed with exactly the correct degree of professional optimism. Two words entered my ears as my mouth tossed them into the air:

"Battleship Row."

No one smiled. Eerier still, no one frowned, either.

The glass doors parted before my badgeless chest, and the thunder boomed dramatically. Drops moistened the dry skin under my eyes. I didn't look back. I was free, and if I had to I would live on dog food in MacArthur Park to stay that way.

The sequel played out several months later:

After several tries and no takers, Rancho Ex-Insurance Department was finally sold off at a loss to Aetna, so named after the mountain under which Zeus had buried the venomous, inflated, hundred-headed Typhon. When the overpriced computers blinked off, the paneled lights winked out, the sprinklers quit watering the foyer garden, and the bells stopped ringing from their ceiling-panel campanarios, all who still struggled to please, to survive, to get something done, to make a difference, to eat lotuses into retirement, to blame themselves for the pressure and insanity, to stay invisible, to feed and house their families, or to seize a niche one step nearer the top of the corporate anthill were suddenly cast out into the cold, not downsized but marginalized, heartless climber and bleeding heart alike, not survivors but casualties, having tumbled from a sup-posedly solid rock of ages right off its flow-charted edge.

> The Euclidean utopia is mapped; it is geometrically organized, with the parts labeled a, a', b: a diagram or model, which social engineers can follow and reproduce. Reproduction, the viral watchword.
>
> — Ursula K. Le Guin

With the aqueduct in place and the oligarchs in firm control, the Valley continued to congeal, grow, and ramify. Lonesome service-men returning from World War II found mates and helped double the population. It takes water to reproduce like this, however, so when the water table fell, the pharaohs reached out for Mono Lake, and the building went on and on.

By the 1960s, the flowering orchards that had made the place famous were all but gone. As growth went supercritical, secret atomic experiments shed their decaying atoms across the Valley, which by 1980 represented the largest deteriorating urban sprawl on the planet. By 1994, aerospace contaminates polluted the aquifer running sluggishly below the industrial parks, shopping centers, aircraft factories, and decaying streets and neighborhoods. The Northridge Earthquake added eleven freeway overpasses unto the ruins. A Mexican man driving on Canoga Avenue toward Calabasas saw Llorona near the wash and swerved into a drainage ditch to avoid her.

The apartment complex behind steel gates painted olive green crouched among shuttered office buildings in the midst of what I later learned was a global capital of pornography: Chatsworth, plat-ted by the San Fernando Valley Improvement Company in 1888. The place had been named after the estate of the Duke of Devonshire the same year Lankershim's son J. B. established Toluca, later renamed Lankershim, later renamed North Hollywood. Somewhere nearby, concealed in what seemed to be ordinary warehouses, Girardian film sets and erotic props hid with the secrecy of urban military laboratories. Owensmouth ran straight south behind my apartment past cracked sidewalks and cinderblock walls like an unforgiven knife slash across a prostitute's cheek. Morning and evening the air smelled of sizzling fat. Film crews had shot part of *Terminator II* just up the street near Plummer.

I was there two weeks when I dreamed about an oncoming rainstorm.

There was just enough time to finish unpacking what was left: books and tattered chairs, an old computer, a mattress, a red Cherokee pipe, a crucifix, and statuettes of Shiva, Buddha, and the Venus of Willendorf I had picked up in LA. A Change of Address for the post office. Phone, electricity, parking, gas, done. I laid down on a small green couch rescued from a dumpster in Calabasas and lit a candle.

As a vast El Niño storm moved in on the world's largest suburb and rain spattered and then pounded on the glass door behind me, a strange salty warmth unknown since childhood began to flow down my neck. Outside, the storm rumbled on, but the salty flow ran almost unabated from night to night until I left the Valley two years later.

Hemmed in by luggage and used furniture, I drove northward on the King's Highway with an old goddess in my pocket, still uncertain of why I had shed what felt like centuries of tears.

Mentored by the Untamed

At first blush, one might think that arriving at long last and after many hardships in the Land of Promise (as California has been characterized since its coastal cliffs were spotted by scurvy-wracked Europeans) would give rise to some sense of gratitude, or at least a pause to appreciate. Yet no sooner have settlers, soldiers, and swindlers disembarked from their vessels, trains, and planes than they set about building over, paving down, and covering up the Golden State's stupendous natural beauty.

In part this might be due to a lingering puritanical dread and hatred of the aesthetic side of life. The American reaction to nature has always revealed an unresolved, fearful ambivalence. We make avid spectators of the once-great outdoors, yet the journals inked by our pioneers refer ominously to what Daniel Boone called "the dark and bloody ground," a diabolical wildness brimming with unknown haunts of sin guarded by mysterious pairs of fire-lit eyes. Incoming Pilgrims waved Bibles and crosses at the shadows lengthening across potentially demonic glades and groves, never suspecting that a deeper darkness already hid within.

Historically speaking, the West's relationship to the natural world has long been that of a conqueror and subjugator, seldom that of a respectful guest. Little wonder people stereotyped as "savage" and "colored"—in other words, earthy—have been so similarly mistreated. California Indian languages contained no word or concept for "ecosystem," but the people who spoke them belonged to the land and sea and knew both well and in fine detail. The rootless newcomers who displaced these dwellers wrote about them with bitter envy thinly veiled as contempt.

Feeling like strangers in a strange land, oncoming wayfarers raised ground-eating surfaces and sky-blotting edifices to wall out the disturbingly alive presences dripping, crawling, and cawing all around them. Such externalized constructs of control work something like the social masks people wear, or like bars in a zoo, locking away the wildness within by hiding its outward signs and shapes. When Father Cyprian Rubio decided to modernize and cleanse the mission church of Buenaventura ("Good Fortune") in 1893, his extensive renovations included whitewashing the walls and painting right over the Indians' original artwork. He missed the arched side door whose Moorish designs had been thought by the Indians to chart the land outside the compound.

"Our people are of the church-going kind," bragged Edbert Newbury in 1876 a year before a drought bankrupted him. "Its concept is slightly snobbish," boasted the Janss Investment Corporation as it laid out Lynn Ranch and The Oaks, "deliberately planned to appeal to highly trained, highly selective, highly paid people." "Selective" may have been an unfortunate choice of word given names like Albertson (who bought Westlake from William Randolph Hearst), Goebel, Adolfo, and Rosenberg. Their master plan sought to domesticate the Conejo Valley as German scientists spirited over after World War II brought their rocketry experiments to Point Mugu.

Yet no matter how much wealth, status, or rebar humans drag into Ventura County, an endemic animal wildness always has the final growl.

Ventura County is not overrun with animals—at least not anymore: an 1866 ordinance banned them from the streets of Ventura, and mushrooming suburbs drove them into the as-yet-untamed hills. But their names and faces do keep showing up here, from the Jungleland lion farm opened by Louis Goebel to groom animals (including MGM's Leo) for Hollywood to wild horses ranging through Simi Valley to Wildwood, a park just west of Conejo ("Rabbit") Valley. The first missile to be test-fired at Point Mugu was named "Loon." In the ultramarine waters that lap between the Channel Islands and the landward shore, many species of porpoise, dolphin, and whale frolic in and out of a full third of Southern California's prolific kelp beds. Profusions of birds land on and take off from the Ventura and Santa Clara Rivers. As a college student I went out in the hills and shot a bird, something I had done before elsewhere; but this time, seeing it still its eyes clenched shut, a wave of pain for the little thing swept through my heart, and I decided never to kill an animal again unless the alternative was starvation.

Often the elements have acted like wild animals: misbehaving earthquakes, fires, and floods like the one that cracked the mission's roof in 1857 and ruptured its aqueduct four years later. Old photographs of the newly built Rincon roadway show heavy surf pounding perilously against the seawall. Raging seas have made use of the Ventura Pier planked up in 1872 to destroy the *Lucy Ann* three years later, the *Crimea* and *Kalorama*, and the oil tanker *Wallace L. Hardison*, named after a Santa Paula oilman and blown to smithereens as it docked. After a quiet spell a salty surge sent the *Coos Bay* right through the pier in 1914, and in 1929 a storm shook the rebuilt pier to pieces.

Even the plants go wild, and not just the columns of waving kelp. The Los Padres National Forest covers 46% of the northern part of a county blessed with more microclimates than any other in California. Deep alluvial deposits from the rising mountains to the north make the county a glory of organic fecundity, with beets and strawberries in Oxnard, lemons and avocados in Santa Clarita, walnuts and oranges almost everywhere, and dry crops where irrigation is not practical. On a visit to the mission bookstore I saw that a branch with a mind of its own had punched its way through a wooden wall.

In a land of so much Artemisian wildness, I suppose it makes sense that my first psychotherapy supervisor's name was Diana and that the second's was Virginia. My first college crush had been Laurel, like the tree. My new bride's name was Ellen, derived from Helen: "Wicker, reed, shoot; torch." Her sister's name, Ramona ("Protecting Hands"), echoed Helen Hunt Jackson's famous heroine whose fictional home could be found nearby in the fields of Rancho Camulos. This Helen had set her novel in California to bring attention to the mistreatment of what remained of its native people.

At CalLutheran College (now University) in tidy Thousand Oaks, my own wildness began to peep from its box when I took literature classes from a man who led me to his office to return a paper I had written. Pressing finger and thumb on his short black mustache, he asked me why I didn't speak up more in his class. This was an invitation rather than a bid for information—his courteous but frank appraisal had informed him of how easily shyness possessed me then—and as our after-class conversations gradually deepened, I learned what it was to be heard without judgments, preconditions, shoulds, or oughts, by a careful listener who leaned back in his chair wholly present. Even his breathing seemed to listen.

What surprised me the most about him I would not understand for years to come. Although dutiful, he did not conform, and although critical, he did not rebel. He simply was, like a rock or a leaf, like a wise animal who knew its way around; and because of that level of comfort with himself, he smilingly refused to be anyone else. In short, he was the first man I had ever met who really accepted himself, including his own refined capacity for wildness.

What is wildness? To a mind that thinks in terms of fences and walls raised against its own impulses, "wild" means "out of control," but that does not ring true for the self-balancing natural world. With the loss of my childhood Lutheran fundamentalism I began to perceive the intrinsic wisdom in wildness, in unchained natural passions allowed to flow themselves to completion. I saw "wild" acting out for what it was: a defense against really sitting down with one's inner promptings and paying heed to them. The bomber, the shooter, the rebel without a cause were not truly wild, they were over-reactive, traumatized, and immature. What they needed (besides to grow up) was to encounter more wildness, not less.

Hermann Hesse was wild, and so was Mary Austin. Shakespeare and Thoreau and Beethoven were wild men. Susan Griffin's *The Eros of Everyday Life* was a wild book. "I have been and still am a seeker," Hesse had written in his novel *Demian*, "but I have ceased to question stars and books: I have begun to listen to the teachings my blood whispers to me."

All this worked deeply on and educated me even after my graduation from college. Out of being well-mentored a desire surfaced to train in psychotherapy, so I eventually went back to school as a graduate student, married, older, somewhat wilder when I allowed it, and inspired by a dream to seek out my birth parents and discover my lost heritage. It was time.

When I called my grandmother after a two-year search for my origins and told her I was Lorna's son, the news fell into a silence that lengthened beyond the interval of surprise I'd expected.

"We were told," she finally replied, "that Lorna's son had died at birth of heart failure," and I could hear the tears in her voice.

Once CalLutheran had consolidated on old farmland left by the Pederson family, Thousand Oaks had found a reputable hook on which to hang. With meadows and prairies pushing in on every side, the town surrounded by so much wildness held onto its conservatism as it grew. Yet the scads of churches, blocky malls, soulless gated tracts in Newbury Park, freshly painted picket fences, manicured street dividers, and giant square Convention Center screening the hills from the freeway could not keep out the presence of the wild.

People not raised in Southern California often look surprised when told how conservative it really is, whether respectable Thousand Oaks, quaint Moorpark, or rather Morecop, that charming capital of police interference with the young, or Simi Valley, home of the Ronald Reagan Library. Some who founded towns in the southland were former Confederates uprooted by the Civil War. Later settlers were "Folks," Louis Adamic's term for Midwesterners riding in by car and train from places like Kansas and Nebraska and Iowa to ease their tuberculosis, read their Bibles, and eat cheap food in cafeterias. Still others were families of servicemen and factory workers displaced by the labors of World War II. Even now revenue from military bases and naval ports bolsters a formidable portion of Ventura County's income.

Regressive, reactionary conservatism has been analyzed as misanthropic, self-divided, authoritarian, power-hungry, intolerant, sexist, racist, aggressive, medieval, and cloaked in rosy denial, but it is seldom recognized as profoundly ecocidal as well. To make a policy of caging or destroying what is wild is no accident. It does not express simple ignorance or lack of education. It betrays a hatred of nature so malevolent and uncontrolled that more than half the plant and animal species in the world are now under threat of extinction

That anyone exhibiting a vested "religious" interest in the end of the world could be allowed to acquire real political or financial power—and this as American election candidates fall over themselves to display what tremendous Christians they are—underlines the pervasive influence and power of ecocidal rage boiling in the unreflective national psyche. Yet no one in the public sphere discusses the prevalence of those impulses of hatred satisfied by crushing a meadow beneath a parking lot. No one points out the basic distrust and paranoia implied by wanting total control over imagined dangers, or how obliterating a hillside also obliterates that much more of one's soul. Objections to such destructiveness are dismissed as politically motivated. To the reactionary mind, however, nature, whether inner or outer, human or nonhuman, is not an ally or mentor, but an adversary.

A core observation of ecofeminism, a socially informed environmental movement that first burgeoned in 1974, is that exploitation of the natural world and oppression of women are both expressions of a will to dominate. Assertions of might and control rely in turn on objectification, which turns the living into things, and a phobic hatred of interdependency, which is one reason why a developer planning to strip mall a meadow always argues for his individual *right* to do so; the community and the land have no say in the matter. Ecofeminists observe that by objectifying women as "closer to nature" and nature as clothed in "feminine" attributes, institutions founded on male privilege extend their control over both.

It makes a macabre and tragic ecopsychological sense, then, that, stationed in a county so determined to leash the elemental and the natural, the mission should be notorious for its mistreatment of girls and women. All the missions observed rigid rules for females, including incarceration, shaming, and the occasional beating; but according to a Native account, priests at Mission Buenaventura regularly copulated with their young charges. One even commanded the girls present to sing loudly to cover up the noise he was making.

To the best of my knowledge, however, no one has argued yet for a parallel between the loss of 80% of the artifacts from the Reagan Library's collection of a hundred thousand and the financial cataclysms that punctuated the second Bush Administration, with foreclosures and bailouts as predictable fallout from the reckless deregulation of credit institutions. "Idiots made me rich," gloated hedge fund manager Andrew Lahde. "God bless America." Aside from numerous belt buckles, the missing items included two that were particularly symbolic, locally and nationally: a hand-made American flag and a figurine of an elephant.

> How few the days are that hold the mind in place, like a tapestry hung on four or five hooks. Especially the day you stop becoming; the day you merely are. I suppose it's when the principles dissolve, and instead of the general gray of what ought to be you begin to see what is. Even the bench by the park seems alive, having held so many actual men. The word "now" is like a bomb through the window, and it ticks.
>
> — Arthur Miller

In the dream a glowing, dark-haired woman confronts me, asks me what the trouble is. I fail to recognize her as Sophia, but I respond:

My marriage is stifling. My job is a nightmare of boredom and bureaucracy. I don't belong where I'm living and don't know where

I'm going. I feel like an animal locked in a cage. It makes me wonder: What has happened to us? Our ancestors worked a few hours a day and spent the rest of it how they chose. And there were men in those days who ran as free as wild horses cantering across the savanna....

She points, and I look down. On my right forearm sits a large circular birthmark akin to one on my birth mother's arm. I've fancied it the head of a bear pointing his nose toward my right hand. In the dream my left hand covers his head.

"Hey Cain," the woman inquires, "why are you covering up your mark?"

Upon graduating I took up the normal routine of a marriage and family therapist intern for two years or so before receiving a phone call from a therapist named Scott who worked in Simi Valley. He had heard I was looking for another internship, but the one he supervised held little interest, he explained, for most of the interns he had spoken with about it.

To some extent therapy training exposes the practitioner to the shadow side of a community. This was how I knew, for example, about the millions in cocaine money pouring through Thousand Oaks. I knew that the highest-paid prostitutes in the county grew up in noteworthy families and often enjoyed the best education and the smartest attorneys available; that an FBI agent who stalked and terrorized his ex-wife would probably never see a day in court; that under a cloud of clichés about democracy and freedom, the government does indeed pay men to quietly assassinate other men in other countries. However—

"Violence," explained Scott, "is one of our best-kept community secrets. On occasion it leaks out, but by and large the public knows nothing about the work I do with the men."

The men?

"Groups of men just out of jail or prison. Ordered into a year of mandatory therapy as a condition of their probation. All arrested for violent crimes. Like to come out and see for yourself?"

"I certainly would."

So I did, and I came away so amazed by his impact on men often given up for hopeless even by therapists that I stayed on for a year of special training. After that I ran groups of my own in two counties for five rewarding and difficult years.

> The drug dealer, the ducking and diving political leader, the wife beater, the chronically "crabby" boss, the "hot shot" junior executive, the unfaithful husband, the company "yes man," the indifferent graduate school adviser, the "holier than thou" minister, the gang member, the father who can never find the time to attend his daughter's school programs, the coach who ridicules his star athletes, the therapist who unconsciously attacks his clients' "shining" and seeks a kind of gray normalcy for them, the yuppie—all these men have something in common. They are all boys pretending to be men. They got that way honestly, because nobody showed them what a mature man is like.
>
> — Robert Moore and Douglas Gillette

"What causes battery?" I was often asked by the curious. Well, batterers cause battery, although our clients included other violent men: bar fighters, gangsters, former Special Forces troopers, the occasional assassin, quite a few rapists, and even a self-medicating psychiatrist. The question implies a determinism, a causal force rather than a series of decisions ignorantly made within a bloodthirsty culture that socializes violence into males. Most of our clients came out of very traditional upbringings. Men frequently protested our lessons on raising children without hitting them by declaring, "My dad beat the holy hell out of me, and it didn't do me any harm"—except of course for blistering self-hatred, numbing out of the body, a violent temper, and ending up in a group for court-referred men. Some clients were mystified by their own violence: "I never, ever, thought I would grow up to act like the men in my family." Part of our work was showing them how aggression, and the aggressor himself, are internalized.

If a culture of ingrained, violent traditionalism provides the keg, what packs it with explosive powder?

Cage a lion long enough and eventually it fights to break free, even if it has to maul a trainer it normally loves. Something similar is true for us as well. Cage human nature in constant admonitions to be good, ring it about with bars of enforced respectability, ram decency and morality and all Ten Commandments down its throat, and make it passively obey and bow and scrape and surrender, and violence eventually bursts forth as a predictable result. As analyst Janet O. Dallett says in her book *Listening to the Rhino*, "Violence is the human spirit's protest against the enforcement of more goodness than it can stomach." One lit match on the wrong day and the smiling powder keg who compliments his coworkers and helps old ladies take out the trash levels half a well-tended neighborhood.

Another consistent pattern I witnessed in those years had to do with the pervasiveness of emotional immaturity in our clients. Some had grown up with at least a modicum of love and affection from their mothers, and many with a great deal more, but not one of the hundreds of men I counseled had enjoyed the crackling warm presence of a psychologically vital father figure. Not one! The key term here is "father figure." The majority of domestic perpetrators I saw came out of intact nuclear families officially headed by a father. What counted early on, however, was whether loving fatherly energies were available regardless of who they came from, whether a birth father, stepfather, or fatherly friend or mentor. Ultimately, our men were here because no one had ever shown them how to hold their fire and tend their wildness.

"I have a question for the group," I said after a morning of confrontation with three recalcitrant members had deepened into a discussion about the wounds that men bear. "I want you to raise your hand if you truly, honestly feel that your father was available when you were growing up in the ways you really needed him to be. I don't mean always available, I mean usually. Hands up."

Not a single man raised his hand.

After a thunderstruck moment, everyone began to weep silently.

On a very low day I parked my car, trudged through the parking lot, and went on up the four concrete steps to our apartment. Newly planted blue and yellow ornamental flowers bloomed within the cement-ringed beds set aside for them. Matching banners flapped overhead like captured battle standards. I opened the door and shuffled in. My eyes were fixed on the tan carpet....

.....and fell upon an enormous pair of shoes. I looked up slowly. The shoes were attached to a long pair of legs that belonged to wide hips set below a stout torso topped by a sandy-haired head more than six feet off the ground. The head was grinning. My mouth fell open.

I had met him once before after contacting my birth families. I took two steps forward and threw my arms around him, deciding right then that we'd skip the DNA test.

Not that I looked much like him, except perhaps in profile. He stood almost a foot taller, lighter-skinned and thinner-haired. My hair was browner, thicker, and wavier, like my mother's. Where his face looked like a cross between Dick Van Dyke and John Wayne, mine was a twin to my maternal grandfather's. I had met that grandfather a few months before his death and regretted not having met him sooner.

"No news from your mother?" my father asked while pouring Chianti.

"No. She won't respond at all. The only one who won't."

"That's too bad. On the other hand, though, the hell with it if we like each other. Here's to us."

"To us."

It was subtler, this likeness between my father and I, yet easily confirmed even without the similarity of our voices. We should not have looked alike, and yet we did. Family and friends said afterward that so akin were our mannerisms and temperament and ways of speaking that seeing us talk together for even a moment was like watching two differently wrought lamps burning with the same flame.

We sat up half the night before he talked to me about the war.

He had been a Marine in Korea in some of the heaviest fighting.

("You can always tell a Marine," he'd joked when we met, "but not much.") His eyes looked inside as he spoke. His presence filled the room with a quiet electric intensity I would come to know as characteristic of him. In such moments a compass needle would have swung about to point at him. No, I will not reveal what he told me; it was his tale to unfold, for my ears alone, and it harrowed up my soul to hear what he had been through.

When the voice so like my own stopped speaking, we shared another silence together. Then:

"A question?"

"Yes?"

"Are you really getting up first thing and making that syrupy Tahitian coffee you learned about overseas?"

He chuckled. "I really am."

He asked me then for a bit of my own history, so I gave him some. Despite the hour he listened intently as I spoke. A quirky half-smile flickered across his lips now and then. I knew that smile.

When I got as far as high school and being picked on by a bully, he asked, "What did you do?"

"I didn't do or say anything at first. When it built up to where I'd had enough, I knocked him out one day at lunch and set fire to the school. Fortunately they put it out in time."

He nodded. "Runs in the family."

I cracked open my eyes at eleven the next morning. When I finally staggered to the kitchen, yawning and blinking, he was already seated at the breakfast table, smiling at me and sipping syrupy coffee.

"You were never in combat?" he asked as we walked together later, shoulder to shoulder, our eyes on the ground, heads down, hands at our sides. I had wondered where I acquired that mannerism. "You don't look military at first glance, but something about you..."

"Not this time around," I told the man I'd quickly grown fond of and was unsure I would see again soon. "Danger yes, combat no. But somehow I feel at war, have felt so for as long as I can remember."

"What sort of war?"

"I wish I knew. It's like my roots were before I met you: unknown, but giving off a sense of something just beyond my understanding....something to do with history, with identity, with things long past and things I haven't done yet. Things that happened here long ago. What I have not understood...but before I leave this earth, I will."

I could feel his mood sadden in empathy. He sighed.

I stopped and looked up at him, willing him to understand this about me in our too-brief time together. Unconsciously I had assumed the military posture known as parade rest.

"You bear scars of a kind I hope I will never know," I told him. "Yet I too am a soldier, if not of 'Truth' or patriotism or save-the-world idealism. I don't think the world as we know it can be 'saved' in its present form."

He nodded. "Then..."

"In some way I can't explain just yet, I know that I'm simply a soldier of Time." The certainty in the saying of it now that I had found the words set me trembling. "I'm a foot-weary grunt on a long, long campaign. And my campaign never ends."

In Ventura I paused to consider the bulky Junípero Serra monument and Camino Real bell in front of the palm-treed City Hall. He faced left as though looking back over his trail, his left hand clenched around a staff. How would he feel about all that had developed out of his efforts in Alta California? We stood one hundred and seventy-nine miles north of Mission San Diego.

At Buenaventura Mission a gift shop on East Main admits the patron to the mission museum. What's left of the mission itself contains a wagon wheel, a bell tower striped like the stack at Mandalay, and what looks like a sundial altered—altared?—to serve as a drinking fountain. Dusty ruins of Chumash houses demolished in 1787 lay scattered and broken just up the street. Raising my head, I saw whitewashed Spanish Colonial apartments hunched over a wrecked adobe factory. Across the busy street homeless men lay face-up in the park or curled sideways on dirty blankets. All in brilliant sunshine reflecting off white surfaces.

My gaze ran along the brown beams crossing the white facade. NO ONE ADMITTED *Beyond This Point:* BURGLAR ALARM. A bronze eagle clutched a globe in its claws. A cello hidden by the "Mission Indians" had been excavated and put on display. The chandeliers resembled upturned wooden spiders. PLEASE DO NOT TOUCH THE CONFESSIONAL.

Maybe Freud was right about what we know as "civilization": one vast colonization of wildness by the superego. I was reminded by all this of the gated sterility of an apartment complex newly stamped upon the landscape in Newbury Park. The spotless whiteness, the perfect lines, the well-tended cleanness, everything in its place and locked down tight. Watchful security patrols in ironed uniforms made sure the neophyte residents stayed in line. Someday, if nothing were done to prevent it, the entire county would feel condemned to that kind of perfectionism. All things considered, it amounted to a perfect cage for making the animal within yearn to smash something.

A large painting of a king and queen at a pageant hung on the gift shop's west wall. Within an enclosed garden, King Solomon intended marriage to the red-and-blue-robed Shulamite. The nameless woman was black like Calafia in legend if not in this depiction. She had dreamed accurately of her future abandonment by the master of the harem and taken steps to escape her abductor, with an outcome far happier than that of spurned Llorona. Blessed are the undomesticated, for they shall inherit what's left of the untamed earth. Good fortune!

A cycle of Cahuilla creation songs tells us that the ancestors of us all melted into being from out of the world itself.

At first they were not human and had no hands, but by transforming into deer, birds, and other animals, looking through their eyes and taking on their roles, the ancestors acquired appendages and, gradually, their humanity as well as their intimate knowledge of their surroundings. This is why it is said that humans learned the handling of tools and the singing of songs from their animal kindred and from the all-giving world, and why an eternal estrangement of person from world is absent from Cahuilla cosmology.

On an overcast summer day I forsook my apartment and the misty streetlamps along Vineyard Avenue in Oxnard and trucked my sea kayak to the beach near Mandalay Bay. A light fog rolled in as I prepared myself. No matter. I wouldn't go far, and anyway my survival gear included a waterproof compass. I watched waves crest and break.

More than a thousand dolphins regularly swim the coast along San Diego, Orange, Los Angeles, Ventura, and Santa Barbara counties. I had yet to see even one up close. The Chumash believed that the very presence of dolphins somehow protected the world. The cold sea breeze made me shiver.

"Time to go," I told a curious little girl standing off to one side, and with that I ran into the surf, boarded my boat, and paddled past the breakers.

It's impossible to describe the sense of well-being out on the water and away from all the noise and smog. In no hurry to go anywhere, I drifted and watched the sailboats go by. Swooping pelicans scanned the sea for fish. A seal poked up his head and vanished.

I was thinking about surfing my boat in when a cloud of birds gathered off the starboard bow. Probably nothing, perhaps a passing school of fish. I moved in anyway, quietly slipping the paddle blades through the water to avoid scaring the flock.

I turned my head at a splash behind me and saw nothing; turning back, I caught sight of a plume drifting skyward. A bird had likely raised it, what with so many plunging into the sea in search of food.

Then there echoed forth a deep exhalation, and a dozen curved fins stood up twenty feet in front of me. I gaped.

The fins came on, and more ash-colored, smiling foreheads than I had ever seen in one place slipped silently forward. Ten feet.

A single thought flashed across my awareness then: *I should get out of the way!* Too late.

Unperturbed, the entire pod passed under me and surfaced, blowing, just behind me. I turned. Even swimming lazily they went rapidly, arching and subsiding, arching and subsiding, almost seeming a part of the sea itself.

The kayak fairly danced over the distance as I dug into the brine to catch up and see what they would do. The courteous swimmers parted like a curtain before me and closed around me.

> If the secret of the plant is growth and place, then the secret of wild animals is embodiment and passage, as though the creature were itself a gesture or a speaking.
>
> — Paul Shepard

For more than an hour I paddled at speed with swooping dolphins on either side of me as we made our way up the coast. After an unsuccessful attempt to close with one of them I respected the small stretch of water they kept between us. It was clear that they didn't mind me accompanying them so long as I followed the rules.

My reverie deepened. An astronaut once wrote that he never understood "round" until he saw the Earth from space. Watching the dolphins fly over and under their liquid medium, luminous foam running off their rounded backs, I realized that I had never before comprehended the word "grace." What was that phrase Bachelard used to describe the movements of the dreaming spirit? "Lightness of being." If angels could swim, they would surely flutter and bend like these sensual beasts, these divine gamesters, these elegant and pliable free associations of God. May they go on protecting the world.

The Santa Barbara Barrier

Frank Herbert, late author of the *Dune* science fiction series inspired in part by conversations with an Indian friend and in part by ecological devastation in Tacoma, also wrote a novel called *The Santaroga Barrier* in which psychologist Gilbert Dasein is hired by a marketing firm to infiltrate Santaroga, an odd little town in California. His mission is to find out why its stubborn residents refuse to buy any products manufactured beyond the city limits.

From the moment Dasein arrives, everyone seems to realize he's from out of town despite his efforts to blend in. Although polite in manner, Santarogans don't like strangers, and they all share a kind of citywide collective unconscious primed to repel potential threats. The hostility of the group organism against outsiders manifests as loose floorboards in Dasein's way, innocently dangerous strips of carpet that trip him, and even cars careening toward him for no identifiable reason. And all the while, the amused citizens maintain their surface friendliness.

There is no town called Santaroga in California, but no sooner did I alight in Santa Barbara, newly divorced and ready to direct a counseling agency, than greetings from all sides—a neighbor, a coworker, the clerk bagging my groceries, a man selling newspapers—invariably posed the same question, over and over: How long had I been in town? I talked and dressed no differently from anyone else. Nevertheless. At a State Street bookstore counter, in a natural foods café in Goleta, in a breezy Stearns Wharf wine shop, at the Daily Grind, where I drank hazelnut coffee and watched the sun come up, "How long have you been in Santa Barbara? How do you like it here? Planning to stay long?" I was glad I wasn't a spy.

To some extent this made sense. I could usually recognize someone raised in San Diego. A surprising openness announces the expressions and gestures of people from my hometown. They exhibit an outgoing informality of a kind I had not entirely suppressed after living in other counties. At times I could tell where in the county somebody hied from. "East County, huh? The chew and boots and T-shirt give you away." Or, "Artistic dress. Buy it in La Jolla?"

But never had I lived in a place where my status as newcomer felt so exposed to public view.

"I'm writing you a ticket," said the motorcycle officer through lips that scarcely moved, "because you ignored the sign."

"Which sign?"

State Street, Santa Barbara's main thoroughfare, is a crowded place, particularly on weekdays, and its shop- and cafe-lined downtown segment is not wide enough for left-turn lanes. This is because the street and many of its buildings preceded the automobile. The sign now brought to my attention declared that between certain hours on certain days, left turns of the type I had just made were prohibited.

"Sorry. I'm new to Santa Barbara"—he nodded abruptly, having known it before I rolled down the window—"and have never seen a sign like that before. I have a clean driving record, too." I loosened my necktie.

"Where are you headed?" he asked, continuing to write.

"The Superior Court, to meet with some of the judges on behalf of my clients." I tried to tell him about my new job running therapy groups for violent offenders. He refused to make eye contact.

"Sign here, please. Your signature does not constitute an agreement with the citation." Which stamped my first moving violation, ever, upon my formerly perfect record.

Back at work a sympathetic colleague asked, "Did you tell him who you are and what you do?"

"Yes. It made no difference."

"Maybe a relative of his is being forced to attend one of your groups."

Junípero Serra gets no official credit for opening Mission Santa Barbara on a swamp-encircled hill north of Ventura—where kindly Chumash had carried him literally on their backs one high tide—because Governor Neve postponed the event until Friar Lasuén completed the founding in 1786 on the feast day of Saint Barbara, after which a rainy winter held off construction even longer. Even so, Serra had performed the opening rituals before becoming the Santa Barbara Barrier's first known victim and heading north in disappointment for Carmel.

Seen from an exclusively human perspective, these first Californian places to be colonized received their names because the padres and soldiers entered them on or near certain religious observance days, yet the names invariably refract some sly glint of the spirit, essence, or future of the locale. Santa Barbara, where the Santa Ynez Mountains now hold white "castles" looking down upon the city, was named after a fourth-century saint locked up in a white tower by her wealthy father Dioscorus to stop her from joining the people down below. Expensive garments, efficient servants, wise tutors, a new bathhouse: none of it dampened her desire to be of service beyond her confinement. One telling has her ordering a window (three windows in some accounts) cut into the tower wall; in another, her prayers opened a hole in the wall so she could escape and hide in a gorge, much like neophytes escaping the local mission hid out in Mission Canyon. Some say her father cut her head off and was incinerated by a bolt of lightning; others, that the lightning saved her life by blasting him first; but however it was, believers looked to St. Barbara as patron of artillery and high explosives. Long before Santa Barbara's founding, its two-tower mission, or Canon Perdido's naming after a fieldpiece lost in the city, paintings of the saint featured towers, cannons, and palm fronds.

Santa Barbara possesses the fabled loveliness of her namesake, but also the restraint imposed by the local wardens of uniformity. In 1851, Alpheus Thompson's house was burned down for deviating from the local adobe style. Today, gazing seaward from the Riviera, the eye cannot evade the waves of whitewashed walls and red tile roofs. This "Mission" architecture, in actuality a cement-surfaced blend of Beaux-Arts, Japanese, Spanish-Moorish, and Chamber of Commerce mixed together by Arthur Page Brown, architect to millionaires, invaded the city in 1884 when Brown designed homes on Garden Street. His popularization of this style at the 1893 World Columbian Exposition in Chicago encouraged its imitation throughout California. In 1922, the powerful Community Arts Association organized a planning division to make over Santa Barbara into a "City of Spain" rather than of California, and Mission-style buildings have been the standard ever since.

As in other mission towns, the elements had something to say about the pretentious colonial architecture. The 1812 earthquake near Ventura destroyed missions all over the state, including Santa Barbara's. The second tower raised in 1831 fell a year later, was rebuilt, and was damaged by the 1925 earthquake. A storm tore off the face of the presidio. The face of the mission chapel cracked and flaked, chemically eaten away from within until expensively and painstakingly restored.

By 1870, the town once attended by vessels with names like Favorita and Princessa began to eject people in groups, particularly harried Mexicans and Chinese. As Joseph Johnson, chief editor of the local Press, boosted Santa Barbara as a seaside health resort and Stearns erected his new wooden wharf, and as the city council prohibited traditional Mexican performances, Californio influence was confined to a single ward. By 1880, not one Mexican name appeared on the list of county offices, although plenty showed up in the vigilant Press in connection with petty crimes.

Californios who did not leave in disgust huddled together in El Pueblo Viejo, a compartment of neighborhoods near the ruins of the old presidio. Some found work aloft in the Butler Belt as wealthy Americanos took to the hills. By the 1920s, the KKK paraded proudly through the streets, celebrants dressed up once a year in Spanish costumes covered with flashing sequins, a second barrio circled the noisy Southern Pacific freight yard, and the Arlington Hotel, rebuilt after burning down, housed two large bell towers.

The force of the Barrier seems to decrease as distance from the city increases. During World War II the military and its industries did not occupy Santa Barbara as heavily as towns like San Diego or Los Angeles, but it did install Vandenberg Air Force Base and its rocketry up in the north county near grassy Lompoc, a city not far from Santa Maria, named after the vessel Columbus wrecked on Christmas. The remains of Mission La Purisima Concepcion doze near Lompoc as well; Mission Santa Ines, site of the hard-fought Chumash revolt of 1824, casts its long rectangular shadow near Solvang. Oil production in this part of the county boosted little towns like Orcutt. Further south, the Barbara's towers of drilling platforms received women's names when first raised along the otherwise scenic coast to pump inflammable crude.

The counseling agency I directed clung precariously to a bend along State Street. From my office window I could see cars and pedestrians and quaint little western-style storefronts. Businesses in the city sometimes hired contractors to give the sides of buildings the appearance of cracked whitewash revealing fake adobe underneath. The mission mythologem of romantic glory days and warm, lazy nights was still hanging on like cheap perfume spilled on sun-soaked rawhide.

To my left: a phone, not ringing. To my right: two expressionless police officers guarding the door. Behind me: a slumped-over client verified suicidal. Above my desk: a portrait of Vancouver's *Discovery* and two other vessels creeping into the harbor a few miles south of State Street. That was in 1792. Like Serra, Vancouver had not stayed long, bounced away perhaps by the Santa Barbara Barrier.

The phone was still not ringing, and I wished it would. The client was silent. The police were not happy. They had better things to do than to wait for me to receive a call. I had no choice but to wait, though, because a social worker had canceled the ambulance summoned to transport the client to the hospital. So I told jokes to amuse the police—"You guys ever think 'mental health' could be this insane?"—until the phone finally rang and I asked the caller to reauthorize the ambulance or provide the wheels herself. She did not want to do either until an offhand remark about the officers waiting so patiently in my office hinted gently at the correct course of action. "I'll be right there."

At any given time I oversaw the progress of three hundred convicted perpetrators of violence, male and female, nearly all of whom had done jail time. I also trained interns and ran some of the men's and women's therapy groups. Other responsibilities included appearing in court, showing up at fund-raisers in a suit and tie, falling behind on client assessment appointments, and talking the occasional maniac out of murdering his family with his at-home arsenal. A depressed, khaki-jacketed man who darkened our door one Christmas Eve in lieu of shooting his wife flowered into one of our wisest and most active group participants, Saint Barbara's gunpowder blessings be upon him.

The part of the job I came to hate was the weekly courtroom visit. For this I had to sit in front of the tall lacquered bench and give oral reports to the judge on each program participant brought forward for the reckoning. Fortunately, the judge who normally oversaw this caseload took a personal, though necessarily brief, interest in the judged. Those working hard to learn from the program and stay out of trouble received her praise and encouragement. Those who fell short were either chastised or, depending on the offense, handcuffed in court by guards with unbuckled holsters and walked off to jail before a roomful of silent onlookers.

The quality of mercy depended strictly on the judge. Many tried to make fair decisions and clearly did not enjoy having someone jailed. A few had no time or patience for whichever "criminal" was brought before them, and on one occasion a happily expectant client with a sterling record of attendance and participation was frogmarched off under harsh white lights to the Graybar Hotel for some unpaid fine. Outside the courtroom, still other judgments imposed life-changing absolutes. Clients convicted on a felony charge almost never returned to their old careers. With the reactionary paradigm of punishment dominant throughout American culture, few employers were willing to give a former Dioscorus a chance to prove he had indeed outgrown his former self.

All clients had to pay a fee for treatment that many could not afford. No public funds covered treatment for perpetrators, not even in a place as flush as dynastic Santa Barbara. Probably the majority of our clients should have been attending a prepaid substance abuse program while receiving group and individual psychotherapy, but no funding could be found for that either. As million-dollar yachts floated off East Beach, anguished people desperate for a second chance lived in the streets until rolled up by the police. Some were prostitutes and peddlers doing what they could to survive. Others did not survive.

It was no surprise, then, when my boss confronted me one day about why I wasn't leaning on a destitute addict behind on her fee payments. A finger tapped a column on the freshly printed spreadsheet of the type I had left the corporate world to evade.

"She's dead," I said.

When we find ourselves inside a repeating story, sooner or later we play all the parts. Born into fabled La Llorona's tale as a child declared dead at birth by a mother named Lorna, I've also felt at times that her sorrow was my own. At other times I've identified more with her departing lover.

A similar dynamic animates the story or "myth" of a place, where all its characters and major events take the local stage and reenact the play symbolically.

In the Barbara story we meet the educators who teach her, the rich father who confines her, the people down below who need her gentle hands. Barbara herself, reputed to be a just and powerful healer, could be thought of as a hidden treasure yearning to be found and brought out into the open.

Oil has been a questionable find, especially when set fire to, with the dire climatic consequences of our internal combustions externalized, but the motif of hidden treasure has taken many forms around Santa Barbara County. One of its grimmest involved a young woman named Barbara abused at the mission by the brutal and lascivious Father Jimenez. In 1881, Giovani Trabucco boasted about his hidden wealth over too many drinks at the tavern, after which he was found stabbed next to a bag containing $650 in gold. Solvang, Los Pinos, Ranger Peak, Aliso Ranch, Veronica Springs, the Santa Ynez River, the San Marcos Pass, and the Solomon Mountain have all been the focus at one time or another of buried treasure speculations.

Llorona showed up in 1835 when the supply vessel *Peor de Nada* discovered an Indian woman on San Nicolas Island. She was looking for her missing child. Located again without the child in 1853, she moved into the center of a legend in which she halted a ship-threatening storm. Wearing black since her husband's assassination (he was the last commander of the presidio), Cipriana Llanos de Flores gave a poverty-stricken mother in need of a skirt the astonishing gift of the Mexican colors hidden since the American takeover in 1846. That was the year the invading John Fremont claimed credit for the peace plan he offered the Californios, but this diplomatic treasure was actually conceived by Barnarda Ruiz of Santa Barbara.

Just south of the city and its palm trees perches Summerland, whose name in 1897 was a euphemism for the World Beyond. Henry Lafayette Williams had started up a spiritualist colony there but switched to oil drilling once crude was seen bubbling darkly from the mustard-covered ground. A local rumor has it that his restless spirit still inhabits the Big Yellow House. Another maintains that he fell headlong into one of his own oil wells—being drunk by the milk shake one might say—and got to the underworld quicker than he expected.

Next door is Carpinteria, named from the indigenous boat carpentry witnessed by incoming Spaniards. Of Carpinteria's spiritual significance a Chumash tale tells us that

> The first Chumash people were created on Limu (Santa Cruz Island). They were made from the seeds of a Magic Plant by the Earth Goddess

Hutash. Hutash was married to the Sky Snake, the Milky Way. He could spit lightning bolts. One of them gave the people fire.

When Limu got crowded, Hutash decided that some of the people had to move. So she created a rainbow bridge that connected the island to the hills above Carpinteria. The people were instructed to walk this bridge without looking down. Some did look down, though, and they dropped into the sea. Pitying them, Hutash turned them into dolphins, which is why the Chumash speak about dolphins as sisters and brothers.

From three hundred and fifty miles up the coast, San Francisco always keeps one pylon planted back in the gold miner days, and sometimes more than one, with trolley stops bridging legendary points between the then and the now. San Diego lives out the fifties, whereas Santa Cruz plays the sixties and seventies over and over and over again. Los Angeles refuses to believe it's been invented yet. But Carpinteria is locked out of time. During the four years I attended graduate school there I seldom beheld an accurately set clock, and on one frantic walk to the train station—running late and unable to find a shuttle—I stumbled past no fewer than six wrongly set timepieces glancing smugly out of restaurants and boutiques fronting Linden Avenue. It would not have surprised me if Rod Serling had stepped out from behind a palm tree: "Picture a man wheeling a suitcase...."

Carpinteria is home to a school up in the hills. Pacifica Graduate Institute was founded in the 1970s "For the Sake of Tending the Soul of the World" with graduate studies in depth psychology and a phenomenological focus on the Other World of the unconscious (or as Jungian analyst James Hillman prefers, "the imaginal," which sounds more like a process than an attic). The road running by the campus is Lambert, the last name of the French philosopher and mathematician who coined the word "phenomenology." Instructors inside the school's white walls are worthy of those who educated Barbara.

Does the hidden treasure ever come down from the ivory tower? Now and again it does, for the social tower wall of the Santa Barbara Barrier remains subject to fluctuation. At its conscious best it prevents harmful influences from entering, such as heavy industries which have set up shop in nearby Goleta. At its unconscious worst the Barrier rigidifies into an impermeable gate guarded by a members-only mentality: Sophia ringed about by powerful archons.

In 1872, the mission garden was still off limits to anyone but true believers and truer blue bloods. The mayor's niece stole inside but was discovered, the gate by which she entered ordered sealed. Nevertheless, more breaches were in the offing, first by royalty—Princess Louise in 1882, Queen Elizabeth in 1919—then by daylight commoners coming through by 1959. The mission itself underwent a series of openings, including renovation to fit it for public services, welcoming of school boarders, expansion of the archive library, vegetables growing in the old cemetery, barriers lowered and removed. A door appeared in the sacristy's south wall. The west church door was enlarged and provided with a window.

In matters therapeutic I felt at home, but in castles and courtrooms I did not. If the judge didn't like me and the castle coterie remained unimpressed with a man who had clearly never played a game of polo in his life, it didn't matter how many men I talked out of acts of do-it-yourself terrorism. The forms must be observed.

Mythologically understood, a nightmare of retreating from a wall of water rushing in from the bay where Vancouver had visited and departed suggested invisible Poseidon, mighty bearer of the archetypal turbulence of nature sending me fleeing imaginally for my life. The next day I noticed a tattoo in the shape of a trident on the back of the right hand of the intern I was training. He would be the last I would train there. Some dream images will not stay in dreams.

Calling an old friend in San Diego, I told him of my unaccountable fear that I would soon be unemployed.

He thought for a moment, then asked a question I would never have expected.

"Isn't it time you came home?"

Maybe it had been my failure to schmooze the leading citizens throwing those expensive hillside parties I'd been ordered to attend. Maybe it was the mythological material I included in the curriculums, and which clients engaged with much more interest than the usual anger-bandaid stuff. Or maybe, just maybe, the Santa Barbara Barrier was primed now to expel me, a foreign element too long at large in the community immune system. But why? Would I go on being pushed by imaginal tidal waves on the backs of the steeds of roused Poseidon? Would I ever understand how California thought?

They were sorry, they said. It was regrettable, they said. I was a fine clinician, but it just wasn't working out. Nor could I say goodbye to my clients—against the rules. Here was my final paycheck.

I took it.

Did I have an address at which I could be reached, just in case?

Yes. I was heading down to San Diego. I had been gone for eighteen years. I would be staying there with an old friend. Here's the address.

Good luck on your journey.

It was only when a book fell off the shelf and onto my head that I began to understand the story I was in. Crouching in the room my friend had made available for me, I picked up the book and turned it over as my eyes went wide.

It was, of course, *The Odyssey*.

It would seem that Poseidon is no stranger to the waters off Point Conception.

Cabrillo had noticed the vicious crosscurrents on his way by Point Arguella, its name bestowed later by wandering Vancouver with a nod to Monterey's commandant. Nearby Honda's name means "deep trail," a fitting description of "the Graveyard of the Pacific." *Edith* (1849), *Yankee Blade* (1854), *Anna Lyle* (1876), *Santa Rosa* (1911), and *Harvard* (1931) all went aground or sank here where warm waters mix with cold. 1923 saw seven destroyers of Squadron Eleven smashed into the rocks as a storm reversed the tricky sea currents. On land, a train paralleling Portolá's travel route north-ward derailed in 1907.

I walked slowly among lumps of dark, sea-washed stone. Nowhere else had I felt so heavy. A large kite spun out of the sky.

That the ancient Chumash believed this place, which they called Humqaq, to be the Western Gate for souls heading into the after-life—a metaphysical portal in the Santa Barbara Barrier as it were—was disputed by a 1997 article written by an archeologist and an anthropologist. The article, which was funded with a grant by an aerospace industry pushing for a California Commercial Spaceport near Point Conception, maintains that only a small band of tradi-tionalist Chumash ever held that place as sacred—and that they weren't truly Chumash at all.

In addition to offending many Chumash, resurrecting the old "divide and conquer" strategy by marginalizing one Native group as anti-progressives, and administering a bitter taste of "here we go again" in many Native people who read it, the article ignored a forceful reminder of the power of lore and place: those hulks bathed in the swirling currents of a portal through which so many lost sailors' souls had flown from earthly life.

> It's only water
> In a stranger's tear
> Looks are deceptive
> But distinctions are clear.....
> There's safety in numbers
> When you learn to divide
> How can we be in
> If there is no outside?
> — Peter Gabriel, "Not One of Us"

Bright white lights shone on the other side of my eyelids. I opened them and squeezed them shut again. Afterimage of three police uniforms aiming three flashlights directly into my face.

"Sir, what are you doing here?"

"Sleeping out under the stars."

"Why?"

"I couldn't afford a hotel."

"Why not?"

"I'm unemployed."

"Let's see some ID."

I handed them my driver's license and asked them to get the lights out of my face.

"This says you live in Escondido."

"That's right."

"What's your business in Carpinteria?"

"I go to school here. Used to live and work here, too."

"Sir, it's against the law to park out here and sleep."

"I didn't know. There aren't any signs posted."

"Get out of the truck slowly. Keep your hands in sight."

An easy thing to do while bathed in a circle of light. I pushed back the edge of my sleeping bag and climbed out of the truck bed.

"Got any weapons on you?"

"No."

"Any drugs or alcohol?"

"No." I had sipped some wine with dinner, but I wasn't telling them that. "And I still can't see."

The light swerved away, and I found myself confronted by what William Hurt might have looked like in his early thirties. Radios chattered on the evening air. Once out of the warm sleeping bag my bare chest was chilled by the sharp Aeolian wind. Good thing I'd gone to sleep with my jeans on.

"Put your hands behind your back."

I did so, shaking my head. It would be an intimidation approach, then. My work with bullies and perpetrators had familiarized me long ago with this psychology.

Hands, not metal, gathered my wrists together.

"Mr. Chalquist, we're going to give you a choice. You can either take a ride to jail or get out of Carpinteria." I almost chuckled. I'd be back again tomorrow for class, and if any police harassed me I would file a very noisy lawsuit.

As my hands were released I reflected that, had my skin been of richer color, I'd likely have been on my way already to enjoying the local guest quarters. I had seen that before, too.

Crunching sounds on the pavement as the officers walked back to their cars.

I drove to Ventura and parked by the sea.

When dawn touched the sky with fingertips of rose, I woke up in my front seat with a cramp in my neck and a parking citation stuck to my windshield.

Of the two missions in the north county, Santa Ines near the Danish fantasy town of Solvang is the most intact in the sense of being the most successfully museumized.

Clouds in the distances beyond a line of spindly wet cotton-woods curled over the range of hills behind the tan walls of the mission. Broken stone mills lay out front in a small plot framed by cacti and agave plants. I entered the long church and walked beneath white gabled beams. Here and there sat worshipers in long pews of darkened hardwood below rounded arch windows cut high in the walls. A Saint Agnes in a niche in the altar was said to have been fashioned by Chumash neophytes. I went outside, passing by pillars along the outer hall. Squared hedges guarding the three-tiered fountain formed a leafy Moorish star.

A sign in the garden informed me that because the Indian girl Pasquala had warned Padre Francisco Xavier in time—"Padre, Padre, war, war"—he was able to organize a defense against a "senseless and most destructive raid" on the mission. Some of her own Tulares (said the sign) from the Central Valley had killed her father for some unstated reason as he worked the mission vineyard, after which the senseless raiders carried her and her mother into captivity. She escaped her people somehow and "ran wildly praying" to warn the faithful of the attack.

The only believable part of this story was that the girl died soon after of a fever. How often the innocent succumb. "It is said that she is buried in the Mission Church," but without the memorial of a gravestone.

An image of Mary stood with hands pressed together in bene-
diction among candles and poinsettias placed within a brickwork
grotto framed with vine-wrapped lumber. What was she thinking
about, I wondered. Her pregnancy, perhaps; a blue sash hung high
about her waist. I walked under a thin metal arch supported by two
cube-shaped pillars and went downhill onto a dirt path. On either
side, sunk into small piles of concrete embedded with round stones,
life-sized wooden crosses marked the fourteen Stations. Each stood
at the foot of square enclosures that reminded the Californian eye,
irresistibly, of parking spaces. Red paint splashed on bases and arms
commemorated the sacrifice of the Lamb of God. At the station of
"Jesus condemned to death," a resigned figure in white was led off
below a rounded arch to the slaughter that awaited him, another
innocent slain by the forces of empire. On my way back to the car,
as I passed a chunk of archway, one of the original twenty-two
ranged around the quadrangle, it occurred to me that what Jesus
had said about praise also applied to sorrow: silence it when innocence is crucified and the very stones cry out.

At Mission La Purisima Concepcion, roughly twenty miles west
of Mission Ines, I walked below a long pink wall and bell tower sitting next to the usual white chapel. Beyond the wooden bridge,
beside the dirt road, and upon the glowing grass was a sheep pen.
After glancing at the usual mission paraphernalia—workshop,
loom, spinning wheel, Indian hut replica, octagonal fountain, square
pillars of white brick—I entered a doorway and saw a cemetery of
grass but no markers. At least it hadn't been paved over. The church
was empty except for an altar, some lamps, the Stations on the
walls, and makeshift wooden benches that loaned the whitewashed
interior the look and feel of an abandoned depot. Cluckings of
chickens and neighings of horses drifted in through the arched
doorway. At the back of the church, in the shadows under a
decrepit staircase, the walls were painted with uncanny, fault-like
designs resembling unhealed compound fractures trying to tear
themselves open.

"Move slowly," advised Neda DeMayo in a low tone, "and don't stare at them. They see animals with eyes at the front of the face as predators. A few steps, stop, look away. Step, stop, look away." The group of eight shuffled up the hill with simulated casualness. Long stalks of grass bent under our feet as we approached a curious herd of horses at an oblique angle. Ears pricked up at our approach. We stopped, just a band of fellow creatures sharing a woody slope.

It had been more than a year since the Barrier and Poseidon had joined efforts to propel me back to San Diego County. During that time I had gradually realized how deaf I had been to the language and character of Santa Barbara. To me it had been a pretty seaside place to live and work and occasionally play. Only after I left had I begun to take her seriously as a being in her own right, with her own style of expression and need for appreciation.

Horses were introduced into North America by conquistadors who favored the Arabians and Andalusians first ridden into Spain during the long Islamic occupation. As Indians were massacred or locked up on reservations, their herds of horses ran wild over the continent until two million mustangs roamed the American and Mexican west by the 1860s.

The Bureau of Land Management claims that if left unchecked, wild horse and burro populations would swell so greatly that forage on public ranges would virtually vanish, threatening not only livestock but the horses themselves. Since 1971, the BLM has collected a hundred and fifty-nine thousand wild horses, with a quarter of them never emerging from the holding facilities. The wild horse population in the U.S. is now at its lowest point ever.

Horses can no more stand confinement than Saint Barbara could. Neda, whose name means "sanctuary," sets them free to roam at her Lompoc ranch Return to Freedom.

I had ridden horses, groomed them, picked their hooves clean and wrapped their legs, visited horses in barns and in stables, and learned to ride them well enough to stay upright in an English saddle, but I had never seen a wild horse in person. Contact here was at their discretion, not ours. If they did not feel like wandering over for a look, we would see them only at a distance.

Horses group naturally into small herds. The band grazing fifty yards in front of us struck me as unusually jovial and lively until I realized that every horse I had ever known had been, in effect, depressed, a product of solitary confinement. These were not. A lead mare circled toward us as a stallion took up a position behind the band of a dozen or so. Their assertiveness amazed me. It was clear that if we posed a threat, that mare would come charging down on us while the stallion drove the rest to safety. We sat down to wait.

Eventually, the mare allowed a female member of her tribe to amble over and examine us. We rose slowly. I put out a hand to rub the visitor's nose—carefully. Before long horses were walking around and through us, milling about, snuffling, scratching each other, tossing their heads, munching stalks of grass, and proudly presenting their brown coats. I could not get over how happy they were. It made me wonder if, freed of hateful jobs and financial obligations and the entire apparatus of an empire in decline, we too would be this happy given the chance to live as we liked, in accord with the resurrected freshness of our repressed original nature.

> Sing in me, O Muse, and through me tell the tale of that many-sided man who wandered far and wide after sacking the hallowed heights of Troy. Many were the cities he saw and the minds he learned from; and many the sorrows he suffered, heartsick on the open sea, fighting to save his life and to bring his men back home.
>
> — *The Odyssey*

When a fellow student asked me if I would help her move from the east coast to a spacious new home in the mountains at Painted Cave, I found myself eager to test the efficacy of my internal shifts of attitude and feeling toward Santa Barbara. At worst I would just be bounced off the Barrier again...

Having carried in furniture and assembled a bed for the new resident, I powered and carpeted a tool shed beside the house to make a hospitable cell for writing and contemplation while I stayed on to help with the landscaping. At night the moist wind sighed and moaned through the tall trees of the Los Padres National Forest. During the day my Barbara's eye view from the heights revealed intricate currents weaving across the Channel below like the cur-sives of a nonhuman language. The angry Barrier pressure had gone. I dreamed once that the gnarled pine tree just beyond my front door burned with a gentle fire that bathed my abode in a kindly light.

"…..So for lack of a better idea I ended up giving a few free 'psy-choeducational' classes to San Diegan parents on welfare. It was worth doing, but it felt no different from my past work with the poor. I was glad to be of service, but for me, it was not particularly transformative." My listening classmates nodded.

"And so ends the official part of my summer fieldwork presenta-tion." My hands clasped each other on the podium a few inches above the Pacifica emblem. Into the abrupt pause fell the neigh of a distant horse.

"I was writing all this up," I went on, "as the final paper for this fieldwork course when the incompleteness of the project came home to me. Too many loose ends, you see, with my job gone, my truck repossessed, a relationship ended, and me broke and roaming the hills in Escondido, Santa Barbara, and other coastal Californian places. I knew intuitively that somehow all this was part of the work, but I couldn't understand at first how it all fit together. And then…."—my throat began to close—"….then something happened." For a moment I could not go on.

The class waited patiently until, with a heaving sigh like that of a sailor blown up on an island of friendly people curious about his wanderings, I found my voice and continued, able at last to speak even if my throat did tremble at first. Only then did I grasp a quiet homegrown truth intrinsic to the place whose beauty I had been suspicious of, sneered at, occasionally appreciated, succumbed to by stages, and finally allowed to enter my heart more fully, softening it and me: Time in lovely Santa Barbara runs something like time in Sophia's version of heaven, called *pleroma* ("fullness"): parallel to an eternal Now. No wonder on my first walk through Carpinteria every clock I looked at had been wrong. The place did not just host a phenomenology of agelessness, it was one, like the Land of Youth in old Irish tales. Beautiful Barbara, a Christian Sophia, soul of renewal to those who would open the door—or the window—and allow her to come in.

Standing in that attentive space, ever so gently embraced by it, I finally told the tale thus far to Pacificans standing by like attentive Phaeacians waiting to hear the drifter speak:

"It started when San Diego spoke to me in a dream...."

Part Two: Homecoming

San Nemesis Obispo

It was a foggy morning at Port San Luis when I ghosted by Fat Cat's Café, with its mission-tile roof and outdoor patio and imitation Aztec sunstone framed in a ring of rusted metal. Sauntering up the pier, one of three thrusting seaward along this strip of coastline, I halted to observe a seal lounging on a wooden platform next to a docked power boat. A man sat in the bow, a cigarette in his fingers. The seal barked at him and rolled over, playful and languid. My camera was in my pocket. A thick forest-green shirt warmed me against the October breeze coming in off the ocean. The throaty squawk of an unseen bird. Are you listening, Calafía? Are you watching how I move within this mist and count the crows?

And I belong/In the service of the queen...

Self-knowledge might awaken with "Know Thyself" and grow with "To thine own self be true," but it ripens only when we see ourselves as part of some larger story. In my case this meant the story of coastal California, whose salty waters rocked the planks on which I swayed while enjoying the cool gray gloom that enfolded me in its SLO murky blanket. Having understood that places have complexes crying out to be heard, perhaps now I could learn the stories without being lived by them. I had come to San Luis Obispo to find out.

> Story is the most essential thing we have. In some
> ways it's the only thing we have. Some people who
> want healing go to a therapist and tell the stories of
> their lives. Then they see the story differently, shift
> the pattern, and that is healing for them. In stories
> you have a shortcut to the world of emotion, a
> direct path to the mythic and unconscious, to
> meaning.
>
> — Linda Hogan

Other, more ambitious wayfarers had preceded me: Juan
Cabrillo in 1542, Spanish galleon pilot Pedro Unamuno chased away
by Indians in 1587, shipwrecked Cermeño in 1595, Vizcaíno the
Renamer in 1603, patrolling Portolá in 1769, and of course Serra in
1772 to bless the fifth mission in California near the northwestern
Chumash village of Tixlini.

A deep breath; the ululation of a nearby buoy. It felt weird to be
broke. Until two years ago I hadn't been out of work since I was sixteen years old. Maybe my late employers had actually done me a
favor. After all that had happened to me so far on El Camino Real, it
was high time I drew up my own mission statement. First, though,
I had more to learn, ponder, and be changed by....starting here.

....And I belong/Anywhere but in between....

Because Christendom has insisted for centuries that its supernatural beings are historical facts, we tend to look at other people's
gods through the narrow filter of the same literal-mindedness. Our
scholars report that the Greeks thought they saw Zeus or Hera seated upon literal heavenly thrones of gleaming gold; our anthropolo-
gists conclude that Native Americans believed cloudbursts to be
inhabited by literally fiery Thunderbirds. Descendents of indigenous people colonized by Christian missionaries often come to see
their own deities that way, "superstition" being another word for
literalism.

For cultures who do not literalize like this, the gods move more
like universal laws or personifications of the qualities of being: Zeus

as an image for the heights of authority, Aphrodite the creative attraction of opposites that weave the cosmos together, Hera the faithful binding that keeps them married. As Joseph Campbell and C. G. Jung liked to observe, the gods might be imagined as holy metaphors of natural processes that exceed human understanding even while announcing themselves to us.

If we consider Nemesis, whose name means "distributor of what is due," in this construct-dissolving light, the goddess of sacred reckoning moves more like what Heraclitus, the Taoists, Hegel, Nietzsche, Freud, and a host of other deep thinkers have observed: extremes of every sort tending to change into their opposites. Heraclitus called this *enantiodromia*. Jung updated that word to mean the conversion of psychic polarities into one another. Freud knew it as "the return of the repressed." The Greeks saw it as punishment for the crime of hubris.

Situated halfway up El Camino Real along a stretch of coast where warm waters mingle with cold, San Luis Obispo County makes a natural temple or altar for a rebalancing dynamism like Nemesis.

SLO rests like a pivot between the relatively liberal (Northern CA) and relatively conservative (Southern CA) halves of the state, although within the county the politics are reversed: conservatives in the north, liberals in the south. The mission lies between two high hills of granite, with Salinan Indians above and the Chumash below further south. Mission and county were named after a bishop cut down by illness halfway through his life. "I am arrived within sight of the port which I have long desired," St. Louis is reported to have uttered at the end, dying at age 23. (Young James Dean would die behind the wheel in San Luis Obispo County in 1955. The black car that collided with his red one was coming from the opposite direction. He was 24, and he probably never saw the ancient images of Nemesis holding a steering wheel.)

Illness struck three padres a year after the mission's founding, requiring them to return to New Spain (Mexico). Two more padres nearly succumbed to poison; a third, Francisco Pulol, died of it.

Syphilis and typhus competed with each other as killers of vulnerable neophytes.

Nemesis has also been portrayed holding a torch. The first of the recurrent fires to plague the mission erupted when Indians shot flaming arrows into the roof two years after the mission's founding. Another fire followed two years after laborers broke ground for the mission church. Another ignited the roof on Christmas two years later. A second Christmas fire broke out in 1881 when a neophyte full of holiday joy fired off a gun. Terrible twos, as if dispensed by the scales of the terrible goddess of restoration. In 1920, an outbreak in the sacristy burned away the false ceiling covering over the original roof beams. Eyes painted on the beams stared downward into the church.

Forceful rebalancings continued into and after the American occupation. A year after Rome Vickers published the Democrat paper *The Pioneer*, Walter Murray unfurled the Republican *San Luis Obispo Tribune* in 1868. Heavily hunted otters rebounded in such a spectacular comeback after the trappers left that they threatened the Pismo clam overcollected by eager beachgoers. Mining magnate George Hearst bought four huge ranchos; to one, San Simeon, William Randolph Hearst would retreat into the ostentatious pastiche of a castle named after himself after years of overspending while making implacable enemies. Below him, the Pacific drowned the *Columbia*, the *Pigeon*, the *Harlech Castle*, and many other bold vessels that never arrived at their planned destinations.

Llorona usually materializes after an attempt at colonization, but sometimes she arrives just before—as in 1875, when a woman named Albinez went to prison for poisoning her three children prior to a boom in housing land sales. She did this to avenge herself upon an unfaithful lover. She ate some strychnine herself but survived. That year rancher/developer Miguel Avila's naked body was recovered near a creek.

The night before I drove up El Camino Real for my first real visit to San Luis Obispo County (I had been through a few times but never stopped), I dreamed of 101 winding upward past tree-covered hills on its way toward the Cuesta Grade. Over this scene hovered the word **CONTAMINATED** like a large black label stamped upon a scenic postcard.

I would learn some disturbing local facts in connection with this word. One involved Avila Beach, once the largest oil port in the Pacific, where leakage from the Union facility had poisoned the ground for ninety years before anyone caught on. The entire downtown had to be dug up to clean up the toxic mess.

At the fishing town and wildlife preserve of Morro Bay I learned from a sign posted near the water that

ALIEN SPECIES ARE
INVADING MORRO BAY
...But From Underwater!

I also learned that nearby Los Osos ten miles west of San Luis Obispo had gone up without a sewer. Aware of the corrosive seepage of proliferating septic tanks, the California Coastal Permission has forbidden further development in town until a sewer system is installed. The cost is estimated at $150 million and does not include a $6.6 million fine for the one million gallons of septic discharge per day.

Passing through town, I noticed a long mural on a concrete wall on the side of a gas station. In the mural a huge, growling grizzly reared up at gun-pointing conquistadors like the ones who had shot *los osos* to feed the mission. The English word "bear" derives from the same Indo-European root as "metaphor." A metaphor of what? The Romans knew Nemesis as Invidia, the goddess worshipped by gladiators and by the *venatores* who grappled with wild beasts.

It was an hour or so after dawn when the chime of the clock and bell outside City Hall reverberated from the white walkways and inlaid red tiles to bounce from the pavement in front of the plaza. Pink grilles barred the square glass windows of the administration building. To keep things in or keep things out? Was there at bottom any difference? Some contagions cannot be stopped by lock and key;

they pollute the mind and heart before they slag the surroundings. Witness the El Camino Real bell guarding the plaza. No reflection, no caution, no depth to mindless boosting. Glancing back through history, the reader mentored by the humanities sees empire after self-promoting empire pushing pawns and castles like those Louis played with in boyhood, only to subside into their own stinking wastes. Yet, "The good man," observed Albert Camus in his novel *The Plague*, "the man who infects hardly anyone, is the man with the fewest lapses of attention."

I got out of my dew-coated car and walked up toward the mission, pausing in another plaza—this one backed by a wall composed of irregularly cut stones—to listen to splashing water stared at by a bear and a long-haired Indian boy, both cast of bronze. The boy clasped his hands around one knee; the bear dipped a paw into the fountain. CREEK ADVISORY. AVOID WATER CONTACT ACTIVITIES warned a sign near the mission. James Hillman has asked what happens to the deep psyche when animals go extinct. Here was part of the answer, these cold statues, here to unconsciously announce the fate of the round pillar in the mission colonnade's square hole. The return of the imaginal animal. Extinguish him and he shows up again in the local complexes, architectural or otherwise.

Above the double-door archway, grape vines curled toward a shield on which two arms—one robed, the other bare—crossed each other at the elbow such that the open hands seemed nailed to the cross behind them. *Checkmate.* I went in.

On one wall inside some artist had left stylized bare-breasted Indian maidens mashing acorns into meal. Five girls at the fifth mission. A jagged king's highway of a crack in the wall joined their studious erotic forms. Glass cases held their stony tools. A closer look to avoid a lapse of attention: yes, the crack did run diagonally, like a bishop's trail across a chessboard.

On another wall hung a painting of red-robed Louis, staff in hand, mitred, white-clad, young, framed in dark wood, right hand raised in blessing. Did he comprehend the seriousness of the game he was playing? "If you keep on excusing," wrote Camus, who understood fascism from fighting it while in the French Resistance, "you eventually give your blessing to the slave camp, to cowardly force, to organized executioners, to the cynicism of great political monsters; you finally hand over your brothers." And become at last their bullying keepers instead of their faithful students, teachers, or servants.

I stepped out into a garden where red, white, yellow, and violet blossoms matched flowery traceries in the L-shaped chapel. A single bell hung in a small brick tower streaked with mildew that the pigeons didn't mind. Two more bells from Lima, Peru had been installed in 1820, a year after completion of the quadrangle in all its linear redoubtability.

Psychology has shown us that when the holder of a powerful position wreaks unintentional havoc on the undeserving, unconscious motivations must be taken into account. The projection of one's shadow upon convenient enemies or "primitives," the unconscious arrogance of appointing oneself trustee and rescuer to those in need of enlightenment, the unexamined state of entrenched judgmentalism hiding behind the parental facade: such are the smiling poisons that spread contagions of hatred and violence under the guise of beneficence. "In the Crusades and in campaigns against heretical sects, Jews, and suspected and/or purely imaginary thaumaturges," remarked Victor Turner, "Christian civilization embarked on its first concerted effort at regeneration through sacrificial violence, offering the mutilated bodies of its enemies as gifts pleasing to a god whose son had once appeared as the Prince of Peace." But far from the last. "I meant well" has ceased to be a valid excuse since Dostoevsky, Janet, Freud, and Jung destroyed it, and was not much of one even before them.

Everyone knows of moments in which the voice of conscience (Nemesis within) whispers an alert. Life itself issues them, and not always in a whisper. Nothing was quiet or subtle about the flaming arrows, the dying children, the vomiting and diarrhea, the welts and blisters, the noncooperation of people robbed of their freedom and ridiculed for their beliefs. To systematically ignore injustices presupposes not only a huge vault of unconsciousness, but a conscious effort to turn away—and therein dwells the accountability. It is human to forget, to miss a nuanced detail, or to succumb to a temporary blind spot—but profoundly inhumane to succumb, decision after decision, to a master plan of endless complicity, abuse, exploitation, and violence. The cheerfully inhumane do not hear the screams and the weeping and, in our day, the cries of dying species because their ears and hearts are plugged with justifications, excuses, hypocrisies, slogans, and easy explanations. The wrongdoers needed it. The savages deserved it. The Lord intended it. For their own good.

Whatever their all-too-human weaknesses and blindnesses, the record shows plainly that missionary "fathers" and many who came after—the slick politicians, the destructive developers and polluters, the industrialists insane enough to build a nuclear reactor near an active fault line—were addressed time and again by cautions, protests, revolts, illnesses, fevers, suicides, explosions, and deaths. Their refusal to stop and reflect on the consequences of their actions is not simple repression or leakage from an unplumbed unconscious, but what Sartre meant by *mauvaise foi:* bad faith, a deliberate refusal to face hard facts, one of which remains the covert satisfaction of indulging an unanalyzed streak of sadism.

Just here the looming figure of Nemesis insists on the difference between punishment and accountability. The record also shows that only when those who commit prolonged, destructive acts of bad faith are held responsible for them no matter what justifications they muster can the healing really begin and the same old invasions—of life, of land—lose their impetus to repeat themselves.

Passing a church sign resembling the headboard of some giant's bed, I noted THE BLADERUNNER DAY SPA. Blade Runner: a movie image of what some on the Los Angeles City Council actually hoped for the future of LA. What was that doing way up here? Let it not be a sign of injustices to come drawing forth still more drastic rebalancings.

As the ostentatious battlements of Hearst's giant new rook looked down on San Simeon, another, smaller castle opened its doors in San Luis Obispo. I stood in a noisy downpour for a few moments to pause and consider the remains.

By 1925 automobiles had grown popular enough throughout California that tourists were driving around gazing at beaches, mountains, and the rest of our then-spectacular scenery. The Milestone Motor Hotel was built around the novel idea of allowing sightseeing motorists to park and spend the night. Because the name packed too many letters to be easily read by car, Arthur Heineman shortened it to "Milestone MoTel," and a new word merged into the busy lexicon of travel. Yet even here, at the first motel, the mission influence of the past was palpable, from stylized dome to rotting cabins. Eerily, the dome resembled the two covering the Diablo Canyon nuclear plant like large round breasts capped by concrete nipples. Like Hearst Castle, like the missions, it was never finished, the tainted milk having run dry long ago.

I followed the Cuestra Grade up over the hill and down again until I reached Atascadero just south of Paso Robles and the Central Coast's wine country. By one reading Atascadero means "place of much water," but by another, "place where one gets stuck." The latter made more immediate sense in view of the thousand-bed Atascadero State Hospital. A sign bolted to the metal railing out front warned me not to do any hunting. Edward Gardner Lewis had laid out the town around here as the first of three utopian communities but, like the other Luis, got himself stuck in a jail. The second utopian, Walter Bliss, manifested the Administration Building if not heaven in 1914. The third, William Kullgren of Beacon Light Ministries, lit up himself with special "lunations" that warned of apocalypse for all who did not live in trailers. This was before the state hospital was built.

I parked and asked a passerby where a bookstore could be found. "Hmmm...don't know of any big ones, just a small place up the road near Ralph's. Probably closed, though. There's an unmet need, huh?" At the Long's Drugs off El Camino Real I browsed bestsellers and camping equipment without finding anything I really wanted or needed for my restlessness. Upon exiting I shook my head at a dimpled girl in her twenties beckoning to survey me or sell me something. "Jesus loves you!" she called out in an undertone of

It troubles me that the love of Jesus often carries with it an undercurrent of hate —

hatred as rolling glass doors snapped shut behind me. Evidently the padres' religious mythos was alive and unwell on this stretch of the King's Highway. A remark by George Carlin went through my mind: "Jesus doesn't really love you, but he thinks you have a great personality."

Back at the hotel I laid crinkling maps on the red-and-blue-checked bedspread to contextualize my reactions to the SLO atmosphere around me. Funny how the streets of this mission town all ran diagonally, platted that way by William Hutton back when the mission served as both courthouse and jail. A skateboarder skidded and jumped and did tricks outside my window for two hours and left at dusk; only afterward did the phrase "boy pope" go through my mind, and these words from a Frank O'Hara elegy to James "Little Bastard" Dean, now safely promoted from bad-boy actor to causeless saint: "Your name is fading from all but a few marquees, the big red calling-card of your own death. And there's a rumor that you live hideously maimed and hidden by a conscientious studio." Sir Alec Guinness had dined with Dean and walked out with him to see his shiny new car. Gripped by a premonition, he sternly warned his young companion that if he drove that car he'd die in it. Guinness felt puzzled by his own remarks until he heard the sad news a few days later. Nemesis issuing a warning?

I thought about what I was doing here.

It had taken a swift return to San Diego County, the county of my birth, to wake me up to the inner reality of place. For much of my life, I now knew, I had followed Serra and La Llorona up El Camino Real without suspecting it. Every county I had ever lived and worked in was a mission county.

Writers, critics, photographers, and artists had been drawn to the remains of California's missions with mysterious constancy for over two hundred years. What was the pull? What was it for me? I certainly had no desire to be near the missions. Going into them made me sick or troubled me with nightmares. I despised the colonialism, authoritarianism, and genocide they represented: the cracking facades, the empty cant, the smell of oppression, the loveless iron bars over windows and doors. No, the missions and their continuing legacy of expansionism and domination felt more like wounds calling out for treatment, wounds that could not close. Something wrong and evil had injured the very heart of my home¬land, and I felt driven by a consuming need to understand what it was in depth.

The only dream I remembered upon waking recapitulated past journeys, past leave-takings. The morning coffee was too weak, the shower was lukewarm, and the switch broke when I tried to turn off the bedside lamp.

When dawn's delicate touch lit the skies with tints of rose, I gathered my things and checked out of the motel, having left the light on for them.

Nemesis had been hard on Mission San Miguel Arcángel, founded in 1797 with a cracked dedication bell. Here padres were stricken one after the other. Antonio de la Concepcion Horra began to rave shortly after the mission was founded and ordered his troops to open fire at nothing. Marcelino Cipres from Mission San Antonio and two other friars got sick to their stomachs, suspected poison, and ordered three neophytes arrested and flogged in front of their families, only to learn that the "poison" was mescal drawn from a tin-lined copper container. Francisco Pujol fell ill here and died in 1801.

Situated thirty-seven miles north of San Luis Obispo, the mission burned in 1806, with much of it left in smoking ruins. After its rebuilding some of the neophytes exited underground via escape tunnel. When Tulares from the east came raiding in response to Father Juan Cabot's aggressive forays into their territory, the attackers were repelled, but the missionaries abandoned all hope of expanding the "rosary" of the mission project any wider.

After secularization in 1834, the mission did some business as the biggest saloon on El Camino Real before subsiding further into a wrecked desolation that continued to exude an aura of death. The first neophyte mortality had been recorded at this mission. Two thousand two hundred and forty-eight more decayed unremembered by name or face in the oft-spaded ground. All eleven of the unfortunate Reed family and staff who bought the mission were murdered by AWOL sailors looking for gold. Local legend claims that a ghostly presence wearing Reed's old coat still paces the hallways accompanied by a woman garbed in black.

A flaked red campanario, acres of moldy walls, and a cheesy plywood friar holding a cross and bell: my eye caught these first as I exited at San Miguel and parked my car across from a small muddy park. Through a square adobe gate and two doors held by rusty hasps waited the mission's inner courtyard. Long streaks of mildew dripped down the eaves of the church. Chunks of fallen plaster exposed cobwebbed adobe bricks mixed with ox blood and bird carcasses. A vandal had scratched "Craig" on an inside wall long ago.

While walking around a wooden carving of a muscular Michael, angel of retribution, hefting a sword over a cowering Satan, I overheard a young woman asking a docent if the priest who conducted healings was in. Someone in her family was ill. I shook my head. *Imagine looking for healing in this ruined place.* Here, though, at least one could view honest mortification. No fantasy towers with masked electronic bells, no whitewash covering up the Indian art, no plaques praising Serra or Nixon, no frocked manikins frozen under glass. Just the holy Eye in the ruined chapel staring out at centuries of colonial devastation.

Outside, the ruinous effects seem to have spread to the town around the mission. My glance took in lots choked with weeds, broken pavement, rundown fences, a tow truck, fields of bare dirt, what looked to be a warehouse, and a few tired construction workers with the dust of their labors still on them.

The real miracle, I decided as I drove toward the freeway, was that we should have been convinced to settle for all this instead of knocking the dust off our feet, turning away forever from the archons who master-planned its chaotic and loveless immensity, and letting their works subside into rot, reclaimed at last by the masterless land.

Confrontation with a Conqueror

King City began as a train stop, and in a way it never ceased being one. I had driven my car here, but the outpost feel of blow-through transience hung in the manure-soured air all about me.

For some reason I hadn't caught that feeling in Jolon to the south, once a busy town and now a dusty crossroads leading off to Fort Hunter Liggett. The fort was named after a general who had fought in the Spanish-American War, during which hundreds of thousands of Filipinos were exterminated for democratizing purposes. Visiting Mission San Antonio de Padua required passing through an Army checkpoint, entering the base, and traversing a gunnery range. *All the missions should be situated thus*, I thought, noting camouflage-colored armor drawn up in tidy rows. Empire psychology never changes, only its costumes and techniques.

After a twenty-mile drive I found myself on a dusty road leading past a series of wooden signs the color of dried blood. The long line of the mission rose up from low tan fields of tinder-dry brush. The remains of a barracks stood choked with weeds out front. Seeing the red tiles (*tejas*) on the roof, I remembered that they were developed here to ward off flaming arrows shot by locals angry over their lands being conquered. Today the curved clay tiles cloak entire southwestern landscapes. An old rumor said they were molded over the thighs of captive Indian girls.

149

At length I came up to a long line of gaily dressed people waiting to get into the chapel. A dance was in progress. Laughing guests paused beneath the brick archways to photograph each other in front of the iron-barred windows, but **No Admittance** to the overgrown garden taken over by spindly weeds and California poppies.

To enter the mission I passed two wooden figureheads and ducked under the Stars and Stripes draped above the front door. Once inside my adjusting eyes recorded:

A length of stretched hide pinned to a board

 Cattle-branding emblems from the various missions

Twists of barbed wire displayed in a case like a

butterfly collection

A painted severed hand with musical notes on its joints

More notes on the wall, set in a grid below which read:

San-to Dios San-to Fuerte San-to Im-mortal.

One of the musical instruments preserved at the mission is a violin that belonged to Jose Carabajal, the son of a Salinan woman and her Spanish husband. The padres forbade him to play any of the mission's violins, so he carved and sanded and strung his own from local materials. He practiced until ready to join the mission orchestra, which he did in 1803 under the direction of Father Juan Bautista Sancho. For the most part mission music confined itself to plainsong, but had the prancing, weeping strings of Mozart or Beethoven ever sounded here, where the first bell in California was cast? I thought about the inmates of Auschwitz playing music for the Nazis while secretly drawing solace from it. A lilting laugh from an entertained guest brought me back to the present.

Where does it come from, this collective trance, forgetfulness, and tolerance of the intolerable all rolled into one? Hannah Arendt called it "the banality of evil," and Robert J. Lifton "psychic numbing." Abraham Maslow wrote about "the pathology of normalcy." William Whyte referred to it as "groupthink." Mark Twain was blunt: "moral cowardice." So was Sartre: "bad faith," the refusal to face unpleasant realities and painful responsibilities. Public deceivers of "the masses" always take care to reinforce it: *Tell them what they want to hear. Keep their attention on words rather than events. Repeat the lie so often that they accept it as truth. Focus on quirks of personality instead of on the issues. Rewrite what really happened. When all else fails, blame the victims, the reformers, the honest bearers of bad news.* Little wonder if distracted and chronically discontented citizens accept what they're told as though it derived from their own benumbed powers of thought and response. When influential people charged with guarding the public good subvert it instead by attacking the very foundations of consciousness, it's difficult to function as anything beyond passive and programmable, giving away freedoms like tickets for a dance.

By contrast, Mission Soledad to the north of King City gathered a steady harvest of disharmony: floggings and starvings of neophytes, three murders and an epidemic in 1802 alone, a crazed padre dying on the altar like a sacrifice to a voracious god, the mission itself deserted, sold, neglected until the restorers and boosters tried to make something out of it, there in the same city as a prison bearing the same lonely name. Fast food joints and gas stations colonized a strip of road fed by the town's main freeway offramp.

Little was left of the mission complex when I made my way around a roped-off mound of adobe ruins to see for myself. A sign near a field under cultivation marked the site of the original church destroyed long ago by floods. In an era of empire and erasure, absences often evoke more than presences. Painted columns above the replicated altar framed a mourning woman in black.

Outside, the impressions subsided into fragments and remains. Square headstones of that familiar carmine hue, one of them for Jose Arrillaga, Governor of California during its Mexican period, his small memorial set flush with the ground on a plain plot of soil.

Straight rows of green crops standing at attention in the distance. A side of the bone-colored mission bulging out like a cyst through the whitewash. My eye moved faster. An octagonal fountain of brick; a bell cast in Mexico suspended from a timber protruding from the church; palms, firs, a Camino roadway monument, a walkway lined with stone. I had seen enough. A camper to outpace on my drive back up the dusty road. A glance to catch the brand of vehicle as I passed: *Intruder*.

I drove back to King City and checked into a motel room wondering what kind of underworld I had stumbled into. As I headed for the bath I noticed a bottle opener fastened to the inside of the bathroom door lintel. Standard equipment?

King City was named after Charles King, buyer of a large Mexican land grant on which he grew wheat. In 1886, when the Southern Pacific reached the town, King City's expansion drained the life and business out of Jolon. The town now covers 2.8 square miles, with dry farming pastures arranged in green squares around it. Most employment here cycles seasonally around the back-bending realities of agricultural growing, processing, and packing. Steinbeck's father worked here for a flour miller as one of the city's first residents.

Viewed from an anti-immigrant stance, King City should be crawling with chaos. Most of its twelve thousand residents are of Mexican heritage, some are illegals, especially the field workers, and few make much money. Yet homicides are rare and homelessness is almost nonexistent. The city is served by one police officer for every thousand people who live here. Nothing seems to be blowing up or burning down.

The leading crime statistic in King City is burglary committed by stealthy young males. The cause is not far to seek. To make ends meet, low-income parents must work themselves to death in the fields and factories. The "family values" image touted these days by wealthy politicians and grinning evangelists stands for little but hypocrisy to families who can scarcely pay rent, eat, buy clothes, or stay together. Study after study demonstrates that as income drops, stress, substance abuse, crime, and violence break forth from families teetering on the hard cold edge of nothingness. Neglected by their overwhelmed parents (when the parents have not been deported), the children of such families bear the additional burden of surviving in a nation that pretends class differences do not exist while the wealthy grow wealthier and millions starve. In desperation some of the young turn to crime, especially if it pays to do so. Education, enough to live on, and good mentoring often end the problem for neophytes not yet warehoused and institutionalized.

Unpacking, I settled down for the night, pleased to be in a place with the gumption to plant its cemetery at the city's northern entrance just off the King's Highway. Beyond my window, two midgets stood swaying next to a Harley in the gusting September wind.

Depth.

Monterey County has been described as scenic, fecund, rugged (especially near the coast), even enterprising, but its essential character, its soul, is depth.

King City dwells in the heart of the long Salinas Valley that bisects the county and grows $3.5 billion a year in lettuce, artichokes, strawberries, and many other crops around the Salinas River and above the longest underground stream in the nation. John Steinbeck, who was born in the north end of the Valley, would have had no trouble identifying its rivers as the tributaries of mist-shrouded Hades or Pluto, whose name means "wealth" and also "the unseen."

The peninsula thrusts westward like the head of a hound, perhaps that of Cerberus guarding the nether world. At its edge, where a wealth of sardines had once poured from the waters, Monterey Bay descends abruptly to the deepest underwater canyons on the West Coast. From them flow upwelling waters bringing mysterious denizens from depths beyond those of the Grand Canyon. Ever a land of extremes, California reaches to the highest (Mt. Whitney) and the lowest (Death Valley) places in the forty-eight states, but her subterranean psyche pulses strongest under the sea near her former capital city.

Here too persisting ecological features carry over into the human sphere as local, recurrent metaphors. As a human quality, depth—as imaginative vision, as heartfelt expression, as probing below bright surfaces—characterizes the artists, poets, and thinkers like Robinson Jeffers and Mary Austin who have always flocked to the county, or, like Steinbeck, who were born here. Some have felt drawn to the spiritual and geographical verticality of Esalen and its cliffs and hot springs at Big Sur, others to yearly conferences at Asilomar in the forests of Pacific Grove.

Still others have confused depth with death. Killing oneself, for example, signals a descent literalized instead of psychologized into loss of an old self ready to die—suicide as aborted initiation; and this fateful door has often revolved here. Big Sur has seen its share of suicides. So has Carmel, so named by a lawyer and a developer, a scenic, flood-washed cove where self-styled bohemians camped out in 1905 to bake clams and write poems, and where Nora May French killed herself, followed by Jack London (perhaps by accident), and, later, George Sterling. Painter Helen Smith was found strangled by a fishing line. The seaside town grew up around the "Devil's Staircase," now renamed Ocean Avenue. New residents expecting housing supplies from San Francisco had to nail together a ship-ment of doors instead. At least these portals weren't painted red, although Carmel resident Jeffers had written the Lloronic play *Medea* and Mayor Eastwood had starred in westerns as "The Man with No Name." In *Pale Rider* he had trotted into town on a pale horse worthy of Pluto himself, pausing to leave his ten-gallon cap of invisibility in the street while dispatching his opponents to the underworld.

The county as a whole has hosted many Pluto stand-ins, from the spy Thomas Larkin to the robber baron David Jacks to the labor-busting "farm fascists" of 1930s Salinas and the businessmen who retooled Cannery Row into a tourist trap. The earliest of them all, Junípero Serra, lies buried at the mission near Carmel. What a con-trast to the Ohlone who welcomed the first troop of Spanish invaders with a wealth offering of fish—and what a difference feel-ing at home in the world can make. A myth lived blindly never turns out well. Depth lived without reflection flattens into self-parody and self-fulfilling prophecy, but when lived with reflection it recolors old stories with new meanings.

Enter Steinbeck, tall, sunburned, gravel-voiced with a smoker's rasp, a bit of a drifter, eternally informal, taciturn like the boy named John healed by St. Anthony, and as rough-edged as the coast he was born on.

C. G. Jung, whom Steinbeck did not know, and Joseph Campbell, whom he did know, insisted that the quest for self-knowledge did not end (♪ trumpet flourish ♫) with successful self-examination. It constituted a necessary but preliminary phase in exploring the deeper realm of personal myth: myth not as falsehood or archaic explanation for wind or rain, but myth as larger story, as plot returned to life and flesh; myth as fabled intersection of the personal, the collective, and (I was having to learn) the geographical. Steinbeck more or less knew his myth. Growing up in an old Victorian house Salinas kids called "the Castle," professing a lifelong faith in the virtue of gallantry, Steinbeck opened a book of Arthurian legends at age nine. His own first novel was *Cup of Gold*; his second wife's name, Gwen; his third's, Elaine, a far happier choice than the doomed Lady of Shallot. The name of the destroyer that drove reporter Steinbeck into the nightmarish heat of World War II was *Knight*. Sir Lancelot had been knighted by Arthur on St. John's Day. Steinbeck tried but failed to rescue Arthur Miller from the blacklists of that mordant Mordred named McCarthy.

The productive confluence in Steinbeck's life of place, passion, and myth deliberately lived appears most dramatically in his awakening to the victims of the Great Depression, especially those rolling into California from the Dust Bowl. He drove to the San Joaquin Valley to investigate their plight and hear their stories, and the result, *The Grapes of Wrath*, set before a galvanized public what the media had ignored. Having learned firsthand that poverty is served up from unequal wealth rather than from lack of food, Sir John had roused the conscience of a nation from its slumber even as the town fathers of Salinas burned the book in front of the library. Literary critics accused him of abandoning art for ideology and turned instead to Hemingway, the morose ideologue of macho. Steinbeck forsook California in large part because of noisy Californian conservatives who labeled him a communist and hated him accordingly.

In Steinbeck's writing, as in his life, identity and place are not separate. Where you live is who you are, whether Salinas, Pacific Grove, Los Angeles, Los Gatos, or New York. What reconnects the two is Story; and when Story takes up the mantle of epic, then we must speak of myth. Wherever Camelot falls again, the turrets collapse as story first and as finance or politics second.

As Steinbeck aged, the post-Camelot commercialization, overdevelopment, and hypocrisy at large in the U.S. offended his sense of gallantry. He came home from reporting on the Vietnam War depressed and disillusioned, a mood that chilled *The Winter of Our Discontent*, his last novel, and peered forth now and again from *Travels with Charley: In Search of America*. He then went to work translating Sir Thomas Malory's Arthurian tales into modern English.

As he researched this project he spent time in England inspecting old castles and haunts to soak up the feel of the land: depth as the soil of a tale, its earthiness a character too. Yet here Steinbeck went astray. In "going into the darkness of my own mind," as he phrased it to his agent Elizabeth Otis, he forgot that it was not given to Lancelot to unearth the Grail.

Entering the Grail Castle to lie down for the night when warned not to, Lancelot was singed by a bolt of lightning. Caught in what he thought was writer's block, Steinbeck set himself on fire by accident while smoking in bed one night. Elaine rushed to his side and put him out. He would never finish his quest, not even with helpful companions like Arthur Strand and Mary Morgan. Lancelot kissing Guinevere was the last scene he was able to type. As he died he heard the drums and bagpipes of his Irish ancestors calling him away.

"An artist should be open on all sides to every kind of light and darkness," he wrote to his agent. "But our age almost purposely closes all the windows, draws all the shades and then later screams to a psychiatrist for light." Depth does not necessarily connote gloom, any more than Pluto's presence must invite plutocracy or sociopathy, but closing the windows and drawing the shades thicken the darkness, literalize the descent, and invite the deadlier plunges. It was in Monterey Bay, after all, that happy-go-lucky John Denver met his end, this Icarian son of an Air Force pilot, when his plane spun down from sunny heights into the watery depths.

Passing through Salinas on my way to the coast, I quickly found that the terrain did not match the map—especially downtown, where several major streets wove together in a knotted tangle. When headed up Front I'd find myself unexpectedly on Market, East or West; down Main, suddenly on Salinas, or Monterey, or Central, or even Cherry. If signs were posted to warn me of all the forced transitions, I missed them and they missed me in the confusion and afternoon traffic.

None of the missions ever succeeded in stilling the organic voice of nature for long, a voice so often interpreted by the padres as that of the devil himself. In years to come, even the vine-wrapped whitewash on the crumbling face of Mission San Carlos Borromeo displayed a splotchy yellow that only highlighted the green hills in the blue-hazed distance. A wall in the cemetery sheltered a bee hive, its buzzing *melissae* mythologically linked to the long-forbidden Great Mother coming forth again from within.

The stone church first planned at the mission in 1793 stood out from the other beads of Serra's geographic "rosary" by displaying a domed Moorish bell tower and walls that tapered inward to close a catenary arch for a roof. One day these heights collapsed, as did the garden wall, leaving a four-pointed Moorish star peering out of the tower-flanked chapel wall. Such a star is called a *mudéjar*, from a Spanish derivation of the Arabic *mudajjan*, literally: "allowed to remain." If the missions were dreams in some nightmarish dream series, the watchfulness of the indoor eyes at San Diego had proceeded northward to convert their indigenous plurality into the monocular all-seeing Eye at Mission San Miguel, transformed in turn into the star-shaped *ventana* here at Monterey, a wide-open window allowed to remain.

A cracked Moorish fountain hunched below the bell towers. Grilles covered the windows near the Visitors Entrance. My eye picked out a greenish plaque commemorating, for some reason, La Pérouse, an outspoken critic of the missions. *If you can't beat 'em...* A gothic arch led into the darkened church, where vestments hung under glass. Mourning bronze padres in the center of one room kept the death watch over a sarcophagus of the prostrate Father President whose remains were interred beneath a marble slab set before the altar. Serra died here in 1784. Through a locked metal grating I saw the grounds of the school named after him.

A two-tiered cross marked the spot where Serra had raised the original in what was now a wide, paved courtyard flanked by cacti and plants in clay pots. Below the wooden arms, a bizarrely crafted statue of St. Francis, patron saint of the organic, seemed for all the world to be flinging out its arms in agony.

> The soil that I dig up here to plant trees or lay foundation-stones is full of Indian leavings, sea-shells and flint scrapers; and the crack-voiced churchbells that we hear in the evening were hung in their tower when this was Spanish country. Where not only generations but races too drizzle away so fast, one wonders the more urgently what it is for, and whether this beautiful earth is amused or sorry at the procession of her possessors.
>
> —Robinson Jeffers

After all I had struggled through, learned, and been seared by on this series of trips up the King's Highway, it seemed only proper to halt and pay my respects here in the land of depth and death.

As I came up to the railing again, placed my hands upon it, faced the altar, and let my eyes go out of focus, I could feel my calf muscles tightening as a fire came to life and began to burn within my travel-worn body...

Hello. Hello! Is anyone else here?

Silence.

Hello! In the blessed name of Jesus, where am I?

Pause.

Where am I? And...What am I?

Silence.

Finally:

Where? Well, you're dead, not to put too fine a point on it. Dead and buried, long ago. But not, alas, forgotten.

What? What do you—

I am pleased to be your tour guide on your too-brief trail of tears. Welcome to the land of Hades, 'Father.'

No. No! I cannot be in Hades. That is impossible!

Where there is faith, all things are possible. I stand here with other devotees before your tomb, four feet in front of the remains. You died, were interred without your underwear, were unearthed three times, examined, and on the third foray descended into darkness once again. To be roused once more by me and whirled without end, more's the pity.

How...how did I come to...this place?

How? Well, in my time our healers employ something called 'active imagina-tion,' you see. Through its operation you possess an imaginal body, a fantasied form, a virtual existence in the interior space I have bidden be open for our encounter. It is here, only here, in the psychic realm between the worlds of mind and matter, that we meet at long last. Think of this place-within as a temporary stage set up for the space of one scene.

It sounds like the Devil's work.

One never knows who will show up, it's true. Shall I send you back where you came from?

Not yet. —Am I truly dead?

You truly are. It's a sin to lie to a priest. This is a man-to-man confrontation of complete honesty, something scarcer perhaps in my time than in yours. One that I've very much looked forward to.

What do you mean by your time?

It's later than you think, padre.

Many years have passed since...?

Many. Many times many.

Has my work in Alta California been completed, then?

Yes. Long ago.

Other missions were founded? The rosary of belief was extended? Broadened?

Lasuén founded nine more after you, and three more rose after that. The final score at the end of the second half was twenty-one.

Twenty-one! And the heathen are all converted?

Not all. Every pasture has its strays.

Even so, blessings be to God!

And to the neophyte grave-diggers, for they shall be called sons of syphilis.

What do you mean?

While you were busy spreading the Word far and wide over the virgin expanse of my homeland, your companions in God spread invisible sicknesses against which your 'children' had no defense. Keeping the flock at the missions increased their exposure, especially for the women and their babies. The blessings thereby conferred radiated outward to shine upon their unenlightened fellows sitting in the darkness of the wilderness. And over the next century—

No! No!

Yes! Yes! Didn't you remember what had happened in Baja? —I really must hand it to you, even if you do resemble Pete Wilson. I really must. 50% is a whopping conversion record by anyone's reckoning. 75% by some accounts. Well, too bad for those poor Moors, eh? Ashes to ashes, door to door...

The beloved neophytes—

'Neophyte'!—was ever a name so perfectly suited to its object? 'Newly planted' to be sure. Six feet under.

This can't be true!

I've looked upon the graves with my own eyes, touched the monuments— where there are monuments—with these fingers—these! Grass now grows over the nameless tombs. But nothing green grows over yours.

This could not have been the outcome of the Sacred Expedition. It could not have been! Our charter was to instruct, to uplift, to lead souls into the Light of the Word—

Say now. Do you suppose any of your laboring 'children' ever made that last, ironic connection between the fruits they were made to pick and the organic metaphors of Jesus? After all, their mortality rate exceeded their navality. Natality, I mean. Or should that have been nativity? Take it from a native, padre:

California life is confusing and doubly so for the down and out, afflicted as they are with economic scurvy, sans oranges. All those outcast Sunkist paupers languishing visibly in the orange glare. Sweet Jesus of the Vitamin C! One could parish laughing.

Surely this is a matter of conflicting points of view...?

'Conflicting points of view' means that you think oranges are superior to apples and I think the reverse. Genocide is not a philosophical disagreement. Attempts to whitewash what you did are not a matter of 'conflicting points of view,' but of the erasure of the victims' history to conceal current machinations. When will you people quit lying? You need saving far more than anybody you invade.

Genocide! But the Lord bid us labor with our hands, avoid excesses of wealth—

He also said something about a well-swept abode being highly inviting to demons.

—and to welcome His Children into His House—

Children? House? You have 'converted' entire self-sufficient peoples formerly fed by their own skills and educated by their rich traditions into orphans— you who once served as an Inquisitor. Now there was an ashy bit of conversion...

I see in your mind the images of the sentenced and the burned, and it grieves me unto death. I must tell you that I certainly had no part in that.

The padre doth protest too much. Your type of innocence made Christians of your day the perfect tools of divine torture, colonization, and, later, extermination. The devil you kept trying to cast out of the Indians was of your own making, a Prince Incognito reflection of your own thirst to dominate.

How should I address you?

My birthmark tingled as I chuckled without humor.

'Ulysses' will do for now.

Ulysses. Very well. You bear a dark name, my child.

Aye, and the mark to go along with it. And the wrath. And the wanderings...I have followed in your footsteps on my own Sacred Expedition up and down the coast of California, living for a time in a particular locale, hearing its tears without comprehension, mingling as they did with my own, and moving restlessly on to the next, as you did, unable at first to grasp why. I have known violence intimately. I have stared into abysses and felt them stare into me. I have watched countless tractors turn verdancy into vacancy, smelled countless dividers packed with BigMac containers, heard the oil-saturated suck of polluted shores, where no birds sing. And at times what I believed was my punishment, my lifelong vandervecken Flying Dutchman exile, was greater than I could bear.

You were born here?

Yes, in San Diego, the first link in your hellish chain. I have been a wanderer in my own land—a land you and yours have so thoroughly converted, unto spoiling the very air, land, and water which cradle us, the commercial blackening of the very ground on which we try to refashion what's left of our distracted lives 'down' here.

What else...

What else has come of your efforts to do good? The entire coastline—remember its unblemished beauty?—is purchased, parceled, fenced, and drilled, much of it sold out into a magnificent desolation of crowded malls spreading psychic soledad. You can't even camp in an unguarded spot without being fined or arrested. Most of the indigenous peoples who tended the land: wiped out. The remainder: witness to a vision of well-demarcated earthicide against which many choose to fight a rearguard action. The quadrangles by which your missions were shaped have become a way of life, thought, philosophy, morality—and even, God help us, spirit.

But how? How in the name of Heaven could this happen?

In the name of Heaven: order. In the name of Heaven: control. And as within, so without. In the all-domesticating name of Heaven you once beat yourself with sticks and scratched yourself with wires and clubbed yourself with rocks, crucifix held high to make an example to followers bent on self-degradation. I've stood in your San Diegan quarters, with their merciless adobe angles, flat slats like those on which you slept, straight lines going nowhere. Private pummelings at midnight, in the bell tower—remember? Bell symbols now line what we ironically call 'freeways' as ringerless monuments to an infinity of malls and maulings, all of them self-inflicted—

And all because of me?

Pause.

No. But you led the charge. And I know where your missions ultimately come from. Do you? Conquerors created missions to make convert-prisoners of their enemies. But it goes back much, much farther....all the way back to the first attempt to wall out the wilderness. What marvelous progress! Fences to walls to forts to stockades to missions, and forward into prisons, corporations, reichs, concentration camps, empires. Empires wall to wall. —And why you? Why not you, who never learned that hatred of self and hatred of others are at bottom the same hatred? You, yes you, because the one thing the soul cannot stand is imprisonment, and you, who submit to rulers and rules and straight lines and business plans, are the least free souls of all. Your missions, your factories of soullessness and death, are the inevitable outcome of watching life through a grid. You manufacture hells wherever you go. What is the mission but heaven in reverse, an externalization of your private inner damnation? And what is hell but the curtailing of freedom? Freedom is not a condition of being human: it IS being human.

Without Christ, we are all in danger of feeling the flames of Hell.

Would you like to know what hell really is? I've learned a bit about it out on the Mission Trail. Hell is the colonizer's lethal occupation of a place in the sun that eclipses the silenced. A hell on earth, a hell of Earth, a hell of casting 'sinners' who will not conform into the outermost darkness. A hell of smog, loneliness, billboards and traffic in what was once a terrestrial paradise. How I long, how I long, for the days before neon, halogen, and piercing florescence, when the sun actually set and rose in noble clarity, when shining stars all came out in his nightly absence, birds filled the sky, fish crowded the rivers, and the shadows were no sharper than pleasant brushstrokes of shade.

Silence. Then:

What is it that you want, my son?

What do I want? What do I want? I want justice! I want someone to pay for making me a stranger in my own homeland. For my growing up devoid of knowledge of location, history, family, and roots! For my growing up a racist, a patriarch, a colonizer—an imperialist! For this hole in my heart through which the wind never ceases to blow. For places wailing in unceasing and unwitnessed and unquenchable anguish since the day you raised a cross over them and declared them open for business. They wail still. I cannot shut them out!

I—

I want whirlwinds of chaos and falling stars. I want to burn this building down around you. I want to piss on your tombstone. I want to infect and ravage and destroy and desecrate as you and yours have done. I want you all extinct or never to have been born, you and all the sanctimonious suitor bastards who came after you and ejaculated plastic and paper and smokestacks and beliefs and asphalt and junk mail and churches and tracts upon the silently shrieking body of the lover of my lovers and the mother of my mothers. God damn every one of *you to your fiery believer's hell!!*

A long silence. A drop of sweat down my forehead. Another....
Then:

It is becoming more difficult for me to sense you, Ulysses. What is happening?

Knees trembling. Jaw slowly unclenching.

The conditions that make possible our contact are losing their alignment.

My sense of myself begins to grow tenuous as well. Is this the end of our encounter?

Not yet. There is one thing more to be done.

What a sigh I perceive from you!

You asked me what I want. What I really want is for you to have some of what I gathered into myself while pacing you.

I see. You want me to hurt as you have been hurt.

There is that. I have chased you 'round Good Hope and round the Horn' and up El Camino Real. Now that I have, I will unstring my bow and settle for a naked, searing moment of truth and reconciliation, for I know too well the displacement and rootlessness that made you what you were. I utterly condemn what you've done here and will protest it to my last heartbeat, but confronting you like this shows me that in the final reckoning, it's not for me to judge the man who did these things.

No. Judgment belongs to the Lord. Is this a confession, then?

In a way. Perhaps for you it will even serve as the best vicarious epiphany I can manage—for here is some of what flickers in the theater of my memory: fleeting images of where I have been in California, and what I lived, and what she has been to me. Now it will be yours, if only for a moment wandering between the worlds.

You would give this to me in spite of how you feel about me?

No. Because of how I feel about you.

Do you hate me?

Not anymore. I could hate a devil or a demon, but this encounter has taught me who you really are: a tired old ghost of a missionary with a heavy cross of unlived life around his neck. No, I do not hate you. I find you pitiable.

I am ready.

Very well....This is me as a boy, and 'he must get it from his mother,' and not knowing who they were talking about. This is being buried in fragrant autumn leaves. Their rustling coolness...Do you get the sense of it yet?

Ahhhhh.....

This is growing up afraid, this is hitting someone in the face, and this, my first kiss—stolen in the middle of a busy intersection. This is summer sage on the wind. And this is not belonging.

It would seem we are not so greatly different. In many ways...

Here I'm almost hit by lightning, twice. There I nearly drown in the Pacific, twice. Learning to swim, sketch, curse, spit, run, tell from the clouds when it will rain. Youthful folly in three foolish acts: Extracting a bone fragment after a botched dental operation. Fetching a companion from a cliff cave just before the eroding hillside slid down on it. Entering an office building in search of a missing coworker during a bomb threat. Yes, this is what we call 'civilization'...

There's my favorite kite receding one windy March high into the distance, so high I can barely see it. See the kite field 'developed' into a parking lot. Climbing a tree, stealing a pumpkin, eating an orange grown a few miles away, fingers sticky with pine sap. Sunday school, confirmation, anger, shame, and the joy-killing tolling of your God-damned bells.

If only they had tried to hear...

Learning my birth mother's name. Meeting my grandmother, grandfather, aunt, uncle, cousins, father, brother. A private ritual for the death of a friend's father; dreaming about the death of my own father, with whom I have lost contact. He was a man, take him for all in all...

This is betrayal, this is rage, and this, the glow of love doomed to fall by the camino real. Sitting with men confessing to beatings, rapes, murders they'd never been caught committing. This is what homeless people smell like. And this is why...

Ah, but seasons of the land, and wafted aromas of fir, wood smoke, star jasmine, fog, snow. An edge to the breeze as autumn steals over Southern California, felt as early as August. Blossoms and buds—do you see them? Red, purple, yellow, orange, white? So beckoning, so fragile, so intensely and vibrantly alive?— whispering of spring in the deeps of January.

Our time, it would seem, grows shorter...

So much to share, and so little possible! But we have heard the chimes at midnight—and here is what earthy Shakespeare wrote; here, the ecstasy of prayer in a tent while camping on the beach; here, the passion to create, circling like a red-tailed hawk and looking for a home, looking for a home, and burning bright and hot until it finds one. Here is dream, here is myth, here is steamy rock and roll. This is losing friends and relatives to death.

So much death...

Here we are at Port Los Angeles, the water thick with who knows what. Smog over the city like an evil demon. Cans dumped off the 101, and no end to them, no end. Rows of houses, duplexes, complexes, apartment buildings, highrises, business parks, where green hills once stood up in a hundred places: South San Francisco, San Juan Capistrano, Mira Mesa, Canoga Park, no outlet....See the grime, breath the rankness, fill your chest with it, pack your eyes with the sunken ships of vast factories; watch the faces of buildings clattering by, brisk and blank, stained with mildew or rust; the faces of inner city children, as brisk and blank as the buildings; here are spotlights, headlights, traffic signals where once the starlight shone.

Can you still sense me?...

But these are hungry gulls still wheeling above Pismo Beach, a crab eaten in Monterey, an earthquake in Calabasas, Fisherman's Wharf, a sailboat doing tricks off Dana Point. Look at these toddlers on a beach near La Jolla rolling their eyes at the sheer funniness of life. And the animals! Cats and dogs and squawking jays, a gaping bobcat, the neck of a giraffe, the rubbery skin of a pilot whale I hugged, a lizard I moved out of the road—feel his marvelously rough skin—and dolphins playing around the bow of my small boat off Oxnard... And this, are you there? Don't leave without this: the sound of the sea, not in your ears only but mine as well, a saltine swish of sparkling fingers curling up on Queen Calafia's shore, her burnished skin that's next of kin to a California dusk.

Very faintly:

May I...ask you something, Ulysses?

Yes...

How...does one... weep...without eyes?

Use mine, padre. Use mine.

I woke in my tent to a trumpet blowing reveille. Another day of maneuvering ahead. Time to get moving.

Veterans Park is a campground just south of the Presidio on its elbow of land angled between the peninsula and the City of Monterey. Walk downhill and you can see the cold gleam and twinkle of the Bay here and there between tall trunks. For about an hour at twilight, low clouds off the water slide over the tops of the trees in white streamers. In the early morning light a pony-tailed ranger collects the fees, then takes his weed cutter into the underbrush. I lit a homemade tuna-can burner to boil water for coffee. The faint bump of marching boots echoed crisply around the dew-moistened trees.

I was headed for Colton Hall to see where the state constitution had been signed in 1849.

The Hall was named after Walter Colton, California's first American mayor, and compiled from pale stone fronted by a two-story portico supported by smooth white columns. The outlaw Tiburcio Vasquez had been born near here in 1835. An unpublicized auction held here in 1859 transferred most of Monterey to David Jacks and Delos Ashley, a starkly plutonic deal it took decades to undo.

Inset into the red brick walkway gleamed the Great Seal of California depicting armored Minerva holding a spear while miners dug in the background. The framers picked her because California had sprung forth from the heads of its fathers. Or had she picked them? The Greeks knew her as Athena, wise warrior goddess of the polis; Montalvo had called her Calafia. I took a photograph and climbed the stairs to the second floor.

I found a rectangular conference room with a polished wood floor below and a candelabrum above. Two long tables pointed to a desk in front of a simple hearth. Robert Semple, chairman of the Constitution Convention, had sat here trying to get forty-eight representatives to cooperate long enough to hammer out an agreement about how to run the state. A portrait of George Washington hung above the fireplace.

On a whim I sat down at the desk in Semple's chair and tried to imagine the convention: the arguments, the happy exclamations, the motions; the gestures and voices of men who truly believed in what they were forging.

There in the capital of a county where words and depths of place and soul either meet together or descend together, I suddenly recalled today's date: November 11th. It was Veteran's Day, once known as Armistice Day.

Kurt Vonnegut had gotten himself born on November 11th, and

some of his words returned to me as I balanced a quill between my fingers:

> When I was a boy...all the people of all the nations which had fought in the First World War were silent during the eleventh minute of the eleventh hour of Armistice Day, which was the eleventh day of the eleventh month. It was during that minute in nineteen hundred and eighteen, that millions upon millions of human beings stopped butchering one another. I have talked to old men who were on battlefields during that minute. They have told me in one way or another that the sudden silence was the Voice of God. So we still have among us some men who can remember when God spoke clearly to mankind.

On his deathbed another writer, Steinbeck, had invoked Ecclesiastes, where it is written:

> The thing that hath been, it is that which shall be; and that which is done is that which shall be done: and there is no new thing under the sun. Is there any thing whereof it may be said, See, this is new?

Perhaps not from the perspective of Pluto, who in 1849 watched smiling conventioneers waddle home laden with big bags of silver. Some of them probably suspected or knew that seizing California had been a goal of President Polk's Mexican-American War ignited by a convenient incident in sister state Texas. The war had broken out in 1846, the year the Liberty Bell's crack had widened beyond repair—on George Washington's birthday.

What good were they, really, these documentary agreements written on fragile pieces of parchment?

A Hadean thought occurred to me then, transmitted perhaps from the spindly throne beneath me:

No one has devised a way to protect a constitution from the

greedy, who quote it to sanctify their greed, the exploitive, who enslave human beings in its name, the fanatical, who force their religion on others by subverting it, or the war-loving, who promise to uphold it and subvert it instead. But by setting down more enlightened standards for the organization of community (a root of "constitution" means "to stand"), this new document and others like it under the sun endured as evolutionary milestones because the ideals they proclaimed remain imperishably precious, a source of social and historical wealth even when stained with blood.

Vertigo

The sign said HOLLISTER CITY LIMITS, I think; graffiti made it difficult to decipher. The one legible word on a peeling billboard, "Hope," hovered near the face of a child.

I drove in from the west, from 101 to 156 until it decelerated into San Juan Road. Past the junkyard and over the gleam of the San Benito River and into Hollister's normally busy Fourth Street. A long, empty bar glimpsed through the large windows of The Vault Restaurant. Evening traffic was light into and through the crosshairs of Fourth and San Felipe downtown. The mission named after John the Baptist waited behind me in San Juan Bautista. I had passed it at twilight shortly after crossing over the border from Monterey into San Benito County. Travel fatigue said: Let it wait.

My plan to stay in nearby San Juan fell through when the hotels I called refused to hold a room without a credit card, and I had none. I lacked even a bank account thanks to the ChexSystems blacklist of people in debt to a bank. My Wells Fargo checking account had fallen $250 into the red during my long spell of unemployment, at which time the bank closed the account and added my name to the fatal list. Paying off the amount owed made no difference to Wells Fargo. The record would remain. Because all major banks consulted ChexSystems, seven frustrating years must come and go before I would be deemed responsible enough to open another bank account: an effective system for jamming a spoke into the wagon wheel of financial recuperation. I yearned to get off all imprisoning grids and depend on nothing but the land and the sun and the seasons for sustenance. My ancestors had known problems of their own, but forced dependency on the empire wasn't one of them.

I found a motel in Hollister manned by a friendly clerk who did not care about judgments or credits. "Sure, we're light tonight—come on in."

After unpacking I lay down on the neatly made bed and got up again. Might as well haunt the town.

I wonder when we will evolve a truly Californian kind of house suitable for our land and climate. Although relieved to see the twisty branches of orchards instead of stucco-filled tracts topped with terracotta "mission style" tiles on this, my first pass through town (the tracts would appear later), the pale wood sidings and slanted roofs of homes reminded me of Nebraska. What about a flat roof to catch and store rainwater and to grow gardens and pleasant spaces for sitting out under the sun? Or native plants and trees and perhaps an herb garden near the kitchen? Walls of brick or stone or clay would hold heat on cold days and keep the indoors cool in hot weather. Ultimately, rising temperatures, more frequent droughts, and vanishing water supplies will force us to adapt, so we might as well do it sooner and more creatively than later.

In a diner lined with red booths covered with drumhead-tight upholstery I received an overpriced hamburger brought by a fat waitress with scraggly black hair. Her smirk informed me that the establishment served no wine. My eyes took in a yellow tile floor, plastic blossoms in a pink ceramic vase, a waitress who was no Salome. What else was there to see, sans adjectives? A Taco Bell and a Quick Stop across the street. A feeling as though the town waited for something to happen. I could almost smell the darkness outside seeping in through the windows.

Named after St. Benedict, torcher of sacred groves, an order-founding monk so rigidly legalistic that his own religious brethren tried to poison him, San Benito County stands geographically surrounded, with the Santa Clara Valley and Santa Cruz to the north and west, Merced to the east, Monterey to the south and west, and the Diablo and Gabilan ranges on either side. Through the most seismically active county in California cuts the San Andreas Fault, aptly named after a monk who died pulled and stretched over a cross of diagonally placed beams. It intersects the Calaveras Fault near Hollister. Tectonic plates grind and crush in perpetual opposition directly below Mission San Juan Bautista, founded in 1797. The 1906 earthquake ran a crack like a streak of black lightning down the center of the church. Most county residents live in either shaking Hollister or quaking San Juan Bautista.

In my journeying up El Camino Real I had often seen how easily ecological facts and features translated into unconscious but highly persistent metaphors. A culture dwelling in conscious closeness to the land would not be surprised by this, but we Westerners in general and Americans in particular had been displacing, uprooting, and pioneering for so long that we never fully arrived anywhere at all, as Wendell Berry has pointed out. As a result, it has taken a Thoreau to know Concord, a Muir to love the Sierras, and a Mary Austin to articulate the arid beauty of the Owens Valley. Today we rely on an Andy Goldsworthy to show us Scotland, a Peter Ackroyd to get inside London, and a Berry to explain the inner life and needs of Kentucky.

We might blink, then, but should not, at the long history of oppositions and ruptures in San Benito County, from those at the mission (where neophytes tried to kill a padre) to melees at the New Idria cinnabar mine (1851) to bursting cannons, marauding outlaws, erupting juveniles (since the 1980s), and even an exploding locomotive when cold water met a hot engine. The cross on Pagan Hill has been burned and axed; Castro revolted against Governor Micheltorena in 1843 and was revolted against by John Fremont; the city council of Hollister, again and again in deadlock, has been described by a former city attorney as "dysfunctional." Thomas Flint and William Hollister, the first Americans to settle here, feuded over who got what land until Hollister relocated west of the San Benito River and Flint withdrew to the east. Another disagreement led to them trading sides, with Flint's family now on the east of Rancho

San Justo and Hollister's on the west. A fight broke out years later over which town got the county seat, San Benito or Hollister. Hollister won....for then.

So when the platter-wielding waitress condescended to bring me a root beer, I realized that the quick surge of anger pulsing through me ran into a larger local pattern of ignition and collision than a touch of travel tiredness might explain. Easy explanations are the sure death of inquiry.

Back at the motel I reluctantly clicked on the television for a bit of local programming, for something that would tell me more about this oppositional place. The evening blare fare included Nicolas Cage in a Mustang flying over a row of police cars, a special on volcanoes, a Dodge ad featuring a smoking dragster, screeching teens preparing to fire a cannon, and a riot at a football game. The resulting sensory mush fell apart into senseless fragments: schizophreniform commercials overrun with anorexic models, leering executives on cell phones, jumbled strains of loud music, and frantic snatches of sleaze designed by unscrupulous psychologists to amuse and persuade the uncritical. Obviously I had repressed all recollection of how jarring TV could be. After enduring twenty minutes of this I turned off the set and stepped outside in lieu of putting my steel-tipped shoe through the picture tube.

> So I bought a .44 magnum in a solid steel cast
> And in the blessed name of Elvis, well I just let it blast
> 'Til my TV lay in pieces there at my feet
> And they busted me for disturbin' the almighty peace
> Judge said "What you got in your defense, son?"
> Fifty-seven channels and nothin' on
> Fifty-seven channels and nothin' on

The Springsteen song thrumbed on in my mind as I took a deep breath and looked around. The motel was not only light on guests, it was as empty as an exhausted mine. Removing a pouch of tobacco from my denim jacket, I filled my pipe, packed it, and lit it. The aromatic smoke mixed pleasantly with the cool night air.

The distant sputter of a motorcycle engine turning over. Since 1947, when four thousand bikers roared in long black-clad columns into Hollister, the motorized Knights Templar known as the Hells Angels have made an annual pilgrimage here. I had missed the event, but in an adjacent parking lot, a leather-jacketed man angrily gyrated his arms and walked on. I craned my neck, lost sight of the shadowy stranger, but remembered another outlaw with an attitude. *You brood of vipers! Who warned you to flee the wrath to come?* Sitting in prison before losing his head, John probably felt that even the Redeemer had abandoned him.

The angry Baptist's tomb was desecrated in turn by another outlaw. Julian the Apostate was a nephew of Constantine, first Christian Emperor of Rome and the man most responsible for welding freedom-seeking Christian sects into a hardened state religion. Brought up in that religion, Julian rebelled against it. When he claimed the throne in 360, he opened his arms and treasuries to pagans oppressed much like the Christians had been before their rise to power. In 362 he passed an edict to enforce religious freedom. If nothing else, rebels remain history's disregarded but persistent example of how repression always strengthens the repressed.

Templar, temple, temper, rebel, temblor. Although not cognate they vibrate in a common frequency. At least in California.

Most cultures revere some sacred personification of the principle of justice, whether a god, a wise animal, or a spirit. For the Greeks this principle went by the name of Themis ("to put in place"), bride of Zeus and born of earth and sky.

In ancient depictions the poised goddess of *law* ("put, lay; something fixed") and *order* ("to arrange") holds a sword in one hand and scales in the other, the sword for discriminating between the opposites, the scale for carefully weighing them. She usually holds the scales higher than the sword. The Romans called her Justitia, and the Age of Exploration blindfolded her. Unlike angry Nemesis, who confronted one extreme with its counterpart, and often to deadly effect, calm Themis judged the extremes together so both would receive just judgment. Where they collide instead of alternating, some version of Themis, the archetypal balancer, is waiting in the wings to weigh the matter.

Peering through the finely ground lenses of myth and metaphor as all our land-centered ancestors did reveals San Benito County as one of her earthly altars. Aside from the goddess's role as an inspirer of oracles like the local Indian woman who spoke of the great 1906 quake before it struck, the dual motifs of judgment and justice radiate all the way back to the naming of the mission and of Hollister's rancho. The county's most comprehensive history to date was penned by a judge and profiles a series of outlaws and lawmen, some of whom change roles, like the mayor on trial for attacking a deputy, and the judge who defended himself by clouting a suspect with an ashtray.

This dream came to me before I made my first visit:

> I am in a hotel room somewhere in San Benito County. Second floor. I keep trying to leave, only to discover I've forgotten something: a shirt, some pants.... Under a table I notice a small sleeping bag and, beside it, a child's toy left by the previous occupants....Outside the window, trees are swaying: there's an earthquake in progress. The building I'm in moves a good ten feet back and forward, but fluidly, without the usual jar of a quake, as a voice over the loudspeaker comments calmly on the motion while it lasts. On one of my returns for something forgotten I meet a woman in her fifties who tells me about a certain storybook I should read. She is very attractive. We embrace..... and I wake up from the dream right then with "This Old Man" jingling through my mind.

To enter into such a dream on the purely personal level would not necessarily be a detour. Forgotten clothes standing in as the attire of a persona left behind but beckoning still, for example, or accoutrements of childhood out of sight but still in mind. Re-collecting pieces of myself on my way through California. But to stay in the personal can be limiting, especially on a journey such as this one.

Bringing in the dimension of place opens up the dream even more. Returning for what has been forgotten was not only a prime task of my odyssey, but an imaginal anticipation of doublings and doublings back in rupturing San Benito County, whose first prominent newspaper was the *Echo*. Scouts had sited the mission next to two wells twenty paces apart. The small sleeping bag and unspecified toy: not just my own from an earlier time, but also left behind by the child on the billboard outside Hollister? By Isaac Mylar, who came to California as a boy in 1852, grew up in this county and wrote about the mission and its surrounding arc of town? Whoever he was, that unseen child, had he slept under the table for shelter from disruptive earthquakes? Where had he gone once the rumbling died down?

"Paddywhack" denotes the midline ligament that allows a four-footed animal—a sheep, for instance—to hold up its head. It is also an archaic word for an Irishman: Irish like the local Breen family, like Isaac Mylar, like descendants of Southern Pacific railway workers who infused the county with a pungent dose of Celtic culture. The word also means a rage, passion, or temper, a trade term spoken by butchers, and the administration of a thrashing. Because so many officers treading the beats of the urban world were thought to be Irish, "paddywhack" is believed to have inspired another colorful law-and-order term: "paddy wagon."

I've forgotten if the dream woman (a personification of the place? A mask of Themis?) ever mentioned the name of the storybook. Perhaps it was one of the history books I studied after visiting the county, including Mylar's. On the other hand, perhaps it was *The Odyssey*.

As for knickknacks, many adorned a film character named Madeline as she found herself tailed by a retired Irish police investigator. One of them, a necklace, tipped him off that she wasn't who she seemed to be.

Climactic scenes of the 1958 film *Vertigo* were shot in San Benito County, and the film as a whole resonates and rumbles with the local vibes right from its opening scene of a pistol-wielding cop dashing after an outlaw scrambling across a red-tiled roof. In the next scene James Stewart, who had hung from a roof by his fingers, tries to balance a cane in the air.

In the film considered by some to be Hitchcock's greatest, an old friend named Gavin Elster hires acrophobic former detective John "Scottie" Ferguson to follow his wife Madeline around Northern California. It would seem she is possessed by Carlotta Valdes, the spirit of her dead great-grandmother. Like Llorona, Valdes was dumped by a wealthy lover determined to take her children; and like Llorona, Madeline wears black and white, gravitates toward water, and haunts the local missions. She also has a habit of vanishing. Valdes had wandered the streets of San Francisco pleading "Where is my child?" before killing herself in despair.

Although the film's original title was *From Among the Dead*, its echoes of La Llorona seem to be unconscious, even the bookshop named Argosy (a reference to Jason, whose wife was sad Medea), the name of the screenwriters' previous novel (*She Who Was No More*), and the question Scottie's jealous friend Madge asks herself after watching Madeline drive away from his apartment: "Was it a ghost?"

The vertiginous motif of doublings and opposites shadows the entire film. Some examples:

- The film's double climax.
- The mission's "double" bell tower (a fire destroyed the original).
- The prominence of Hitchcock's double spiral emblem.
- Several reflections in mirrors, windows, and paintings.
- Judy and Madeline, Madeline and Carlotta, Carlotta and Llorona.
- The deliberate contrast of Madeline's white coat and black scarf.
- The famous "contra zoom" technique invented for this film: a shot that pans forward while tracking backward.

- The McKittrick Hotel doubling as the old Valdes home.
- Madeline's visit to two missions (Dolores and San Juan Bautista).
- Scottie's traumatic repetition of being up high while someone screams and falls.
- Gavin's ditching of Judy, repeating the fate of Carlotta.
- The double makeover of Judy at the hands of male lovers.
- Kim Novak jumping into San Francisco Bay repeatedly during filming, with James Stewart going in after her.
- The film itself was released, shelved, and then re-released. Its restoration amalgamated old and new colors, sounds, and types of film.

Why do we repeat unsatisfying relationships and destructive old patterns? Freud, who called this syndrome the "repetition compulsion," thought we were all prone to a streak of self-destructiveness, but perhaps we should nominate Themis over Thanatos. A century of psychoanalysis has clarified the deep human need to polish and replay old plotlines we never got to finish, especially when they encompass an injustice inflicted on us or by us. Those caught in the replays might feel as though the goddess who regulates relationships and power, judges and assemblies, were recreating past wrongs and wounds to inflict punishment, but instead she might bring a chance for redress.

Her sword of psychic justice gleams with a double edge, however. Without healing, without reflection, victims so easily find themselves revictimized or turn into victimizers themselves. A perpetrator is an escaped inmate who finds a new prison and accepts a promotion to warden. And so the cycle of injustice grinds on relentlessly as would-be avengers inflict new wounds. The virtuosity of *Vertigo* demonstrates this dizzying spiral of the blind compulsion to repeat, over and over, in the absence of the kind of Lloronic night vision that sees the cycle through to its end.

Does the same dynamic apply to the land and the restless ghosts who haunt it? Do the padres still play "The Devil's Waltz" on a broken pipe organ to attract curious natives? Do the Indians still play sad songs here from inside the walls of "the mission of music"? Does Llorona still drift aimlessly in the plaza as Kim Novak did for years after *Vertigo* was shot?

> She looks like a princess in somebody's rags,
> She dreams of a world without danger,
> Climbing a stair to a room of her own
> With someone who isn't a stranger,
> But now she eats what she can,
> And accepts what there is for a man,
> This nobody's child, this precarious girl,
> Who lives on the rim of the world.
> — "On the Rim of the World," by Malvina Reynolds

It was too early to enter the mission, so I sauntered around the Alameda. A spring breeze off the fragrant emerald hills carried some of the dampness of a recent rain. Two-story shops of wood, brick, and even adobe preserved the sense of walking down the planks of an old western town. Junk shops and clothing stores and coffee shops, yes, but nothing like the shrieking red and yellow of a McDonald's. GALLERIA TONANTZIN, read the white side of one mission-style shop. WOMEN'S CONTEMPORARY ART. Tonantzin, undivided mythic sister to bright Guadalupe and dark Llorona.

> My Virgin de Guadalupe is not the mother of God. She is God. She is a face for a god without a face, an indígena for a god without ethnicity, a female deity for a god who is genderless, but I also understand that for her to approach me, for me to finally open the door and accept her, she had to be a woman like me.
>
> — Sandra Cisneros

After I had visited the mission, filing away my impressions—a sculpture of mission founder Father Fermin Lasuén sunk up to the waist in concrete and stone as though they had opened up to swallow him; high ceiling beams stretching above a wood floor that gave off echoes; small high windows unable to relieve the gloom in a chapel dominated by repeating arches; a lonely graveyard of crude crosses nodding over anonymous weed-covered plots; a cluster of picnic benches on the tall grass—I stepped outside onto the wide veranda. Walking a wide dirt path to the front of the mission, I stopped to photograph a statue of an Indian holding his arms aloft, evidently in prayer. Viewed from this angle, however, he looked like he had been stabbed in the back.

I circled around to the plaza, once a stage stop and now a grass-covered bus stop circled by facades from out of a Hollywood western. The heavy sense of being watched by unseen presences reminded me of Stephen King's novel *The Shining*. Perhaps every prettied-up history-repressing mausoleum raised to sanctify a massacre operates as a kind of Overlook Hotel, not just for a cursed Shining few, but for everyone caught in its ecohistorical field. I could almost hear Llorona moaning. A shudder went through me. If anything, the green plaza smiling upward at the sun felt even creepier than the dank corridors of the mission.

Behind the bronze Indian, before the ORIGINAL ROUTE EL CAMINO REAL sign, between the plates of the San Andreas, below the mission campanario, I stared out across neat rows of expectant soil to the line of distant mountains; and as the gloom I had outpaced all morning caught up with me, I finally admitted to myself that nothing I could persuade myself to do, push myself to do, or bleed to do would bring that weeping ghost back to life, or remove a single broken-hearted tear from her tormented imaginal face.

I am sorry I'm too late, I thought at the place around me, the graves, the fields, the peaks. *I would do anything to reverse it all, put it back the way it should have been. But in spite of everything I have done and been through and been given, I am insufficient to the task.*

Not so heroic after all, I squatted condemned to that dismal reverie of self-judgment until a bus pulled up to disgorge tourists at the south end of the plaza. Time to go be depressed somewhere else. And there was always the highway ready to bear me still farther north.

Lingering, I tried to focus my mind on a blurred snapshot of memory, glimpsing the face of the child on the billboard I had passed.

What is innocence? "Unless ye become like children," Jesus observed, warning of influential men—"wolves in sheep's clothing"—who lured seekers and followers into a distracted and childish state of pseudo-innocence, the tool of the cynical tyrant. Jesus had also recommended taking the beam from our eye before removing the splinter from our brother's nineteen centuries before Freud wrote about projection. Both saw idealism's shadow side. They saw that pseudo-innocence invites in oppression and opens the dark door to injustice. Every institutionalized horror begins with the words, "It could never happen here," or, "to me." As psychologist Rollo May stated baldly, the ultimate mistake is the refusal to look evil in the face.

Considered in the harsh clear light of Themis, consciousness can only mature by outgrowing pseudo-innocence—and whatever heroic impulses hover nearby waiting to be "helpful."

In the end, I reflected, we are judged not by what we ideally intend, but by the consequences of what we do in this world. Themis consciousness is a painful acquisition. It quakes pleasant assumptions into dust, runs deep cracks through denial, stands calmly between supposed absolutes without succumbing to either. It is not impressed by waving flags or crosses. Reading between the lines of sermons and speeches, it does not sign up for social programs that impose salvation or improvement on the unwilling. Consciousness, like charity, begins at home.

Rupture hurts and terrifies at first, but from between the cracks new possibilities rise into view as decrepit authorities both inner and outer find themselves deposed. One can almost hear the archetypally authorized judgment pronounced above old idols littering the floor, toppled from the scales that found them obsolete: *Not innocent, but not guilty either. Case dismissed.*

Lines from Arthur Miller's *After the Fall* returned to me as I departed the plaza and walked back to my car with a certain new lightness in my step:

> You know, more and more I think that for many years I looked at life like a case at law, a series of proofs. When you're young you prove how brave you are, or smart; then, what a good lover; then, a good father; finally, how wise, or powerful or what-the-hell-ever. But underlying it all, I see now, there was a presumption. That I was moving on an upward path toward some elevation, where—God knows what—I would be justified, or even con-demned—a verdict anyway. I think now that my disaster really began when I looked up one day—and the bench was empty.

As familiar ground gives way, glimmerings appear in the dark to hint at a new kind of innocence uncrucified by cynicism, disen-chantment, nausea, or despair. A fresh, imaginative innocence for balancing on shifting surfaces not described in any rule books.

I was a long way from understanding its source, but a decrepit billboard losing its face had suggested a word to go forth with: "Hope."

Escapade Velocity

Santa Cruz said to me, "Live in this balmy pleasure
dome and you'll never age, at least not much," and
the head shops, students sharing joints, trouba-
dours singing "Blowing in the Wind," Volkswagens
plastered with college parking permits, radical
broadsheets covering utility poles, and women in
granny glasses walking with that sixties sidewalk-
scraping shuffle did make it easy for a middle-aged
man to imagine himself a quarter century younger.

— Thurston Clarke

To me Santa Cruz said, "Hear my story or I'll kill you." A white van
out of nowhere missed my car by a few feet in the first of several
near-collisions during my time in town.

It was breathtakingly lovely here, I saw coming in on Highway 1
past Aptos, where a fishing pier at Seacliff Beach faced off against a
sunken concrete ship. The S. S. *Palo Alto* started sea life as an oil
tanker and then did time as a casino and dance hall before a storm
washed out its midsection. I would soon learn that it was only one
of many wrecked transportation experiments in this high-velocity
county. A few miles west in Capitola tottered the ruins of Rispin

Mansion, home to a ghostly woman in black.

As with other places along the King's Highway, I arrived without having studied the local history, so I couldn't understand at first why I kept getting lost in a twelve-square-mile city for which I carried adequate maps. No matter how carefully I drove, I could not go straight to any consciously selected destination. My car had detoured onto an invisible roller coaster winding up and down through forested, sea-facing Santa Cruz, its deceptive youthfulness glowing seventy miles north of the Plutonic depths of Monterey.

From Ocean Boulevard I made my way west to Pacific, pulled over, and stopped. My head ached. I locked the car and went for a walk in a downtown vaguely reminiscent of Santa Barbara's State Street.

A man on a skateboard whisked by me. I looked again. He seemed to be in his thirties. A woman in her forties with a well-pierced midriff drifted by, followed by a lean cyclist with a billowing mane of snow-white hair. Quite a few young surfers milled about, some having a smoke, but other standers by in their twenties laughed loud laughs while fingering chains dangling from their roomy pants. Some of these looked at me as though casing me for a street crime. I took care to keep my face blank and my manner confident as a Tom Petty song tripped through my mind:

Well, they're putting me out on the old King's Road/I didn't know which way to go....

A psychological case could be made that the American phobia of aging demonstrates an unconscious reluctance to embrace the role of the seasoned, initiated elder. "Phobia" because those caught by it go to any lengths to avoid the physical weathering of getting old, from paying for plastic surgery to dressing like a teen. They would flee aging itself if they could.

It isn't always like that. In many cultures the elderly hold an honored place as mentors and keepers of wisdom and history. Members of these cultures do not assume that adulthood, let alone wisdom, befalls as automatically as wrinkles. Over many generations they and their ancestors have evolved elaborate rites of passage and initiation to discipline and mature and dance the young into being caring, responsible elders. These procedures, which weave art, song, ancient lore, a sense of place, and the gratefully gathered fruits of the earth into an effective ceremonial whole, not only strengthen the harmony and knowledge of the community, they solve the problem of how to keep immature, ambitious people out of positions of power. By contrast, cultures without effective rites of passage into adulthood or adequate public models of wise, balanced elders—the sort of sensible people who learn from their mistakes and manage their feelings instead of acting them out—crank out large numbers of parentified, neuroticized, angry young people and emotionally childish adults.

The world of myth reflects in its stories this troubling polarization. Where the magical child appears, especially a Divine Child, the old man is not far behind. Because they belong together and need each other, splitting them apart, or trying to repress one of them in favor of the other, pathologizes both. It would be like trying to have height with no depth or vice versa. Everyone knows of daydreamers so impractical and airy that only an unseen snake wakes them up, and of curmudgeons with their eyes on the ground who walk into a tree branch lit with bright blossoms. The psyche resists being torn into opposites, insisting instead on expressing itself as a whole. The self-appointed moralizer crusading against "indecency" secretly sleeps with the devil. The cynic is a closet idealist who has not found his road to Damascus.

The Roman poet Ovid gave the magical child the name *puer* ("poo-air") *aeternus*—"eternal boy"—in the *Metamorphoses*, where he wrote, "Behold puer aeternus, with his angel-seeming face / But oh, those invisible horns!" C. G. Jung used this term to describe the psychological syndrome of the idealistic, dreamy, unconventional charmer who jumps from enthusiasm to enthusiasm but never settles into psychological adulthood. Evoking a figure from popular folklore, psychologist Dan Kiley published a book in 1983 called *The Peter Pan Syndrome: Men Who Have Never Grown Up*. A male under the *puer* spell promises much but seldom carries through, finds practicality difficult at best, loves ideas but ignores details, and sometimes dreams about flying above the ground. His female counterpart is the *puella aeternus*, the wistful girl with her head in the clouds.

In life and myth these dreamers are shadowed by the ancient figure of the *senex* ("old man"), a wise elder when positive and a cranky authoritarian when not.

Viewing Santa Cruz through this mythical-psychological perspective reveals a coast upon which the tempestuous *puer* energies come out to play, idealistic and energizing when tended consciously but angry and impulsive when combated, ignored, or otherwise unconsciously identified with. The place itself was named after the Holy Cross on which the Redeemer died, a Divine Child not destined to mature into an elder. The same might be said of Villa de Branciforte, a small pueblo dug in across the San Lorenzo River from the mission in 1797. Just as *puer* attracts *senex*, *senex* also attracts *puer*—much to the consternation of the padres, who looked with loathing at their gambling, rowdy neighbors. Equipped with a racetrack and abundant alcohol, Branciforte lived hard and died young, but not before its denizens looted the "hard luck" mission where more than one lecherous *senex amans* had mistreated a young Ohlone or Yokuts inmate. (Like "Miwok," "Chumash," and "Pomo," the names "Ohlone" and "Yokuts" are exonyms imposed by outsiders to cover large groups of culturally and linguistically diverse native people.) After the festivities a *puella* was seen darting by with a padre's socks on her feet.

Models of development under the *puer*'s influence strenuously emphasize the literalized metaphor of growth. In Santa Cruz, with its luxuriant stands of cottonwood, fir, pine, alder, sycamore, and redwood, the metaphor is hard to miss even before climbing among the Santa Cruz Mountains. In keeping with liberal culture there, a redwood planted by William Jennings Bryan and Charles Caldwell Moore in praise of peace refused to sprout until after World War I. Axel Erladson did better with his Scotts Valley "tree circus" of hardwoods forced to grow in bizarre loopy patterns. For a time the Valley also sheltered a theme park called Santa's Village manned by little green-suited men. The bobsled ride carried onward the local motif of high velocity while the Christmas tree spun completely around. The park closed in 1979, one of several failed carnivals around the county to echo the fate of spent Branciforte.

Fruits and vegetables in nearby Watsonville have been known to reach impressive sizes, particularly potatoes, pumpkins, apples, and strawberries. Local Stephen Martinelli learned how to lock cider into a state of extended youthfulness. In a fateful *puer* moment the *senex*ian hand of Judge James Logan accidentally crossed a European red raspberry with an American blackberry to produce the berry named after him.

If growth be a piling of one thing atop another, Friar McNamee's 1884 proposal for a new brick church might qualify. He wanted it where the old mission church had stood, but a hardware store and lumber yard eventually claimed the site. McNamee also wanted to make over an old wooden church into a boy's school.

High above Watsonville, a more successful school for children sits within a fog-drenched redwood forest towering on and around the Mount Madonna Retreat Center. Radiating from its shrine to Lord Hanuman, stairways guarded by icons of flying monkeys run level by level down to the road. The monk Baba Hari Dass, or Babaji, occasionally rides up in a modest silver Taurus to bless visitors and daub red dots on their foreheads. He knows several languages but speaks none of them, having taken a vow of silence in 1952.

Boys will be boys, but sometimes growth gives way to a tree circus of obstacles that twist it out of the shape of its original nature. When growth goes wrong, the community must deal with the likes of real estate and mining crook Isaac Graham, who showed up in the mid-1800s to marry a woman half his age, chase her after she fled to San Francisco disguised as a man, and win custody of her daughters after his son (nobody had known he had a son) killed her brother. Locals also had to reckon with Judge Joseph Skirm, one of the town jail's first occupants, who won the love of Mary Burger after shooting at the man who was dating her. The Santa Cruz gallery of boyish acting out includes mountain man Charley McKiernan, who lost part of his skull in a fight with a bear; Jason Brown, a Ben Lomond resident who collected aircraft parts he never assembled into a plane; Kenneth Kitchen, bricklaying builder of a submarine repeller and a Court of Mysteries to outlast the Apocalypse; and Father William "The Comforter" Riker, polygamous master of Holy City in the mountains, founder of radio station KFQU (think about it), and inventor of Hawaiian Punch. In town one salesman of a concoction called Vigor of Life hired a singer for what must have sounded like the definitive *puer* anthem: "Don't Leave Your Mother, Tom."

Here follows a brief and possibly nonrepresentative gathering of more or less random quotations uttered in my presence by Santa Cruz residents when I first got to town:

- "Sure, sugar. Over there." — a waitress in response to my request for a payphone. Glitter flashed from her eyelids.
- "How busy we are depends on....well [giggle], business, and that depends on the season. It's kind of a mood thing, I would say." — the lip-ringed owner of a restaurant.
- "You're on the wrong Soquel. There are two of them, you know." — a helpful gas station attendant.
- "What?" — a teen being asked the way to the hardware store. Judging from the tone, hammers and saws might never have been invented.
- "Who gives a shit? I hope the whole damned station burns down. Then I can collect the insurance money. Piss on it." — a service station owner asked what it was like to work in speedy Santa Cruz.
- "$%*#@!!!!"— a trinity of drunks singing as they wobbled through a hotel parking lot and out onto Ocean.
- "These things really go. Wanna take a ride?" — the leering employee of an electric car business established near the beach.

Of course, the county has also seen its share of examples of the negative *senex*. Among the earliest were Father Ramon Olbés, who ordered a female neophyte lashed for refusing to copulate with her husband in front of him; Father Quintana, who handled his iron-tipped whip so frequently that desperate inmates strangled him in his cloak; and Olbés' replacement, Father Gil y Taboada, famous for having sex with young Indian women until one of them—a rape vic-tim—bestowed on him the gift of syphilis.

As for the positive and creative face of the *puer*, it shines out here with unusual brightness in the *puella* arena of women's bold tran-scendence of convention. Picture Eliza Farnham—determined suf-fragist and co-builder with Georgiana Bruce of El Rancho La Libertad—bumping over the Santa Cruz Mountains in her horse-drawn buggy, the first driver with the nerve to go up there. Or Eliza Boston, the first woman to hold public office (school trustee) in Santa Cruz and a founder of the first local suffragist society. Her colleagues included Elizabeth Stanton and Susan B. Anthony. Another bold driver, stage coach and horse expert Charley Parkhurst, was believed to be a man until her wardrobe came off at death. By some accounts she was also the first woman to vote in California.

As far back as 1883, Martina Castro gained notoriety as one of the few women to own land in the state when she took the reins of the Soquel Augmentacion Rancho. This was a year after Josephine McCrackin welcomed her new husband to the ranch she had pur-chased from Lyman Burrell. McCrackin would found both the Sempervirens Club of California in 1901 to look after the redwoods and the state's first bird protection society. Her lifetime's worth of writing and speaking and leading and organizing would inspire the 1902 preservation of Big Basin as California's oldest state park.

Feminism has taught us that "the personal is political," and psy-chologist Carol Gilligan that "to have a voice is to have a self." The political raised its voice in 1969 when Shameless Hussy at UC Santa Cruz rose to the status of the nation's first feminist press. Its con-tributors would include notable and provocative writers such as Susan Griffin (*Woman and Nature, A Chorus of Stones*) and Pat Parker (*Womanslaughter, Movement in Black*). Papier-Mache Press and HerBooks Feminist Press followed this lead over the next two decades.

Now in her sixties, Susan has taken on the role of an elder, as I saw while greeting her at an academic conference we attended in Santa Barbara. Her wistful smile and unbending candor still gave off the archetypal sparkle of the ageless struggle for a just and inviting world where everyone feels at home.

From Santa Cruz I drove rapidly north up 17 and wound back and forth on the two-laned 9. Tailgaters looming in my rearview mirror were not impressed by my velocity. I pulled off into almost every turnout below Big Basin to let thrill-seekers risking their necks zoom by until two cyclists weaving uncaring in the very center of the road delayed my approach to the ranger station.

In Santa Cruz that old Branciforte racetrack turned out to be paradigmatic. It reincarnated as the chute fitted together by Edwin Penfield for sliding freshly pulled potatoes down into waiting boats, as another chute converted into a platform for tram cars carrying lime, as redwood pipes channeling water over Mission Hill, as a lumber flume fourteen miles long, as a toll road built over the mountains by two companies in frantic competition, and even as the Santa Cruz Railroad. It's as though the admirable surfing qualities off Lighthouse Point extend inland as well, there to mingle with the water streaming from the mountains down through the San Lorenzo Valley and into the flood-prone, nitrate-polluted river that finally splashes into the Pacific.

Flight is perhaps the *puer*'s most characteristic quality, signature, and mode of being. It multiplies at will into flights of ideas, flights of fancy, literal flights off the ground. *I can fly, I can fly, I can fly!* exults Peter Pan in Disney's anticipation of *Homo aeronauticus*. But what comes up must come down, as the old *senex*ian saying insists like a sternly wagging finger.

Jung thought of this law as *compensation*, the psyche's attempt to balance out its extremes. Caught in the inhuman power of *puer* enthusiasm, heedless flight is apt to end suddenly and sometimes tragically, as with the ever-soaring patient Jung warned against mountain-climbing after hearing the man's dream of plummeting to his death. As the subsequent tragedy confirmed, to wish away limitations in a grandiose power-climb of narcissistic omnipotence only tempts the gods to apply stringent grounding measures. Imagine the terror of Icarus when he realized too late that his wings were melting. Apple Computer co-founder and innovator Steve Wozniak must have felt a similar terror when his Beechcraft plane crashed on takeoff from Sky Park.

By 1876, trains and horse cars were already getting in each other's way. Within a year Frederick Hihn, funder of the redwood pipes supplying water to the city, set up shop his City Railway Company to compete with James Pierce's Pacific Avenue. Contrary to the doctrine of free market fundamentalism, neither operation ran well, primarily because of insufficient spending for maintenance. Hihn's red cars stood stranded and soaked during winter rainstorms. Pierce's yellow cars ground to a halt in the unshoveled mud.

The eventual end of the red and yellow feud did not stop the city's transportation ups and downs. When the South Pacific Coast Railroad came to town in 1880, a train leaped from the tracks to kill fourteen celebrants where they stood. A tunneling operations disaster carried off sixty-five Chinese laborers. When Fred Swanton, eventual builder of a failed casino, set up the Santa Cruz Electric Light and Power Company in 1889, the debut street car broke down on opening day at Walnut and Mission. Electrical failures persisted until the cars came humming to a stop in 1926. Buses had replaced horse-drawn streetcars two years before, when a bus collided with a grader.

Pageantry and disaster met off the coast as well. In 1869 the steamer *Columbia* crashed south of Pigeon Point and dumped a load of Christmas packages into the sea. In 1955, a flood swamped the Water Carnival, rushed under bridges decked out in shining red bells, and carried off red and green decorations on the morning of Christmas Eve.

Cars leaping off the rails or colliding with each other, trains jumping tracks, loose explosives blowing up sections of roadway, boys riding bicycles recklessly down the rails, engineers run over, dismembered, or electrocuted: the eerie ferocity of human accidents met its match only in the elements. A tidal wave, flood, and earthquake had destroyed the original mission. In 1906 a fire burned down the magnificently named Neptune Casino, and a storm washed out a wharf a year later. In 1912 storms halted rail passage between Santa Cruz and Capitola, and in 1915 winter weather stopped construction teams chopping at the Glenwood Highway. On the day it was finally finished, a girder hit Supervisor James Harvey in the head near where a streetcar had leaped from its course. The celebration was cancelled, but when the Glenwood did open, cars struck a sharp drop-off that smashed the spokes out of their wheels.

Stormy Neptune has also visited the Los Gatos Highway (17) on occasion. It opened in 1938, and in 1941 winter storms closed it down to two lanes. In 1974 winter rain sank the surface seventeen inches near Alma Fire Station and snow slowed and then stranded unhappy drivers. But most of the mishaps along "Blood Alley" (or "Killer 17") circle around the fact that its 16.5 miles wind through two hundred and eighty-four tight turns: the equivalent of thirty-six full circles. Of the hundreds of accidents reported on its curves by Caltrans, speeding retains the lead in frequency.

Why has nothing been done about all these hurried catastrophes? "Bureaucracy" always offers an easy explanation, but perhaps they have more to do with the *puer*'s unbreakable faith in his immortality. Buoyed up by timeless flights of inspiration, he cannot be troubled to remember every bump in the road down here—even if they do add up over centuries.

I thought about all this as I slowly unpacked my tent Eureka for a night in Big Basin. Even here things felt intense. As hungry mosquitoes tried to dive-bomb through my jeans, a man's shriek rose over a neighboring campsite to ricochet among the trees: "We are here to take a VACATION!!" Alert rangers promptly removed the happy couple.

I felt at odds with Santa Cruz. I had not planned to come here. My business, or so I had told myself, was confined to the missions founded by Junípero Serra. That made ten counting Santa Barbara. After that I was through with traveling up and down coastal California letting these wounded places thrash about inside my well-bruised psyche. I was here only because I had been hired as a contractor by Golden Coast, an insurance quality control outfit based in Colorado. They sent me around Northern California to conduct routine safety inspections of gas stations, restaurants, and other small businesses. Some of these businesses happened to be in Santa Cruz County.

The county knew it, too. Had these red waves of antagonism come at me from a human being, I would have used the word "hostility." The very air felt angry. I had lost count of near-misses by cars, buses, and even bicycles since coming here.

Against my will, it was becoming increasingly clear how far I would have to go to understand in any deep way what ongoing conquest—military, religious, political, industrial—had done to my once-paradisiacal homeland and therefore to its occupiers, settlers, natives, and inhabitants. This odyssey would not end when I reached San Francisco and the last of the Serra missions. No. Nor would ghostly Llorona leave off haunting my imagination and my dreams. The Mission Trail led farther: all the way to Sonoma, site of the last mission founded in Alta California.

I emerged from my tent after dusk and sat down in a circle of redwoods. The mosquitoes had gone, and a refreshing coolness emerged from the shadows and worked its way around bushes and trees. Trunks too massive to fully embrace formed a woody Stonehenge round about me. Jungian analyst Marie-Louise von Franz believed that trees enter the dreams of *puer* patients because *pueri* are momma's boys and the trees symbolize the archetypal Great Mother. With "truth" and "tree" sharing common etymological roots, there is some validity to this claim. But if the psyche does indeed self-balance by compensation, then perhaps it grows its nighttime trees as a gesture of what a healthy joining of *puer* and *senex* might look like, with open arms raised toward the sky and roots sunk deep in the ground.

The branchy beings looming over and around me did not feel maternal. They felt like a circle of wise elders. I was unable to say what subtle goodness passed from them to me, seeping into me like vapor into thirsty pores, but when I changed position to place my back against one of them, I hoped it could feel my budding sense of gratitude.

When you were little you believed that everything
had feelings. Nothing less than that is worth believing now.

— one-time Santa Cruz resident Peter S. Beagle

When I got up I patted the ridged bole of a mighty tree whose
upper branches seemed to lift right into the heavens. No indoor
service can match praying in one of nature's cathedrals. Spend
enough time among these leafy kings and you can almost hear them
spinning out their stately green thoughts. To protect them for
human enjoyment is a commodity-driven view. To protect them for
their own living sake, these gentle giants who breathe foul air and
give back pure oxygen in moist, invisible exhalations: only then do
we leave egocentrism behind to feel part of the web of life that sup-
ports our increasingly fragile existence as one of many.

Having decided to study the town after all, I drove up Mission
Hill and parked.

There wasn't much to see through a light rain, just a blocky
white building with a bell tower, square windows, and the usual
red *tejas* on the roof. The Indian cemetery lay out of sight below the
parking lot of an adjacent church. Everything else had been wiped
away. In 1989, the quake from Loma Prieta had leveled most of the
town, the Holy Cross Church along with it. Of the mission only a
small replica remained, a homunculus left orphaned by its parent
creator.

In the dimly lit chapel three old women chanted Hail Marys. The
sound gave the room an aura of ancient maternal peace. I stood still
in it for a moment, breathing it, letting it breathe me. I thought
about Mary, perhaps history's most misunderstood figure. Her son's
qualities of leadership had not come to him from nowhere. Mary,
who could hold her peace but also raise her voice. *My soul doth magni-
fy the Lord....* A fourth woman joined the group as I departed.

On the way out my restless eye noted engraved lettering above
the chapel door:

O CRVS AVE
SPES VNICA

O Crux, ave spes unica: "Hail, O Cross, our only hope." Outside, the sign on the corner countered with NOT A THROUGH STREET. I sought around for an alternative and saw a black and white post at the edge of the park across the street. *Paz a Todo El Mundo* ran up on one side of the post and *May Peace Prevail* on Earth down the other. In Santa Cruz, town of many standing truths, the seeker can always find another pathway forward.

I looked up. A woman was driving the wrong way on High Street. I couldn't help laughing as I got behind the wheel and head-ed down to the water again. At least cars weren't coming at me any-more. Before ever setting foot here I had dreamed that everything seen in Santa Cruz was reversed in the world of the spirit, such that in writing about it, one must ETIRW EHT SRETTEL SDRAWKCAB.

On a bench overlooking a bank of yellow-blossomed ice plant, a pile of rocks, and foaming waves, I read a characteristically *puer* inscription:

IN MEMORY OF GEORGE KENDRY.
THE STARS IS OUR DESTINATION.

As I gazed westward down the shoreline, I reflected that Santa Cruz perched at the top of the reverse-C of Monterey Bay. To stand here I had passed through three counties, yet I had also explored the interior curve of a single psychic body, with Monterey at its depths, quaking San Benito pivoting at its center, and Santa Cruz at its summit. From the deeps to the middle to the heights. Poetic, realis-tic, idealistic. Classical, Baroque, Romantic. Even the treasures drawn forth from them corresponded with their animated topogra-phy: fish from the waters of Monterey, silver and cement from ground-level San Benito, and celestial truths in True Cross town, where the polyphonic whistling of its breeze-brushed trees sang a natural chorus, charming to the ear and uplifting to the spirit.

Haunted

Although visiting a mission nearly always made me feel sick, a fever caught me before I even set foot in Mission Santa Clara. It ran so hot that I woke up the next morning wrapped in sweat-soaked hotel bed sheets. Dream fragments of children's voices echoed through my tired mind. I would eventually find out that more Native Californian children had died at this mission than at any other. In 1777, the year of the mission's founding, Father Palóu wrote:

> By the month of May of the same year the first baptisms took place, for as there had come upon the people a great epidemic, the Fathers were able to perform a great many baptisms by simply going through the villages. In this way they succeeded in sending a great many children (which died almost as soon as they were baptized) to Heaven.

When the padres first came here they found a paradise with an attitude. With the Santa Cruz Mountains well behind them and the San Francisco Bay ten miles to the north, they walked through a vast, pleasant valley of meadows whose grasses waved between Pacific-swept shores and the woody slopes of the Diablos farther inland. But when the invaders ordered their mission constructed,

199

the Guadalupe flooded five times, driving them back but avoiding the nearby village and its labor pool of heathens. When Serra had laid the church keystone four years later, his mule threw him to the ground. His diarist and colleague Father Juan Crespí succumbed to a fatal illness, and a quake rattled apart the unfortunate church in 1881. Its replacement burned down.

In 1771, however, the padres' biggest surprise walked into the valley as five travel-dusty families led by Lieutenant José Joaquin Moraga from San Francisco entered what is now San Jose ("Saint Joseph") six months after the mission was founded. And just as the mission lands would grow an unthinkably vast supply of fruits, vegetables, and goods of every kind, so would San Jose radiate its many layers and labyrinths of development in all directions until the Valley of Heart's Delight that blossomed all around it lost its bloom and gradually solidified into silicon.

The overgrown valley floor reminded me depressingly of another urban wasteland, the San Fernando Valley, as I drove to and fro inspecting gas stations, strip mall restaurants, and car repair businesses. I had not seen so much asphalt, stucco, and neon crowded into one place since leaving Los Angeles. Sunlight rebounding from the endless maze of roadways heated car exhaust and fryer grease fumes into an overpowering stench. It permeated my shirts and slacks even on days when work did not force me into mission-style fast food joints packed with sweaty customers.

Some people think that when you pave over a landscape, that's the end of it. Not here. In 1950, when Anthony "Dutch" Hamann arrived from Orange County, the oil executive surveyed a county still given over to agriculture. Enlisting the local newspapers, the San Jose Chamber of Commerce, and a dedicated staff nicknamed Dutch's Panzer Division, the conservative former manager of General Motors oversaw a quadrupling of San Jose's population as roads were laid, heavy industry lumbered into town, highways stretched over the valley, and malls rose up to cast angular shadows across its darkening face. He believed he was turning the valley into Los Angeles, and he believed that this was good. On the surface he succeeded.

He succeeded because the ninety-eight thousand acres once known as the Valley of Heart's Delight will grow anything, anything at all, from prunes, olives, almonds, grains, grapes, apricots, apples, plums, and pears, to microchips, networks, housing tracts, business parks, genetic engineering, and high-tech weaponry. Where canneries and chapels had stood, women scrubbed cleaner than nuns or neophytes inspect silicon wafers in sealed rooms. On a map the old valley roughly resembles a heart, from the air a giant circuit board. Its vast, resonant cavity has birthed the vacuum tube, the audio oscillator, the silicon transistor, the integrated circuit, the microprocessor, the personal computer, the spliced gene, and the Internet—and this in the county named after visionary St. Clare, founder of a cloistered order and patron of projected imagery.

As I drove through stifling summer heat intensified by store windows and white facades, it occurred to me that Llorona too might be a kind of afterimage of some prior trauma haunting the troubled present. She had been sighted in all the mission counties, places of maximum social and ecological trauma. Little matter whether frightened eyes had actually glimpsed her. She was here, undeniably here, as a dreaded, vital being of folklore, history, and image.

What nightmarish event had sent the ghostly woman in white or black howling in despair beneath the full moon? Who had exiled her? Would she ever find her lost children? Not here, I thought, glancing around at the shivering concrete and broken curbs. Here they would have evaporated without a trace, without leaving even a shadow.

Sarah Winchester did not come to California to improve her health, outrun a creditor, abandon a family, or corner the market on paradise. She came because a medium had warned her that doing otherwise would expose her to dangerously vengeful spirits from beyond the grave.

At one time, she whose first name means "princess" had possessed everything a high-society woman could ask for, including a beautiful daughter and a wealthy husband. William Winchester was heir to the profitable Winchester Repeating Arms Company. It manufactured "the Gun that Won the West," a smooth lever-action rifle that fired several rounds before needing to be reloaded. John Wayne sported a version of this gun in his cowboys-and-Indians movies.

When her husband and daughter died unexpectedly, the light went out in Sarah Winchester's world. She consulted a medium who apparently told her that her family bore a curse for producing the weapon that had blasted down so many lives. As a result, she must flee New Haven for the West, where she would order a house built and keep it under continuous construction. If the hammering ever stopped, the angry spirits would finally claim her.

In 1884, then, Winchester used her "blood money" to hire workers to raise a redwood-frame Victorian mansion on four and a half acres in San Jose. With no building plan except the bits and pieces she wrote down on pieces of paper and the occasional tablecloth, they enlarged the eight-room farmhouse she had purchased into seven spire-topped stories (reduced to four by the 1906 earthquake), one hundred and sixty rooms (estimated: no one knows for sure), forty bedrooms, forty-seven fireplaces, ten thousand window panes, nine hundred and fifty doorways, fifty-two skylights, forty staircases, seventeen chimneys, three elevators, two ballrooms, two basements, an aviary, and a conservatory. Railroad cars were diverted to carry in materials. Gas-powered generators supplied electricity.

Construction went on twenty-four hours a day and did not end until 1922, when the wealthy widow departed the earthly plane.

According to local legend, Winchester sought to be difficult to find, afraid of capture by angry ghosts. If true, this would explain some of the labyrinthine mansion's odder features, such as staircases leading nowhere, stair posts planted upside down, closet doors without closets, cupboard doors set in walls, hallways that double back, skylights positioned above one another, a window on hinges, a chimney that does not reach the ceiling, and a flying buttress buttressing nothing. Winchester was known to sleep in different rooms, perhaps to avoid supernatural detection. The blue "séance room" where she received building plans from the spirits (friendly ones, presumably) contains an exit concealed behind a closet door. Another door leads to the kitchen—eight feet down.

She also seems to have been obsessed with three symbols that repeat themselves all over the mansion.

The first is the number thirteen. Panes of glass in windows, panels in walls, windows in rooms, steps in staircases, cupolas in the greenhouse, and other features of the house total up to thirteen, an unlucky number since before Judas sat down as the thirteenth guest at table and dark Loki showed up as the thirteenth guest at bright Baldr's funeral. Satan is sometimes spoken of as the thirteenth angel. The second recurring symbol is the spider web cut into so much window glass, and the third is the prominent daisy. Female guides at the Mystery House sometimes wear it as a tattoo. In antiquity the daisy symbolized innocence.

The gods are visible here too. A statue of the youthful Hebe, bride of Heracles, vanished for a time but was recovered. A brass plate fashioned to hold a gas lamp wears the face of Zephyrus, god of the west wind of springtime and abductor of the flower goddess Chloris. Outside the house a statue of Demeter mourns for her abducted daughter Persephone, goddess of spring and the underworld. She had been out picking flowers when Hades erupted from below and pulled her down into the gloomy depths.

Of all the ways to interpret this thirty-eight-year-long tragedy, the scientific is the narrowest and neatest. Sarah Winchester, it could be argued, was suffering from a brain abnormality, perhaps schizophrenia or a mood or delusion disorder triggered by the loss of her husband and daughter. There we have it, a simple, literal, causal explanation that stops the inquiry without satisfying. William James had a term for such an explanation, which he called a "nothing but." Nothing but brain chemistry—but why daisies? Which chemical quirks translate into spiraling stairways ascending nowhere? Which is the spider web molecule? Which is the circuit for playing the organ at midnight?

A psychological explanation pushes things a bit farther forward. Decades of Family Systems therapy have demonstrated how families act like single psychic organisms that balance themselves by unconsciously assigning certain roles to family members: Hero, Rebel, Lost Child, Ambassador, Martyr, Comedian. Families also channel unbearable loads of stress toward one family member, an Identified Patient who acts out the family's hidden pathology as human lightning rod and circuit breaker rolled into one. Winchester joined a family sitting on two generations of repressed feelings about how their wealth derived from mass murder. When denied expression such feelings do not disappear, they ferment. Something had to blow. The imagery of her psychotic break (certainly a break with neurological correlates) translates a thick legacy of denied guilt and self-hatred into retaliatory ghosts clamoring for a breakthrough into consciousness. Against this state of possession the formerly innocent belle found herself as helpless as spider's prey caught in a web. Externalizing the web by giving it form as a Victorian maze lined with wall paper could not free her from its coils.

Seen through the window of myth, Sarah Winchester's lifelong sorrow replays the story of Demeter falling into deep despair over the loss of her innocent daughter Persephone to Hades. For Sarah, however, no clowning Baubo was at hand to cheer her up, and boyish Iacchus was busy leading pageants down in Santa Cruz. As a kind of Christian Persephone, Clare had been abducted by Francis and enclosed in a monastery, from where she had fought off invaders by projecting the powers of the Host at them. Sarah was frozen like one of her statues in a cloistered tableau of perpetual warding off. Some say she died right after another séance, a Demeter turned Persephone and carried off at last by Hades.

The two goddesses occupied places of honor in the annual Eleusinian Mysteries of the ancient Greeks. For almost two millennia adult Athenians made pilgrimage to Eleusis to enter the Telestrion and emerge transformed by what they had witnessed and sworn to secrecy about it. Born into a culture that makes no place for sacred mysteries, least of all those branded "pagan" by missionaries and "superstitious" by scientists, Winchester entered her own built-up temple but never emerged from it into the light.

When I went to see this ersatz temple, the strains of Tori Amos's

Talula playing in my mind, I took many pictures. When I checked the camera afterward, they were gone. Not blurred, not dark, just gone.

Countless visitors have photographed the Winchester Mystery House, so this wasn't the old story of the spirits avoiding exposure, nor had anything touched, jolted, or bumped me on my tour there. Among the misdirected hallways and melancholy towers I beheld no apparitions unless the place itself counts as one, a mystery tradition waiting to happen.

Instead, perhaps the absence of photographs was itself a presence. *Empty*, it seems to say. Spent, unsustainable, bankrupt. Falling down, falling apart, and going away forever. And why would a present absence say this?

I suspect that the Winchester Mystery House is a giant Clarevoyant premonition, a nightmare dressed up in pretentious Queen Anne architecture. When Sarah Winchester moved to California, the Valley of Heart's Delight still bloomed with fruit trees and green living things, especially in the spring. It ran with open water soaking lush vegetation. Pink blossoms filled the sky above it when a cheerful west wind came along. The mansion going up and spreading out in their midst mirrored with eerie accuracy the overdevelopment to come in all its unplanned overgrowth, with the crazy winding and twisting of streets and highways, the living spaces arbitrarily demolished to make way for the new, the squandering of incalculable wealth on appearances, and the helpless isolation of people forced to move without rest from one enclosed niche to the next. Caught in the historical shadow of the mission, Winchester found herself pushed from room to room like a Silicon Valley resident before there was a Silicon Valley.

At present roughly 70% of the Mystery House is open to the public. The rest is closed because the sagging stairs and ruined walls, so like the mission in their inevitable deterioration, are not safe to walk through. If this too offers a hint of things to come, then one day the loops and twists and towers beyond the carefully shaped hedges will fall to saner possibilities—such as sensible, land-friendly, multi-ethnic communities, perhaps, that locals would actually enjoy living in and being part of. With the cocking of a gun nowhere to be heard, perhaps the specters of a murderous past will find their own rest and no longer trouble the living.

Once upon a Northern Californian time, Martin Murphy Jr. of Sunnyvale—formerly a flourishing ranch, now a suburb compartmentalized by business parks—had been a generous friend to squatters. Instead of expelling them, he fed and clothed them without asking them to repay the loans he gave them.

Would he have felt differently about hoards of consumers? Clerks I spoke with at the Sunnyvale Toys R Us built on Murphy's old stables along El Camino Real repeated a story I had already heard: that his upset shade, still in the vicinity, had whispered to an employee, "I hate crowds."

I was shown to a wall of shelves packed with shiny boxes of olive-skinned "Dora" dolls in tidy purple smocks. "When I came in for my shift," the clerk told me, "all three rows were bouncing around and crying. Nobody else was here."

"When does Murphy normally show up?"

"Either late at night or early in the morning. He has been known to whisper, pull on people's clothes, knock things off the shelves, kick balls around."

"How many of the staff here believe in Murphy?"

"Everyone he's pestered."

"How many is that?"

"Most of us."

I walked around the store for a while and stared at dolls, model airplanes, video game controllers for future fighter pilots, fake cell phones for turning children into reliable buyers. No Murphy, though. Testing, testing, one, two, three....

Finished with the inspection, I paused in front of the sliding exit door. A glance around. No one was watching.

"I hate crowds too," I whispered as I left.

As I negotiated the arteries and bypasses of this well-swept geographical atrium through which blood money ran to fund gene labs and advanced weapons factories, I remembered a novel I had used for a grad school paper. Frank Herbert's *The White Plague* was not one of his better books, but its premise is terrifying. After seeing his family blown to smears by a car bomb in Dublin, molecular biologist John Roe O'Neill invents a scientific monster of retribution in the shape of an unstoppable plague designed to eradicate humanity. What's particularly fearful is that, as one of the dangerous "patient men" Herbert says the world is full of, the scientist writes his viral DNA cipher with ordinary lab equipment costing less than $2,000.

In an open letter to world governments he blames for being part of the problem, O'Neill writes:

> Terrorists are like bomber pilots who need never look upon their tortured victims, never see the faces of people who pay in anguish. Terrorists are kin to the rack-renting landlords who never once stared face-to-face into the countenance of a starving peasant....I know there are links between the IRA and the Fedayeen, links with Japanese terrorists, the Tupamaros and God knows who else. I was tempted to spread my revenge into all the lands that have harbored such cowards. I warn those lands: do not tempt me again for I have released only a small part of my arsenal.

This fragment sounds strangely topical for having been written in 1982. Herbert's point is clear and compelling. No mass surveillance and no conceivable security apparatus can ever winkle out all the patient men working in their hidden labs. We will never be safe from them so long as the injustices that sear them remain institutionalized.

Open heart surgery, commercial lasers, nuclear magnetic resonance imaging, and computer disk drives are only a handful of the scientific marvels birthed in Santa Clara County. A flood of technical engineers pours into the market every year from San Jose State University. Yet here in the county whose name appeared on an 1886 Supreme Court decision to project the rights of individuals into corporate bodies, Intel wired together a computer to test nuclear weapons. Geron took out a patent to transfer a nucleus into a stem cell while acquiring Roslin Bio-Med Ltd., a firm involved in cloning the sheep Dolly. Do the inventors really grasp what they set loose upon the world? Several Silicon Valley names appeared on a 2002 United Nations Security Council list of high-tech firms that had supplied Saddam Hussein with equipment for biological, chemical, and nuclear weapons development before those programs were shut down. Biotech and weapons money continues to feed a sizable current of the crimson capital flowing into the county. The labs and schools in which these industries operate work for larger and larger international corporations whose influence is everywhere and whose center is nowhere—and whose ruling bodies give no thought to the risks of unraveling the stuff of life or tearing at the essence of matter itself.

The science labs, the boardrooms, the classrooms and the polished conference tables where university regents and industry captains meet are cleansed not only of unsightly infectants, but of any talk about the dark side of the heart. Like high finance, science for sale is considered a practical affair of objective minds. The human past demonstrates otherwise, illustrating time and again that dangerous technologies developed by scientific enthusiasts vastly amplify the irrational passions analyzed in detail by deep psychology and by the humanities, the poets and the storytellers. Sweep these unacknowledged greeds, jealousies, hatreds, and power drives under a sterile rug, exile them from the disinfected halls of education, and they break in through the back door with redoubled force. For more information refer to Freud's discussion of World War I, consult the history of weapons development, or read Mary Shelley's *Frankenstein*.

No idealist is safe from this inner source of danger. Most of the young scientists who went to Trinity to tinker together the first atomic bomb considered themselves liberal patriots. Their enthusiasm for the project did not fade once they learned that Germany had surrendered. Afterwards men on the scene would use words like "blinded," "carried away," "swept away," and "frantic" to describe the swirl of emotion in which these rational-sounding splitters of atoms found themselves caught. In hindsight Project Director Robert J. Oppenheimer would quote from the Bhagavad Gita to describe the godlike destructiveness they had tapped. His colleague Kenneth Bainbridge used a less elevated turn of phrase: "Now we are all sons of bitches."

Promethean enthusiasm might be a workable name for this syndrome, after the god who failed to anticipate the eventual results of his innovative drives:

> **Promethean Enthusiasm:** an unconscious identification with and inflation by transcendent inventive powers like those of Prometheus, resulting in a reckless, manic mood of creativity leading to disastrous consequences.

Symptoms and Indications:
1. Overvaluation of intellectual power accompanied by emotional self-alienation.
2. Underlying overconfidence, arrogance, or narcissism.
3. Uncritical belief in technology as a source of salvation and redemption.
4. Unconscious rage and destructiveness seeking for an outlet.
5. A high level of professional ambition with a desire for fame.
6. Impatience with anything emotional, nonrational, or nonscientific.
7. Lack of reflection, especially in terms of taking the unconscious into account.
8. A tendency to consider oneself more rational than other people.
9. A tendency to rationalize, mute, or sidestep the ethical dilemmas created by one's work.
10. A near-total disregard of possible negative consequences of one's work.
11. An appropriation of creative powers and symbols that

properly belong to the feminine.
12. Intense remorse afterwards once Pandora's deadly box
has been flung open.

The cure? There is none in the medical sense, but the pathological split of self from world can be managed and monitored with a
home-brewed blend of thoughtful humility, emotional reengage-
ment, respect for human limitations, sharp awareness of ethical
responsibility, a well-tended sense of belonging and emplacement,
unremitting self-examination, and education of the heart as well as
of the head. As Dr. Frankenstein himself expressed it,

> If the study to which you apply yourself has a ten-
> dency to weaken your affections, and to destroy
> your taste for those simple pleasures in which no
> ally can possibly mix, then that study is certainly
> unlawful, that is to say, not befitting the human
> mind. If this rule were always observed; if no man
> allowed any pursuit whatsoever to interfere with
> the tranquility of his domestic affections, Greece
> had not been enslaved; Caesar would have spared
> his country; America would have been discovered
> more gradually and the empires of Mexico and Peru
> had not been destroyed.

As uninitiated young Psyche carried some of Persephone's beauty cream to Aphrodite, she thought to try a dab herself. It killed her,
but loving Eros brought her back to life. Better to suffer the psychic
deaths—of egotism, separateness, intellectual superiority—than to
let loose the fearful literal ones. If our colonial past teaches us anything at all, it's that the sleepless offspring of our heedless interventions always come back to haunt us.

Time to close the circuit. Back once more in Santa Clara, I was
laying on a motel bed, head against the wall, arms crossed, images of
missionaries, techno-nuns, and crying black-haired dolls passing

back and forth through my weary mind, when the lightbulb above my head blew out with a sharp snap.

I saw nothing in the blackness, but the room got noticeably colder. I waited. Had Murphy followed me home? I wondered, half-joking with myself.

No. Whatever it was I sensed, it definitely wasn't masculine.

"Llorona?" I asked aloud. "¿Éres tu?" A pause to listen to the growing coldness. The chill worked its way up my forearms. "¿Qué quieres?"

No words, no images, no frights. Just that crouching, brooding waiting, dolorous, agonized, and intense.

> The Aztec lady crying down in creekbeds
> ran into a concrete wall and, puzzled blank,
> stopped her wailing for her children
> and just stared realizing
> that hope was gone
> — Victoria Moreno

Sitting there in the dark, I gave myself over to listening, outwardly and inwardly, wishing I remembered how to say "I will keep you company" in Spanish. I sat there with her until the chill went out of the room.

The Workshop of Daedalus

The tracker of local traumata arrived just ahead of the storm, parked his car, unpacked it, and, seeing nothing wicked this way coming, at least for the moment, drove out for dinner and a look around.

I had taken 84 from East Palo Alto, crossing the Dumbarton Bridge over the south end of San Francisco Bay to approach Fremont through the salt farms of Newark. A line of darkening clouds marched in from out of a Bradbury novel and took up a threatening position over southern Alameda County.

Fremont incorporated out of five local towns, including the one containing old Mission San Jose, and then, as befitted a city named after a conqueror, tried to grab Newark as well. Turning their attentions inward once more, ambitious city fathers gradually fashioned Fremont into a business hub which by the early 1960s included offices, factories, retailers, and a fat General Motors plant.

The blurred rush of traffic, the too-small street signage, and the absence of places to stop made it hard to view the city. Deliberate? My hurried glance located large stucco houses staring down from a green crest (from which a sign pleaded, "Save Our Hills!"), a transition to Civic Center Drive, ads for joint replacement surgery, radiation labs, and a library housed in what looked to be a former corporate office building. Colossal metal towers like skeletal three-armed giants carried thick wire overhead in their immense downward-pointing hands. As I made my way along palm-lined Fremont Boulevard past Starbucks, storefronts, ethnic restaurants, a mall, and a cemetery, the street names—Mission View, Grimmer, Sabercat, Boone—did nothing to lighten my mood. Angling back toward Central Park, I caught the name of a show at Broadway West: "Woman in Black." Was that a rumble from overhead?

None of the several people I passed on my walk around Lake Elizabeth looked me in the eye. I stopped and watched a man struggling with a kite designed to resemble a barn-stormer as light drops of rain moistened my face—"spitting," my Nebraskan grandmother would have called such weather. Wet goose prints crossed the concrete.

Alameda is Spanish for a cluster of cottonwood trees. Having budded off from Contra Costa County, its northeastern parent, in 1853, Alameda County stretches west along San Francisco Bay, jutting up against San Joaquin County and the Central Valley inland. Alameda's coastal location keeps most of it much cooler during the summer than the Contra Costa cities landward of the Berkeley Hills. The Hayward Fault runs northwest through Fremont and Oakland and Berkeley and beyond.

By the time I got to my hotel room a downpour was in progress. I opened the door and stepped outside to listen to the rain and was astonished at the wet cacophony cascading down in sheets from the roof to drench the balcony. I went to bed imagining gargantuan waves breaking over the hotel from behind.

When I reached the mission the next day the rain had lightened considerably. Timber visible from across Mission Boulevard tapered to foliage cropped into domed hedges like so many man-sized umbrellas. Raindrops spattered the pavement around a U-TURN NOT PERMITTED sign. Up a ramp of stone, then on into the museum behind walls coated with white plaster, past a bishop replica, past the clover he held out, then on to a green-framed painting of Jesus on all fours, a cross slung onto his lacerated back. Another bearded man, this one high up on a balcony, doubled candles on either side of him, leaned forward as though preparing to sing an operetta to the barn-like church.

When the soldiers and missionaries turned up in 1772 (wrote Father Crespí), the "heathen" ran away in panic. The site seemed more inviting, with its valley of oaks and sycamores, its abundant wildlife, its available water, and its nearness to Ohlone and Miwok villages. Fermin Lasuén opened the mission in 1797, ostensibly to save souls but also to finish enclosing Northern California in a far-flung missionary net while providing a staging post for retaliatory attacks on Native raiders from the San Joaquin Valley. Faced with crosses, guns, and swords, the Indians escaped eastward and survived, except for those pursued by the relentless Father Narcisco Duran. Father Altamira filed a useless complaint that Duran was murdering those who would not convert. The church's policy was to ignore such complaints, blame the complainer, or quietly reassign the offending priest, depending on the degree of potential negative publicity.

At secularization Jose and Mariano Vallejo plundered the mission at will, for its extensive crops covered thousands of prolific acres and its cattle herds wandered as far as Livermore and Oakland. In 1845 John Sutter's men rode off with what was left, and the 1868 earthquake wrecked everything but part of the monastery. Later repair parties used Oakland timber for restoration, an altogether apt operation for a mission named after a carpenter.

Turning about inside the church, I saw a circular fountain that held water but poured none. Small wooden chairs were parked in rows as though waiting for a tardy orchestra. Their amphitheater was richly, almost lavishly decorated with a lacquered red brick floor, tall white arches, framed Stations of the Cross lit from below, a flat ceiling striped with diagonals done in pink, red, and blue.

Outside again, in the graveled cemetery, a statue of Serra stared at a row of houses across the street as his robed and hooded companion lifted her sorrowful hand above the tombs. The monuments and caskets were arranged with precision. Did they parallel civic construction in Fremont as the Winchester Mystery House had done in San Jose?

I considered St. Joseph, carpenter patron of housing and real estate, this mission, and the missionary project itself. Had you known of the murder and chaos to be perpetrated in the name of your son, you might have been tempted to put tool-thickened fingers around his neck one night and strangle him in his bed. He predicted that his fame would be used badly by wolves in sheep's clothing and righteous preachers he compared to handsome crypts packed with corruption. "Spread the Good News," he ordered, not, "Destroy and loot entire societies and load generations of trauma onto their descendents." "Love your enemies," he commanded, not, "Invent rationalizations for killing those who disagree with you." Were he to return one day and see these polished markers of the legions of the dead and buried, so many slain by privation, violence, or venereal disease, he would doubtless see himself crucified countless times over by cross-wearing murderers claiming to follow the meek Lamb of God. And he thought the first time hurt.

Christians call him Joseph, but the Greeks might have compared him with handy Daedalus ("Clever Worker"), the artisan who staged the mythic Labyrinth on Crete and stocked it with one Minotaur. One of his sons, whom he lost to death, was the divine child Icarus. In some tellings Daedalus invented the first sails to carry ships out of sight across the sea.

With the highest concentration of Victorian construction in the Bay Area, Alameda the city's outline when viewed from above resembles that a nuclear aircraft carrier: one more ship among the many that have docked there or been bolted together in the yards of nearby Oakland. The northernmost gangway hooking Alameda's 'midships to the continent is a downward-dipping tunnel named the Posey Tube after a county supervisor from the 1920s. One of the southern gangways, a trellised bridge of green metal, reaches across a narrow stretch of Oakland Estuary.

Leaving the bridge, I drove past a chunk of concrete, half-sunk in opaque water, painted to resemble a slice of melon. On the south side an overhead tram roared by above signs in Vietnamese. Passed in review were decaying Victorians, a long red wall with more graffiti than bricks, East 12th, so like Wilshire near Brea, and then, flying by, King Kovers, Mama's Royal Cafe, Holy Guacamole, and

God's Gym ("We Care") as I passed into Oakland.

Daedalus has had a free hand in woody, well-logged Oakland, where the town's first mayor was a land-squatting lawyer named Carpentier. To quiet rioters protesting his seizure of the town from Contra Costa County, he ran on a "law and order" platform and decreed that a wooden wharf embellish the waterfront he now owned. In the election he tallied up more votes than the population of Oakland.

In keeping with the constructive spirit of the place and its people, progressive projects nearly always do well here. Mills College, founded in 1889, awarded the first bachelor's degree to a woman living on this side of the Mississippi. In those days Oakland's electric railway was the most efficient in the nation, and water and electricity flowed abundantly even after the Southern Pacific disgorged a flood of people into the city. Cheerfully busy Chinatown flourished, as did art and culture in general. In 1906, when Moore Shipbuilding came to town, Oakland was recovering well from the great quake. None of its seven banks capsized during the Great Depression.

But construction ("pile up together") is easily co-opted by the problematic mythos of Progress. Oakland's first skyscraper, widely touted as a temple to that mythos, rose in 1903, an eleven-story Beaux Arts office building on Broadway. With the harbor dredged, ship manufacture moved into high gear as cranes over the Port of Oakland swung their shadows across the fattening face of Alameda County's largest city. In 1927, the aerial figure of Charles Lindbergh gave the dedication to open the Oakland Airport from which Amelia Earhart would launch her final Icarian flight a decade later. By the 1930s, the brutal machinery of lumber king and newspaper owner Knowland, first name Joseph, would clear the way for rapid countywide industrialization.

World War II brought a huge influx of laborers seeking shipbuilding work. They found it, but they and their families also found cheap prefab housing thrown together by local contractors paid by wartime federal loan money. Temporary housing would do fine for the extra half million people, insisted smirking men of business staunchly opposed to permanent building as ghettos crept over

Oakland, food supplies dwindled, and elected representatives of the dispossessed held their tongues for fear of being branded disloyal to the war effort. This silence cost them the 1945 election they should have won with ease given rising unemployment, hordes of returning veterans, mismanagement of money, and withdrawal of federal services piling onto the list of overwhelms. As the president of Southern California Edison issued a startling call for *less* government involvement in people's affairs, bulldozers demolished entire prefab neighborhoods, and displaced residents hit the noisy streets.

Oakland recovered again as well-grounded and carefully rethought plans took flight. Robert C. Maynard had joined the *Oakland Tribune* as an editor in the mid-1970s; by 1983 he owned it, the first African American to take charge of a top-ranking metropolitan newspaper. BART (Bay Area Rapid Transit) constructed a new station to connect Oakland with San Francisco. The Port of Oakland was up and running and overflowing with international shipping steaming in under colorful pennants. In another two decades Oaklanders were ranking high nationally in educational achievement, with over a third of residents holding a college degree. By 2002 the African American Museum and Library opened its doors in the renovated Charles Greene building.

From inside the brickwork coolness of the family-owned Montclair Egg Shop, all this history felt of a piece. It also matched the décor around me, with a toy clown riding a high-wire, an electric train running on a track behind the kitchen, photographs of locomotives on the walls, and antique wooden furniture stacked upstairs behind a parked motorcycle. Daedalus would have liked eating breakfast here. At any rate I did, I mused while sipping orange juice and looking around.

As I thought about Oakland's past and present, I felt troubled too. For the most part the complexifying urban labyrinth of innovation, renovation, revitalization, and rebuilding made sense to me. People had to live somewhere. But did it make sense to the land? At City Center, a hub of revitalization, artist Roslyn Mazzilli raised up *There!*, a 1988 sculpture meant as an answer to former Oakland resident Gertrude Stein's complaint that she could not find the house she had lived in—"There is no there there"—although at last report the house was still missing. The sculpture balances what look like pairs of interlocking wings. Trust an artist rather than a desk-bound urban planner to catch the spirit of a place.

Unaccountably, I found myself thinking about Frankie, the white-garbed woman who had ridden the bus until she died in 1982. Her husband had abandoned her for someone else in 1962, leaving her destitute and alone. Locals had referred to her as the White Witch. I shook my head.

If Oakland be a workbench in the busy shop of Daedalus, Lake Merritt undoubtedly serves as his bellows. Sitting in the city's southwestern corner, the ten-millennia-old lake has seen it all, development, Depression, colonization. Local Ohlone once fed on its shores. The "lake" is actually a shallow lagoon flushed out twice a day by tides. The former Laguna Peralta gets its current name from Dr. Samuel Merritt, a mayor of Oakland who installed a dam in 1868 to regulate water flow between the lake and San Francisco Bay. Because of his efforts the lake was declared the first wildlife refuge in North America two years later. Herons, ducks, cormorants, geese, and egrets could land there now unmolested by hunters' sky-sweeping shotguns.

As towers went up almost at water's edge, toxins from runoffs nearly killed the lake. Pollutants from the surrounding watershed still contaminate it, especially when the first rains of the wet season flush garbage into city storm drains. Today a plan is in the works to close the dam only when flooding is imminent. Drains have been fitted with filters, fountains churn and oxygenate the waters, and volunteers educated by several local organizations turn out with nets to skim trash from the surface. Islands in the middle provide roosting and fresh water for migrant birds. At night a necklace of lights encases the lake in a pearly glow for the benefit of appreciative human visitors.

As developers continue to battle for the "right" to dig up lakeside land for still more skyscrapers, the lake presents a cyclical reminder that the pulse of life between land and occupants nourishes both when allowed to, but strangles in both when thoughtlessly choked off as life and spirit depart with the fading breath. No inspiration if no expiration, for lakes as well as lake-dwellers.

"Idealism" is a multi-purpose word. In common usage it refers to possessing and acting upon ideals, aspirations, even dreams. This is the sense of the word most often associated with Berkeley, California.

Philosophy knows of another meaning, however. Idealism represents a school of thought for which reality is dependent on the mind perceiving it. Pushing this even farther, George Berkeley argued that we perceive reality only as ideas or collections of ideas. The world has no needs, no moods, and no substance because the world is what minds make of it. When Bishop Berkeley visited the American colonies, he was so impressed that he wrote a poem to extol the virtues of expansionism. "Westward the course of empire takes its way," he cheered. For him, a philosophy that yoked existence to the pretensions of the inner man went well with colonial designs on mind and matter.

Standing on Founder's Rock in 1866 while staring out at the Golden Gate, attorney, railroad president, and mining financier Frederick Billings recalled this line of "poetry." The College of California men gathered there with him agreed that "Berkeley" would make a fine name for the school they wished to manufacture there. They had climbed atop the same rock six years earlier to dedicate land purchased for the future "Athens of the West."

Widely publicized images of tie-dyed hippies and shouting Free Speech Movement organizers have convinced many that UC Berkeley is a radical school, but it has always been quite the opposite. Clark Kerr, the president whose corporate style of bloodless manipulation had helped ignited the Movement, would have firmly agreed with Bernard Moses, founder of the Department of Political Science, that students should be "missionaries of a mechanical regeneration," preferably under corporate control. In both World Wars the regents were quick to offer the school's considerable resources to the U.S. Government. Berkeley laboratories and scientists were involved in devising the world's first atomic bomb.

For every reaction, however, there is an equal and opposite reaction. Hearing of Bishop Berkeley's philosophical idealism, Samuel
Johnson, compiler of the first comprehensive English dictionary,
kicked a rock and exclaimed, "I refute it thus!" Fixed firmly in place
at Hearst Avenue and Gayley Road, Founder's Rock is an outcropping of the Hayward Fault that splits the city and county. The
school's Memorial Stadium sits squarely on top of this clashing
together of differing ages and varieties of contending stone, with
Jurassic Franciscan mélange on one side and Cretaceous Great
Valley Sequence on the other. So do a golf course and a Buddhist
monastery and several dense neighborhoods. Unlike the San
Andreas, the Hayward creeps continually as the crustal plates
below it grind past each other in opposite directions. It is an ever-
active source of constant, unrelenting friction, a perpetual collision
of worlds.

And so a traditionalistic school where protesting students climb
trees or towers (perhaps like the one from which Daedalus escaped
on improvised wings) finds itself contending with a liberal town
prone to periodic outbreaks of conservatism. The same school that
accepts lucrative pledges from companies like Dow Chemical, sup-
plier of silicone breast implants, napalm, Agent Orange, and
Dursban, and BP, the official worst U.S. polluter of 1991, also fronts
constructive projects like "Helios" to research solar energy collection. Time will tell if that project can keep its wings intact.

The local rule of friction holds whether the colliders are social-
ists and capitalists, soldiers and pacifists, yuppies and activists,
bohemians and businessmen, or—as in the case of strife-torn
People's Park—conservers and developers. "Rock 'n Roll Berkeley,"
as resident and graduate student Sarah McCaleb expressed it in an
unpublished paper. Thinking like a rock, she imagines new forms
and fresh ideas broken out of a quaking landscape demolishing previous structures in very brief amounts of time. Citing Jung, she adds
that consciousness depends on holding in awareness the confrontation of opposites, however painful, not on dismissing them as unreal or insufficiently spiritual to bother about. Only in a consciously
tended field of tension can structures of reconciliation arise.

Table 1:

Examples of (Huey) Newton?s Third Law
in and around Berkeley, California: 1950 ? 1970:

Conservatives block the school from building do that would diminish lan lord profits; in 1956, families are thrown out Codornices so the schoo can take it over for ma students.	Jack Kerouac visits Allen Ginsberg and Gary Snyder in their backyard cottages (1955); Snyder introduces them to Zen, Ginsberg writes poetry, Kerouac starts writing The Dharma Bums .
Politics as usual; dis agement of protest and dissenting opinions; th Cold War atmosphere spreads fear, suspicion and political and relig	In 1961 a biracial coalition comes to power in Berkeley; the first black councilman is elected. Bohemians gath er in the coffee houses and bookstores along
Residents living in the above Berkeley complain about a proposed ordi ? nance to outlaw discrim tion in real estate sal rentals because the go ernment shouldn?t tell? ple how to sell their h	Proposition 14, the Rumford Fair Housing Act, passes; it outlaws discrimi nation by race, marital sta tus, income, ancestry,? sex ual orientation; as such, it is the state?s first fair? housing act.
Led by Ronald Reagan, opponents of the Rumfor Act succeed in having i	Widespread protests, jail ings, violence; the Watts Riots in Los Angeles.
The city council system cally recruits people o	White conservatives emi grate from the county.
Junior high school inte tion fought at Garfield where the hill people?s	Integration successful at Willard and Burbank as of 1964.
HUAC comes to the Bay Area and begins hearing that amount to loyalty?	Jerry Rubin shows up for a 1966 HUAC meeting dressed as a Minuteman

Table 1 (continued):

DuBois club bombed and VDC building dynamited, possibly by the FBI; Re campaigns with help fro wealthy businessmen against reformer Pat Br and wins the governorsh partly on promises to e the Berkeley?style rad	Max Scherr sells the Steppen?wolf bistro and launches the *Berkeley Barb* its Esplandian?themed logo is Don Quixote on a steed, with a lance tipped with UC Berkeley?s campanile. Little Eagle Charlie Brown Artman is arrested at a
The city tries to drive hippies from Telegraph police cite them for mi offenses. The relativel eral city council does for black housing, and one point favors conden nation of Oceanview. Th city begins to demolish	Communes and collectives gain in popularity. Around the county: war protests at the Oakland Induction Center; Joan Baez arrested, visited by Martin Luther King Jr. Black students riot in Berkeley after King?s assassination. Riot at
Governor Reagan sends Meese to arrest activis and protesters, claims allowing Eldridge Cleav teach would motivate ch dren to slit their pare	African Americans, Chicanos, Asians, and Indians form the Third World Liberation Front. They want student?con ? trolled minority programs.
Reagan sends the Highwa Patrol to control a str the TWLF. National Guar called in. At a riot ne People?s Park, 100 are	Protesters give flowers to law enforcement personnel and plant more even though police pull them up. They also fly kites to dis
The Regents refuse to l the park to the city be Reagan opposes it. They turn part of it into a	No one uses it, however, so weeds and grass gradually reclaim it in successive acts of silent, organic protest.

I sat in a booth in Spats on Shattuck Avenue sipping a Borneo Fogcutter. Dry ice swirled forth mist from the base of a white ceramic mug cast in the form of a lighthouse. "This delicious blend of rare liqueurs, exotic extracts and magic mutterings soon worked its wonders on the grimly shroud missionaries," read the ad for the cocktail. "After a couple of drinks and a few silly grins, you could distinguish the missionaries from the natives only by their pink skin." If only.

Part of me did not want to continue the journey northward. To the extent that one can, I had grown used to being in the liminal space, the threshold, the crevice between polarizations of past and future, self and surround, mythic and material, and that part of me liked it here. The rest of me felt worn out from too much soulseeing.

This being an analytically themed county, it seemed like a good place to take stock of something.

That the style, discourse, or soul of a place works its way into us seems to be inevitable. Stay in Berkeley long enough—even a short visit might be long enough for some—and its jolts and frictions will polarize in you and yours. A geopsychic lesson of Alameda County as a whole is that continual sunderings of false unities and outworn structures demand continual reconstruction and creative adaptation. No totalization! Nothing complete! No finished, single Truth for all time to come. Keep your tools clean and ready, then, for the next earth-shaking jolt.

There is a crucial difference, however, between resonating to a place and being possessed by it. Until I reached San Luis Obispo on my long Californian odyssey I had acted out and been inundated by recurring syndromes of place resonating across multiple dimensions, including the ecological, the political, the historical, and of course the psychological. In Alameda County, split by a fault and stocked with timber, the aura of friction and flame around and within me softened as my knowledge of their significance here gained clarity.

The deep psychologies have discussed in detail the destructive effects of identifying with anything less, or more, than ourselves, whether with a superegoic judge or persecutor internalized from outside, the alienating norms of a dominant culture, a tyrannical set of perfectionistic ideals, a voracious messiah complex, or a mythic tale unconsciously relived. Taking any of these for one's genuine self risks possession and overshadowing by something inhuman and uncanny. Stepping back from them does not make them go away, but it can open up psychological space for a freer set of responses.

Something similar is true for coming to terms with the presence inhabiting a place. Instead of picking up a hammer or trying to meditate away a permanent fissure, for example, I could do my analyzing here with some hope of focus. I could draw respectfully upon the energies of this or any other place instead of being used by them—but only once I knew what they were: one of many benefits of a gnosis of place. If only we had one...

As I got up to continue my northward trek I thought about UC Berkeley, named after the philosopher who denied life and substance to matter, and Lawrence Livermore National Laboratory, named after a father of the atomic bomb, and wondered how this county would ever deal with the terrible Daedalus-shaped shadow of having been ecopsychologically involved in nuclear mass murder, a Cold War, and perhaps even the future extinction of life on Earth. What sort of ceremony of collective soul-retrieval would it take to welcome into the open, let alone heal, so wide and radioactive a wound? Would it require volatilizing some uranium? Reworking a mockup of a cyclotron into a mandala? Was I joking, or was I bitter? What did the armorer and carpenter within have to say?

As I walked to my car, a sudden memory of a dream just before I came here sprang to mind as though from the rocks below to offer me some consolation. As I drove for San Francisco I got stuck in southbound traffic, but in my mind's eye a giant woman named Alameda caught bombs in her wide-flung apron.

Five Hundred Years of Resistance

With lowered eyes I slowly walked the outdoor labyrinth in the rain. The black umbrella I held deflected some of the wetness. I stepped right, shifted about, left step, shift...

At the moment little of this occupied my attention. I was thinking rather about the Mission Trail, and about the years spent negotiating its twists and curves, rises and drops without knowing the nature of the invisible lodestone drawing me into a forty-year pilgrimage grasped consciously only in the last two years, and dimly even then. I walked and turned, wondered and turned, the rain-blurred path below me indistinguishable from the path drawn step by step to be inscribed within me, behind me, and before me. I thought about the mission I had just visited.

> It is stories—narrative formal or informal, elaborate and detailed or offhand and telegraphic—of what happened to people in a place, of what they have done with the things that they found there, that best reveal the "real geography": geography, that is, experienced and understood as place.
>
> — Kent Ryden

Little was left of the original mission named Dolores with such tragic accuracy. The central courtyard had been obliterated to make way for a precipitous basilica. The mission had been fumigated recently to drive off powderpost beetles that dined hungrily on old artwork. A wedding was being shot in the chapel as a light rain fell outside.

I did not find the graves of the neophytes who died here at the mission founded and armed near the village of Chutchui, but a circular statue had been commemorated IN PRAYERFUL MEMORY OF THE FAITHFUL INDIANS. From its apex rose a robed gray woman of mournful countenance. From across the cemetery a reflective statue of Serra gazed downward, hands behind his back, in the same bent pose as his likeness at the San Diego Presidio.

Even now the church makes much of its civilizing influence on the Native Californians. According to Malcolm Margolin, however,

> LaPérouse, who visited Mission Carmel in 1786, compared it emphatically to the slave plantations of the Caribbean. Louis Choris said of the Indians at Mission Dolores in San Francisco: "I have never seen one laugh, I have never seen one look one in the face. They look as though they are interested in nothing." Another early visitor, Otto von Kotzebue, likewise noted of the Indians that, "a deep melancholy always clouds their faces, and their eyes are constantly fixed upon the ground."

Sunlight broke through the clouds here and there without halting the gentle rain. A white plaster woman with bird droppings on her head stared steadily—reproachfully?—at Father Serra from over a hedge. It is here, in a moist, moody land of draft and fog, that Llorona seems most openly sad, wherever and whenever she flickers into being. She is powerful here, was even before Juana Alicia painted a large mural of her in the Mission District. When Juan Manuel de Ayala arrived on the San Carlos in 1775, his crew saw three Indians weeping at Mission Bay, or La Ensenada de los Llorones as they named it then. Little wonder that the first signs of measles that silenced so many neophytes forever included reddening eyes and runny noses.

> *Salias del templo un dia Llorona*
> *Cuando al posar yo te vi*
> *Hermoso huipil llevavas Llorona*
> *Que La Virgen te crei*

> *No se lo que tienen las flores Llorona*
> *Las flores de un campo santo*
> *Que cuando las mueve el viento Llorona*
> *Parece que están llorando*

> You were leaving the temple one day, Llorona
> As I passed I saw you
> A shawl so beautiful you wore, Llorona
> That I believed you to be the Virgin

> I know not what the flowers hold, Llorona
> Those flowers from the graveyard
> That when the wind moves them, Llorona
> It looks as though they weep
> — from "La Llorona" (traditional)

I passed back through the chapel on my way out. In a painting of the Mournful Mother even the angels seemed to weep. Lavender streamers fluttering from a circular hole cut high in the roof fastened onto the pillars below. I squinted at a picture worked in tiles and recognized the *San Carlos* heading in, its sails bearing the words Rey, Dios, Pueblo, Muerte (that last above a staring Indian couple), and ¿Quien Sabe? A good question. Who would win here, Thanatos or Eros, El Muerto or El Amor? An earthquake had struck when workmen had filled in the stream Dolores with concrete. Though banished underground, it flows on.

Turn, straight, then turn again. My feet knew the way more surely than my mind.

The labyrinth ("place of power") is ancient, so ancient that Jung believed it to be a universal symbol of wholeness. "Mandalas," he named such centered and bounded patterns, borrowing the word from meditative Tibetans. The one below me was cast in a medieval design copied from the eleven-circuit pattern at Chartres Cathedral in France. Many Gothic cathedrals had housed such patterns winding sinuously below bright steeples and flying buttresses. The one traced at Chartres in 1201 had gone ignored for dusty centuries until Reverend Lauren Artress rediscovered it. The classical design which Daedalus was said to have inscribed at Crete represented yet another style of the ancient pattern winding itself toward a foreordained center. Straight, turn, straight. A flickering of the air pattered a few drops of cold rain against my cheek.

I still wanted to stop. But as I rode cable cars through banks of fog, inspected feminine figureheads in the Maritime Museum, watched the homeless crouching near the United Nations landmark (Does any national government truly care about the homeless? I couldn't think of any), wound my way down signless roads through the dripping mists of Golden Gate Park, and snapped a quick shot of a lone white lady in a mural in the Castro before hopping a bus, I remembered where the lodestones and trolleys and cables and grids were leading me: all the way to the top.

> I, too, have been in the underworld, like Odysseus, and shall be there often yet; and not only rams have I sacrificed to be able to speak with a few of the dead, but I have not spared my own blood.
>
> — Nietzsche

When I reached the middle of the design, I halted for a moment. Physically centered, but still so far to go.

It seemed to me then that my entire Californian life had amounted to a passage through an unseen labyrinth intangible but impermeable, and that I had learned only enough to walk it deliberately. So be it. I would see it through no matter what awaited me at journey's end.

Now if I could just negotiate these unexpected mood swings...

When the Greeks put on one of their famous plays, they made sure that the watchful gaze of a certain moody god oversaw the drama.

According to Aristotle, the pageantry of Greek theater emerged out of songs sung at an annual festival to honor Dionysus (Bacchus to the Romans), bisexual god of drama, ecstasy, and expressive liberation. The lush vines growing out of him, and the drunken, nubile maenads following him, link him to ecstatic states of intoxicated revelry.

Dionysus is sometimes held out as the opposite of cool, orderly, harmony-loving Apollo, but because creative expression partners passion with form, these gods are more fruitfully regarded as a pair. When Apollo was elsewhere, Dionysus took up temporary residence in his brother's shrine at Delphi.

His wildness is not that of Artemis, patron of untouched nature, but of the mobile variety that can explode in the heart of the polis. If a city failed to pay homage to him and his dancing, deer-skinned revenue, he destroyed it with a heated ferocity exceeding that of Mars, about whom a certain businesslike coldness clung even in battle frenzy. Dionysian rage wrought dismemberment, rending, shaking, and flame to send innocent and guilty alike running in terror through the shattered city gates.

When the 1906 earthquake recalled the fate of dismembered Pentheus by destroying much of a city tarnished by heavy industry and captured by plutocrats poised to redesign it in the image of Washington D.C., one observer watching the conflagration spoke of an angry dragon belching fire and brimstone. One of the survivors, a statue recently erected to patriotize the bloody Spanish-American War, bore the likeness of Bellona, fierce destroyer of cities. On Filbert Street, residents saved a row of homes from the flames by draping them in blankets and bed sheets soaked with wine.

Sitting in the San Francisco Opera House for a performance of Beethoven's *Fidelio*, an opera commemorating a wave of revolution sweeping over Europe, I was reminded of how Dionysian a virtue *liberty* (same root as "liberal" and "liberate") really is. Mozart was too much the Divine Child to have written about it except with an aerial lightness like that of Papageno's magical bells. For Haydn, the great cheerful realist of the classical period, it already stood accomplished by tradition as the emotional backdrop to whatever melody he produced. In the music of that day, only Beethoven's soaring fury could break the metal cuff from the imprisoned wrist. Opera was not his medium, but this one announced in soaring tones his signature effrontery nevertheless. "You are who you are through the accident of birth; I am who I am through my own efforts," he had written in a rage to turn down a patron demanding a piece in Napoleon's honor. "There have been many princes and there will be many more—but there is only one Beethoven."

It should not baffle us that Jesus, who preached so eloquently about liberation, would keep company with maenads and drinkers shaded by Dionysian vines and wines. Just look at his mood swings, from the heights of heavenly cheer to the sorrows of Gethsemane, from compassion for an old woman giving her last coins to the temple to whip-wielding fury driving businessmen forth from it. His teachings could not be institutionalized until their transformative passion was muted by writing it out of his story. Only in the Gnostic gospels does Jesus actually laugh.

Dionysus has sometimes been mythologized as patron of the psychotherapeutic arts, but in North America this linkage is tenuous at best. The real patron of American therapy is Procrustes, master of the quick cure and the swift elimination of what makes one different. Dionysian counseling would listen for the song in the symptom, but Procrustean clinical work closes down the symptom with methods and medications in order to swaddle in silence the underworld racket that disturbs peaceful slumber. As a result, the racket externalizes itself as smiling, functional, therapized people wonder why things on the outside seem to be breaking down, blowing up, spiraling away, and selling out. Self-silencing sufferers don't need a pill or a diagnosis, they need a stage and an audience. They need an Epidaurus Theater in which to reanimate their troubled stories, face them once again, and see them witnessed by active participants.

Who among the busy psychotherapists inhabiting California and jammed into the Bay Area pauses to ask whether the subjects of a dying empire need therapy less often than therapy needs Dionysus, expressive god of inner and outer liberation? As for the clients, let those who are ready try out the three-step Beethoven method: give the finger to the oppressors, smash an occasional bust, and write, "I will take Fate by the throat; it shall not wholly overcome me" into the margin of a sheet of fearsome music.

Few do not know of San Francisco's dual reputation for liberation and libertinism. Originally called Yerba Buena ("Good Herb") after an aphrodisiac spearmint that grew here, the city was renamed to pay homage to the ecstatic St. Francis. As one of the few standing out from Christian tradition in his love for the natural world, he is often imagined circled by chirping birds who loved him back. Like the city named after him, he believed in taking his ideals outside and putting them into practice in a world of lowly strugglers unblessed by wealth or nobility.

However, every extreme either casts a shadow or attracts one. When Francis the Pure-Hearted insisted on a strict rule of poverty, Innocent III, the pope who attacked the austere Albigenses of France and launched the Fourth Crusade, worked behind the scenes to dilute the rule. It was actually Francis who was innocent. He seems never to have accepted that the elite of his beloved church epitomized what Jesus had preached against, soaked as they were in money, power, corruption, and violence. (St. Clare ran into a similar dilemma with Innocent IV, but she took it by the horns and held her ground.)

On the geographical stage of San Francisco, with its steep hills and jagged faults, dolorous fogs and summer sunshine, salt water and fresh water mingling in a sixteen-hundred-square-mile estuary draining more than 40% of the state, battling extremes of Franciscan idealism and Byzantine shadow return vividly to life. Long ago a priest judged insane for complaining about how his colleagues treated the native people was shipped back to New Spain along with a priest gone genuinely psychotic after a month of missionary work. By 1817, in a dreadful foreshadowing of future epidemics, a local padre notified the governor that sexually transmitted diseases were mowing down the neophytes. Frenetic 49ers used the church they built for a dancing hall.

"Byzantine" derives from Byzas, son of Poseidon and the nymph Keroessa. He was a mythical Greek notable mainly for the city named after him before it became Constantinople under Emperor Constantine and then, eventually, Istanbul under the Ottomans. Constantinople was also the city defended by Crusaders fighting off pagans in Montalvo's novel *The Exploits of Esplandian*, the novel that gave California a name. "Byzantine" had acquired its air of devious political amorality long before John Fremont saw the wide entrance to San Francisco Bay and was reminded of the Golden Horn and the harbor at Byzantium. By these two routes, then, literary and oral, the gaudy auric nomenclature of Near Eastern corruption crept into the Golden State and lodged in moody San Francisco.

If the city could be imagined as inflicted by an economic bipolar disorder, with doses of 49er gold and Comstock silver stabilizing its alternating manias and depressions like a potent drug, the list of pushers would grow far larger than this byzantine sampling from the late 1800s, when record transactions did nothing to anesthetize the 33% unemployment rate and a powerful quake rolled through the city: George Ensign, key player in bottling up a Spring Valley water monopoly in 1862. William Ralston, center of "The Ring" of mining speculators and doomed president and co-founder of the Bank of California. William Sharon, manipulator of the San Francisco Stock and Exchange Board (whose founding members were known as the Forty Thieves) and devious claimant of Ralston's pile. Silver Kings James Flood, William O'Brien, William Mackay, and James Fair, who married and dumped one Llorona after the next and died in a San Francisco hotel room in 1894. The

Big Four SP barons Collis Huntington, Leland Stanford, Charles Crocker, and Mark Hopkins, who paid for their railroad with inflated stock and won federal funding by redrawing the map of Northern California. "Captain" John Sutter, who set up his paltry little empire in the Fort named after himself and died poor and drunk. James Marshall, discoverer of the famous nugget of California gold and spurned sharer of Sutter's fate. Abraham Ruef, a San Franciscan Karl Rove type of back-stage sociopath who arranged the election of the extravagantly corrupt Eugene Schmitz. William Herrin, a Southern Pacific man who controlled much of the city from his office at Fourth and Townsend. Charles Crocker, brutal railroad magnate and strike-breaker of Chinese laborers. And of course the infamous William Randolph Hearst, son of a miner and spoiled tycoon of yellow journalism.

Llorona had been haunting the city from its colonization, but she resurfaced in 1863 as Adah Isaacs Mencken, opera star, lover of many men, and mother of a child who died at birth. Although widely worshipped, especially by star-struck men (even the St. Francis Hook and Ladder Company gave her an honorary membership), she died curled up into herself, unloved and bitter.

On the other hand, Joshua Norton managed to pick up the golden thread so often lost in the byzantine maze. After going bust in one of the city's periodic financial mood swings, he reappeared on the streets in a top hat with a jaunty peacock feather and a patched admiral's uniform donated by the Presidio. Without preamble he referred to himself as Emperor of California and assigned himself the task of conducting regular inspections of the police and fire departments. Even those San Franciscans who regarded him as crazy treated him with delighted respect. Restaurants accepted the money he printed as the official coin of his realm. He died at his post out on California Street in the shadows of the rising towers, to the last a noble mockery of the city's uncaring captains of industry.

Norton's compassionate idealism soon found effective company. Native Californians had never been accepted as equals by the Californios, but neither were they debased into unpaid servitude.

With the coming of the Americans, Indians were sold at the auction blocks as slaves along with kidnapped Chinese. Donaldina Cameron saw to it that many girls and women escaped the bloody chains of this indignity. Mary Ellen Pleasant won civil rights cases in the courts and brought the Underground Railroad into California during the Gold Rush. She also provided funds for James Starkey's opening of the San Francisco Athenaeum Institute. This was in 1853, and in two more years Mifflin Gibbs gathered up personnel, paper and ink for the new African American press *The Mirror of the Times*.

By 1879, Henry George had argued in *Progress and Poverty* that, rather than amassing wealth that trickles down to the poor, industrialized civilization actually creates widespread poverty. As Mayor Phelan boasted that San Francisco was "destined for Empire" and courted the long-term presence of the Navy to prove it, the American Anti-Imperialist League raised its voice to protest the flagrant injustices of the Spanish-American War. Although Phelan's "Save Our State from Oriental Aggression" campaign foreshadowed the paranoia driving the shameful incarceration of Japanese American citizens during World War II, the League set the stage for many later demonstrations of the cosmopolitan humanitarianism for which the city is so well known.

In the Mission District not very far from the mural of Llorona, another stood boldly painted in tints of red, orange, blue, and green. In it strong-armed laborers shouted out against a horde of warriors ancient and modern. I bent to read the title. *Five Hundred Years of Resistance* by Isaís Mata. I could not imagine a more suitable statement of the city's long struggle against Byzantine corruption, a dark, toxic trend that must never be tolerated, let alone excused or "integrated." Near the mural's right border, the figure of the conquistador had mutated down the war-torn ages into a soldier armed with an automatic rifle. Soldier, marine, cossack, trooper, janissary, samurai, commando, legionnaire, fedayeen, ranger, bandsman, Crusader, conquistador....The names are many, the job description unchanging: to kill under orders in support of organized banditry so often religiously supported. It had been so since bands of fearful men began their long and bloody campaign of centralizing power.

"Homeless men urinated in this corner so often," said the Precita Eyes tour guide while pointing under a wood-framed balcony as we stood in an alley, "that talk of calling out a police patrol went around. One of our artists painted that Guadalupe instead." From one side of the corner, the glowing, blue-robed figure pointed directly out at the viewer. Fingers of yellow light shone from her head and shoulders. "Nobody pees there anymore." I sighed as I pondered this ingenious solution. No cuffs, no police dogs, just a sacred feminine presence invited back to life underneath a rickety balcony. For the first time in my life I understood why men in prison tattooed her image on their back to keep from being stabbed. Some included a humble plea: "Forgive me, Mother, for my noisy life."

> Our Lady of Guadalupe appeared and restored the indigenous peoples by coming to them within their cultural/symbolic system. She came as one of them (*mestiza*), speaking their language (Nahuatl), bearing their symbols (her image), and bringing a message of hope, presence, and love that restored and strengthened them, thus giving back to them their will to live.
>
> — Jeanette Rodriguez

Precita Eyes Mural Arts & Visitors Center leases a suite in the Mission District. Founded in 1977 by Susan Cervantes, it is one of the three original community mural centers in the U.S. The art projects it sponsors catch eyes all over the world. Once street artist Kenneth Huerta finished his alterations, for example, a Marlboro billboard announced "Mal burro" to the passing traffic. "Precita" because some of the artists who painted the plywood mural *Masks of God, Soul of Man* for the Bernal Heights Branch Library lived in Precita ("preappointment") Valley. "Eyes" for the capacity to envision and appreciate what remains of the world's cultural plurality. Examples of Precita art enliven walls and alleys throughout the district.

A mural before me painted on a slatted fence depicted a group of hooded, brown-skinned women. Two were in the foreground, one with a broken chain in her fist. The other wept into her hands. An Aztec sunstone winked from the white-brick side of Dominquez Bakery. I nodded at this conscious remembrance of things ever present and moved on.

Young people jumped over strands of barbed wire hung with keys. This was *When Doves Cry*. Another mural declared **We Remember** in purple letters on a yellow background. Tears ran down the face of a black woman with rose-red lips and a sky-colored shirt. Art as collective therapy, the cathartic truth that speaks us free. Indoors, a paintbrush of collective recollection had left golden hands cupped around a golden, sleeping infant hanging peacefully beneath a ventilation grille.

Outside once again, I stopped in wonder before a garage painted into a magical forest crawled with red salamanders, green snakes, and a curious monkey. The tree in the foreground spoke to the street through a wide-open mouth.

Five hundred years of resistance. Observe ye the lilies in the field.

Jasper O'Farrell had done his best to grid down the geographic highs and lows, but by following the precedent of surveyor Jean Vioget, he left generations of San Franciscans with a persistent if reluctant feel for the place's fluctuating mood by platting roads straight up and down the sides of steep hills. Not until ore skips were transmuted into cable cars—in effect recreating the underworld minescape aboveground—would the wealthy populate heights like Nob Hill, where tourists rode trolleys while snapping pictures and a spectral young woman haunted the Fairmont Hotel.

Although the city's manic depression was swinging to and fro long before the Gold Rush, the bizarre alchemy of mining and its aftermath stamped such an unforgettable example of destructive bipolarity into the land that the scars and wounds linger even now.

The myth of chemically formulating immortal life and wealth started as any myth does, through oral tellings anonymously handed down. Alchemy seems to have risen in part as an unconscious collective response to the loss of animistic frameworks for living in a sentient world. It also represented an earthy counter-reaction to ascensionist-perfectionist Christian metaphors that had hardened into materialist precepts.

The more thoughtful among the alchemists were research scientists and philosophers devoted to discovering the Philosopher's Stone, a luminous substance that could transmute base metals into gold, glass into gems, and illness into health and even immortality. They labored at this not merely to improve themselves, but to participate directly in the evolution and awakening of the world itself. Such work required exceptional devotion and study because, as the alchemical spirit Mercurius warned the novice, "For healthful I can be, and poisonous," especially when performed unconsciously.

In California, where some among the miners nicknamed themselves "puffers" without knowing it to be a term of alchemical derision, impulsive Jasons abandoned their wives and families for the chance to drag pans and shovels and tents into gold-seeking camps in the Sierra foothills. These unreflective Argonauts did not stop at panning for wealth: they tore up hillsides and destroyed streams and ecosystems to plunder the "Mother Lode." Some died of mercury poison while trying to distill their takings; others shot and stabbed each other in juvenile quarrels. Not one in ten came out even.

Nevertheless, by 1859, the manic assault on the earthly mother's body had poisoned the Yuba, Feather, American, Sacramento, and Merced Rivers, cleared the skies of game birds and the mountains of large animals, and cut down centuries of forest growth. Californians used to today's thin fringe of riparian vegetation never saw the miles of luxuriant jungle sawed and hacked away before their grandparents were born. In and around the city, estuary lands shrunk to a fourth of their size to make way for urbanization. Mud flows buried discarded mining implements that temblors would spit out of the ground one unstable day.

Native Californians would have been devastated by all this wanton desecration even without a campaign of deliberate genocide. The manic miners who killed them collected bounties as newspapers all over the state cheered on the murderers in print. In a vicious distortion of the "projection" process described by the alchemists, names like "savage," "primitive," and "childlike" were hurled at native groups to justify their decimation. The reservations mapped out to contain the savages would inspire the system of apartheid in South Africa.

Straddling geographic and historical extremes, the Golden Gate Bridge, that preeminent landmark of San Francisco, captures a picturesque suspension between lethal mania and deep descent, a red metal vine undulating outward as though sprung from the head of the god of ecstasy and madness. According to an ancient tradition, Dionysus was another version of Hades. Through this lens the Golden Gate expands into a gateway between worlds, and the jumpers off its Bridge into unfortunate entrants into the nether region. According to Bay Area resident Corey Hale, the piles of coins left by visitors at the center of the Bridge pay a symbolic if unconscious debt to Charon, the ferryman of Hades, who carried across the river Styx only those shades who came to him with a coin placed under the tongue. The Bridge's first laborers, having survived the long fall toward the iron-hard Bay waiting hungrily below, dubbed themselves the Halfway to Hell Club after being hauled from well-placed safety nets.

Primarily, however, San Francisco has been known for the sea-salted brand of Dionysian generosity and progressive idealism that prompted restaurant owners to install plaques commemorating where Emperor Norton had eaten their ham and eggs in exchange for his funny money. Snapshots of this face of the city's dual character would have to include the peaceful takeover of former island prison Alcatraz by local Indians offering to buy it for the original price paid for Manhattan, the Summer of Love and its call to peace and justice on Earth, Mayor Gavin Newsome throwing open the doors to City Hall to welcome ostracized gay couples eager to wed, and homeless Mark Bittner feeding parrots on Telegraph Hill, a contemporary Francis filmed by Judy Irving, a contemporary Clare. Of late the vine god's return to the city has sprouted urban sustainability movements all over the Bay Area. It would seem that this time he's being welcomed in, food and fiber and all.

I stayed in a Nob Hill hotel during an emotionally up and down visit on the very street where Norton had died at his post. Walking over the sloping pavement he had surveyed so diligently, I uttered a silent prayer for the only emperor whose claims I had ever recognized. A gentle rain spread a multitude of lights over the sidewalk below my wandering feet.

Crossing once more the vermilion lattices of the Golden Gate Bridge, I pulled over on the Marin side, got out, and stood shoulder to shoulder with the bronze Lone Sailor placed there to remember the fighting men and women passing through this port during their tours of duty, one and a half million during World War II alone. We looked back at the cloud-capp'd spires of the city together, the mortal Driving Dutchman and the metal man with his satchel. I was less like him now than when I first met San Francisco: less insulated, more flexible, and with greater reverence for the dramatic impulse, especially when creatively unchained.

For a rowdy moment I wondered if he too had once believed in the fifty-minute playlet of indoor psychotherapy. Who knew? Maybe a well-meaning shrink had given him a session or two for his battlefield trauma, dispensed pills, and sent him forth to the wars again, yet here he stood, firm in a coat of alchemized bronze, his dunnage still at his side. I could think of worse vistas to drop in on.

Mythic Marin

When Padre Luis Gil y Taboada, who was pained by a faulty heart, opened an outpost in Marin to nurse sickly Coast Miwok neophytes perishing at Mission Dolores, he did not know of the place's long history as an ancient center for ceremonies of healing, or that his outpost would enlarge into Mission San Rafael, named after the caduceus-bearing archangel of health. On the door to the mission chapel, situated in a county torn slowly in half by two crustal plates, granites on the west and serpentines on the east, hands crossing at the wrists point fingers in opposing directions. The church parking lot covers the nameless bodies of those who never revived.

If you were to gaze at a map of Marin County through half-closed eyes, you might dream you saw the head of a coyote there on the coast, with Point Reyes marking his nose, Drake's Estero his mouth, Abbott's Lagoon one eye, and one long ear paralleling Tomales Bay, where the county-splitting San Andreas runs into the Pacific, to point northward toward Bodega Bay. While still in a state of reverie, turn the map clockwise until the Golden Gate is on your left. Imagine it a nose instead, a mouth out of Richardson Bay, upper jaw as Sausalito, lower as Tiburon (named after the toothy shark), eye looking out of Bolinas Lagoon, Point Reyes now an ear, and before you might shimmer into being a second coyote, this one looking southward instead of westward.

Here we have Coyote doubled like a dream repeated, his Native Californian Trickster character a mythological parallel to caduceus-carrying Hermes, god of healing, thresholds, commerce, travel, alchemy, oratory, wit, and thievery: Hermes the herder of cattle, guider of souls to and from the underworld, bearer of messages, bringer of dreams. The Romans called the holder of the twinned-snake staff Mercury and asked him to make them eloquent and guard their money, although sometimes he lost it or made off with it. Alchemists prayed in their laboratories for Hermes Trismegistus ("Thrice-Blessed") to help them transmute lead into gold, illness into health, and wrinkles of age into youthfulness.

Trickster was on hand in 1775 to welcome the *San Carlos*, an unfortunate vessel nicknamed the *Golden Fleece* because of her Medean knack for killing those who sailed in her. Its captain had been relieved because of insanity, while its second in command, one Juan de Ayala, was bedridden from having shot himself in the foot. In 1595, Trickster watched an unusual wind blow Sebastian Cermeño's galleon ashore at Drake's Bay and smash it on the rocks. Sixteen years earlier, Drake himself had anchored his *Golden Hind* under Coyote's nose at Point Reyes after losing two ships of his flotilla. When the Miwok women saw him, they screamed, believing the pale newcomers to be malevolent ghosts. In time more than fifty stricken galleons would lie below the waters lapping the peninsula along Coyote's gullet. Collecting fragments of porcelain washed ashore, the Miwoks worked it into jewelry.

Perhaps the fingers on the chapel door point to two different versions of how Marin got its name. Some say it derives from Marinera, a native leader at the mission who excelled at handling boats; others, that it echoes the bay's two "Ysla de Marinera," or "Islands of the Mariners," eventually shortened by cartographers to "Marin Islands." That was in 1850, although the name "Marina" reaches all the way back to the Conquest of Mexico.

> She. A flower perhaps, a pool of fresh water...
> a tropical night,

or a sorrowful child, enclosed
in a prison of the softest clay;
mourning shadow of an ancestral memory,
crossing the bridge at daybreak,
her hands full of earth and sun.
— from "Marina," by Lucha Corpi

Strange things unfurl when a legacy of colonialism inflames local motifs. Here those of healing, travel, and confinement play out in uneasy relation to the mission itself, where sick neophytes were transferred and held. Angel Island: site of a disease quarantine station built at Ayala Cove in the late 1800s; then a detention center for captured Indians and excluded Chinese, some of whom scrawled poignant poetry on the confining walls; then a World War II troop quarantine station. The island was closed to the public until Caroline Livermore headed a movement in 1955 to grant the island state park status. Treasure Island: scraped and piled together from fill collected during the Golden Gate International Exposition of 1939, then made over into a World War II naval base and primary port of debarkation for the Pacific Theater. Today traffic speeding over the Bay Bridge runs over the island and through it. Nearby Yerba Buena Island marks the boundary of San Francisco County and has been occupied by a post-Civil War fortress and a naval training station. Alcatraz: site of a former gold storage fort and two prisons. Law enforcement confined the Indians who took it over in 1969 until they were forced to depart. Cunning Sioux had dropped in five years earlier. And San Quentin: a forbidding installation that took its name from Quintun, a former rebel who traded coats to work as General Vallejo's boatman.

Will the colonial, martial, and imperial ever overpower the local, ecological, and mythical? Has it already? Not likely: for all four islands, and even San Quentin, remain firmly confined in the southward-facing gape of wily Old Man Coyote.

I found my motel in Novato right off 101.

Once unpacked I strolled outside and turned my head. My neck cracked sharply. On one side of the hotel was Nero's Firewood. On the other, the North Marin Water District. In a twilit space between water and fire, I stretched my legs and lit my pipe to consider the twinned motif of health and sickness in Marin.

Marin excels in four spheres of health: the environmental, the somatic, the psychological, and the spiritual. A walk through Muir Woods or Point Reyes is sufficient to confirm the first even without the impressive local record of containing local development (or "maldevelopment" as scientist-activist Vandana Shiva calls it) or the proclivity of Mount Tamalpais for burning up railroad tracks laid upon her flanks. When even Sonoma County failed to block the entry of genetically engineered crops, Marin held firm. The Marinite obsession with physical fitness sends joggers up the trails, cyclists up Mount Tam, rowers into the bays, women into yoga classes, and elders with young faces and shapely legs into the organic grocery stores. Psychotherapists offering fulfillment, inner harmony, clear communication, and self-esteem sit in pastel offices throughout the county, as do gurus of all stripes who dance, massage, contemplate, meditate, sage, smudge, ritualize, and ceremonialize—and the more exotic the discipline the better, as always here in the altared state of California, land of tradition-hungry seekers and wanderers after belonging.

At first I could see no down side to all this exertion, even when I learned that an embalmer had founded the town and health resort Hygeia at Tiburon Point, where medical historian Ilza Veith would buy property just before taking ill. Marin, home of the towering breasts of the sleeping maiden Tamalpais, is also home to unusually high rates of breast cancer. Sudden Oak Death plagues Larkspur with sweating, feverish trees, heavy medication surges through Fairfax and San Rafael, and fish caught in Tomales Bay and in the Bon Tempe, Nicasio, and Soulajule Reservoirs seethe with elevated levels of mercury. A hike on lovely Mount Tam left little time or breath for conversation with the woman who had brought me there, with even less when another avid hiker and I rapidly circled Phoenix Lake in the Ross Valley. Yet even in congested San Rafael traffic I felt embraced in waves of bliss despite a nagging sense of separation, not from the place, but from certain of its inhabitants.

In search of conversation, I accepted an invitation one evening to attend a local spirituality salon. On the floor of a spacious living room overlooked by scenic paintings and impressive Buddha statues sat Michael Murphy, co-founder of Esalen, spiritual pioneer, author of many books, and key Human Potential figure. I remembered reading favorable comments about him in the journals of Abraham Maslow. About a dozen people were there to hear what he was up to. One recent exploration, he explained, involved trying to stay lucid all night while asleep. In this way one could access purer and purer states without succumbing to nightly unconsciousness.

After listening to his explanation and thinking it over, I raised my hand to ask a question: "I appreciate your commitment to the exploration of consciousness, and I'm wondering whether the deep psyche needs consciousness to sort of stay out of the way at times so it can go on about its business, whatever that ultimately is. Could you please say something about your thoughts on this?"

I thought I had been polite and respectful, but to my surprise Murphy stared at me for a moment and replied with what sounded to my ear like a defensive, impatient tone: "I am only offering a new method for people to try out for themselves. Nothing more than that. You are free to try it or not to, as you wish." Eyes were beginning to glare at me from above smiles of taut placidity. I rephrased my question, got a similar but even shorter response, and decided that even the enlightened could have an off day. Maybe he wasn't sleeping enough. I didn't mind that, but the feel of pack hostility left me with a disturbing feeling in the pit of my stomach.

After encounters like this, it seemed to me that quite sincere strivings toward health and wholeness could be accompanied by an underlying need to extend the conscious mind's dominance. In such cases I saw little patience with conflict, fragmentation, the mystery of unconsciousness, or inevitably messy emotions like sorrow, remorse, and anger. It was as though the psyche were a resource to mine, and the body a mechanism to control with ever greater precision. Some who spoke to me about the need to cultivate constant "mindfulness" seemed anxious and hypervigilant and hamstrung by an unspoken perfectionism. I wished them luck calming themselves down but was not surprised at how many had, like me, been Christians. How easily we unknowingly smuggled religion's super-egoic demands into new pursuits! A Catholic nun turns into a Buddhist nun but never questions the need for a wisdom-dispensing authority higher than herself. The devoted convert who once sneered at non-Christian for being "non-believers" now looks down on others for being "unevolved" or insufficiently "integral," and next door the ardent recycler ministers to the housemate who throws away cardboard, whipping up a sermon backlit by the cold fire of a Puritan. I was reminded of narcissistically wounded couples who started therapy by insulting at each other before eventually passing on to, "You're invalidating [silencing, marginalizing, what-have-you] me!" Here again theory-challenged Freud had made an acute observation: So often when we uncover a gleaming new insight we chisel it to fit an old neurosis.

In a culture addicted to power and control, it requires great courage to allow the powers of nature—nature as psyche, as body, as once-natural world—to work their healing magic by themselves, in accord with their own mysterious magic. Without the frantic overuse of drugs and interventions, we might actually end up much less jittery. Better perhaps to gather at the lip of the San Andreas and hurl our self-help manuals into the melancholic depths than make ourselves ever sicker by stretching colorful bandaids over the abyss.

After making a winding descent through firs and bishop pines I sat on the sand at Point Reyes National Seashore.

I looked for but did not see any migrating whales, but gulls wheeled by in abundance, their hoarse cries a melody to the harmony of wind and wave. Almost half of North America's endangered birds and plant species dwelled at peace within this scenic sanctuary. I tried to imagine the hundred or so indigenous villages that once gathered here, their inhabitants running, laughing, fishing, cooking, singing, loving, praying...

After millennia of enslavement and oppression and managerial restriction, "freedom" has inevitably come to mean freedom from restraint. When Mariano Vallejo, Californio commander of the entire northern territory, officially granted Olompali near Novato to the Native Californians who had lived there since before the invention of writing, they probably assumed themselves free of the weight of his influence—until he took back their land. He would in turn find himself displaced, first by a drunken band of robbers calling themselves Bear Flaggers, then by invading Americans who turned a blind eye when squatters relieved the General of his land and cattle. He died still complaining of the injustice of it all, but then imperials have never been known for appreciating irony, perhaps because they generate so much of it.

The restraints of oppression, however, are not the same as the limitations that condition our existence, limitations of time and place, of mortality and strength, of the traumatized landscape and its disregarded myths. Let us always fight resolutely against oppressive restraints, but recognize in our impatience with life's natural limitations a childlike omnipotence, a hunger for control, even a narcissistic rage at the implacable principle of reality. Some would rather blame a sufferer's misfortune on "negative energy" or "karma" than give up the self-inflating delusion that reality is only what we make of it, as though wishing things up with "intent" were enough to make them so. As though life were so easily put under our command! Fortunately, this kind of neo-Calvinism generally lasts only so long as the blamer's life goes pleasantly. It's a pity that we never learn the fate of Job's comforters, although we can probably guess it from examples provided by their pontificating Californian counterparts.

Joseph Campbell, C.G. Jung, Rollo May, Hermann Hesse, and a host of other deep thinkers and doers have insisted that so few ever stumble upon our personal fate, archetype, or myth because we lack a fully conscious working mythology, a collective story for guidance into our deeper story. That is true, but we must also reckon with the revulsion of so many seekers to whatever looks from a distance like a threat to their carefully organized autonomy. Freud noticed this fear behind the widespread disparagement of the discovery of the unconscious and the institutionalized refusal to take it seriously. Marin resident Alan Watts had dreamed as an English child of names and images out of California's troubled history, but when he arrived here he preached about the unconditioned life and called himself a shaman, which he never was. Archetypally speaking, he was a natural priest, but doing priesthood literally by joining the Anglican clergy had soured him to the role and to Western spirituality in general. We are free, he maintained from behind his beard and black kimono, free to cast off all authority, discard the past, and be whatever feels right to be—even down to drinking oneself to death, a failed priest of Pan floating in a Sausalito houseboat named *Vallejo*. He never understood that freedom opens out of the discovery and elaboration of the story one comes in with, not from rebellious attempts at its dismissal.

Such a tragic descent is Trickster's doing, of course, or rather the undoing he prepares for the undiscerning. Lore all over the world attests to Trickster's impatience with hubristic self-assurance. Give him a map plotted to be total and he will change the territory to escape the meticulous gridlines. Inflate a balloon beyond its natural size and Trickster will stick a pin in it. Many Native people, including the Coast Miwok, believed that Coyote fashioned the world. This would mean that the entire grand flux and curve of the cosmos manifests not as an intelligent design, but as a funny story told by a trickster, a vastly extended joke echoing with the laughter of interstellar static. In such a cosmos the cardinal "sin" would be tyrannical perfectionism, and its prime virtue a talent for imaginative play.

I watched the sunset-colored waves roll in. What would health look like from the altar of Coyote, creator as well of the human frame?

It would look like the rake in the grass that stops your walk down a path your soul cannot tolerate. The melancholy that punches holes in your schedule long enough to plunge you into your own depths. The slip of the tongue that pukes into a roomful of sham friendliness, the misdirected email that lands on target, the surge of anxiety that keeps you from making a foolish mistake all bear the writing of Dr. Trickster's prescription. Like consciousness itself, Coyote health deflates what overextends itself and raises up what has fallen too low. Stock a Marin neighborhood with whitewashed McMansions and packs of coyotes descend from the hills to knock over all the garbage cans.

On a drive northward through Marin my car battery went dead and refused to recharge. I pulled off 101 not far from where I had stayed in Novato and, lighting my pipe, waited to be rescued. A stand of sturdy oaks gave me shade on this warm afternoon.

The last time this had happened I was passing through Santa Maria. A moment of reflection offered no easy answers for what the two places shared in common. What was Trickster telling me through this inconvenient malfunction? Why plant me here? Suddenly I chuckled. I had taught a bit of psychology in Santa Maria. What the hell. Maybe someday I would live up here in Northern California and teach a class on the power of myth and place.

A few years later, from the Novato hilltop neighborhood where I took a breath of twilit air before starting my seminar on myth and place, the joke seemed even funnier, perhaps because it was on me after all. From somewhere higher in the breezy hills rose the *yip yip yip* of a coyote.

Odyssey's End

> We feel ourselves to be outsiders, uprooted, in exile
> here below. We are like Ulysses who had been car-
> ried away during his sleep by sailors and woke in a
> strange land, longing for Ithaca with a longing that
> rent his soul. Suddenly Athena opened his eyes and
> he saw that he was in Ithaca. In the same way every
> man who longs indefatigably for his country, who is
> distracted from his desire neither by Calypso nor by
> the Sirens, will one day suddenly find that he is
> there.
>
> — Simone Weil

When the unruly band of dusty drifters rode into the plaza at
Sonoma and put General Vallejo under arrest, thereby marking the
end of Mexican rule in California, they followed a precedent of stealing a march that pointed back to the mission raised in 1823 without
the permission of church authorities.

Jose Altamira had worked at Mission Dolores and seen the neophytes languishing there. His plan was to set up a mission in what
is now Sonoma, warmer and farther inland, and transfer all the

Indians in from Dolores and San Rafael. Governor Don Luis Arguello looked favorably upon this plan because of its potential for checking Russian expansion. Alert Spanish soldiers had already frightened off Russian trapping incursions in Northern California.

On July 4th, Altamira opened the mission with his seven hundred neophytes and spaded into soil rich in volcanic ash to plant the first vines in Sonoma wine country. The church let the mission stand but declined to close the other two.

Alas, "Father" Altamira belonged to that grim group of parentified punishers who confuse fear with respect and equate education with breaking the will of one's "children." Learning nothing from the organic generosity pulsing in the fertile land all around him, he beat his charges with such viciousness that they rebelled and set the mission on fire. After fleeing to San Rafael, Altamira was sent back to Spain, but his replacement, Jose Gutierrez, belonged to the same old boy's punishment club. By the time the mission was secularized only eleven years after its founding, the neophytes were glad to cooperate with General Vallejo's plan to found Sonoma in the Valley of the Moon until he absorbed their land into his already vast territorial holdings.

Having bear-flagged the Indians, Vallejo was bear-flagged himself on June 14, 1846, when thirty-three trappers and mountain men in bandanas and buckskins pounded on the door of Casa Grande at dawn to demand Vallejo's surrender. Led by William Ide, Henry Ford, and Ezekiel "Stutterer" Merritt, the "Osos" ("Bears") had been fooled by John Fremont into believing that the ruling Californios, who were normally genial hosts of American settlers, were now burning down homesteads. Fremont had been leading his men illegally around California in the company of tracker Kit Carson, scalper of Indians, and he wanted to do his glorious part for the coming American takeover.

Vallejo had trouble understanding what the marauders wanted. When he asked who was in charge, they kept insisting they all were. Some of the confusion had to do with the Vallejo estate brandy casks they were tapping as they shouted "Get the loot!" while trying to figure out how to emulate the Texan revolt against

Mexico. At last they settled for running a rudely designed Bear Flag up a flagpole. CALIFORNIA REPUBLC, it announced like a drunk skipping over a syllable. The star gave a nod to Texas. Vallejo took the bear for a pig.

With William Ide busy organizing a new government to free the oppressed masses of California, Fremont arrived to take Vallejo into custody and imprison him in a fetid cell in Sutter's Fort while making off with most of his cattle. When Commodore Sloat sailed into Monterey on July 7th, however, Fremont found himself in custody for exceeding his authority. The resulting court martial judged him guilty on twenty-two charges. At its end, Fremont resigned his commission to campaign as the Republican candidate for President.

As for California, it passed quickly into American hands. Soon it would be the only state with an extinct animal on its flag.

> It is to be hoped that this lesson, showing us as it does how much of conscience and even of personal sincerity can coexist with a minimum of effective morality in international undertakings, will some day be once more remembered; so that when our nation is another time about to serve the devil, it will do so with more frankness and will deceive itself less by half-unconscious cant. For the rest, our mission in the cause of liberty is to be accomplished through a steadfast devotion to the cultivation of our own inner life, and not by going abroad as missionaries, as conquerors, or as marauders, among weaker peoples.
>
> — Josiah Royce on California's takeover

As Table 2 illustates, "Bear-flagging," whereby a small band of men hijack what others own or need, would play out repeatedly in Sonoma County in the coming centuries.

Table 2:

Examples of Bear?Flagging in Sonoma County, California:

- Mission San Francisco Solano (Sonoma Mission) the last mission founded, and the only one founded ahead of authorization.
- General Vallejo reclaims land promised to local Indians.
- Bear Flag "revolt."
- Bear Flag replaced by Stars and Stripes.
- State offices suddenly moved to Sacramento instead of to Vallejo.
- County seat appropriated by Santa Rosa (1854) before Sonomans can protest.
- Greedy growers mine so many immature grapes that the bottom falls repeatedly out of the wine industry.
- Vallejo steals Sonoma's city charter (1860) to prevent the city from buying adjacent land.
- The Sonoma Valley Railroad Company plants tracks through Sonoma overnight to bypass citizen protests.
- When New Town is founded to steal residents from Petaluma, Petaluma counter-bear-flags New Town by encouraging its residents to relocate to Petaluma. New Town vanishes.
- Vallejo loses most of his land to incoming squatters. *His History of California* dies in a fire. The same incendiary fate had befallen the Bear Flag and the mission.
- Vintners put French and Italian brand names on bottles of immature California wines.
- Gallo Wine acquires Martini as one of a series of controversial expansions.
- Wine industrialists turn Napa into a resort and push the poor off the busy thoroughfares. "Doctor" Edward Bale buys Rancho Calajomanas and warps the name into Carne Humana, "Human Flesh," for the amputations he had performed as an inebriated army surgeon.)
- Santa Rosa developers push their agenda so forcibly that the city once gardened by Luther Burbank drowns in asphalt and glass as traffic jams 101 and smog haunts the Sonoma Mountains.
- Measure M to ban genetically altered crops passes in Marin but is bear-flagged in Sonoma County by cold callers pretending to be organic farmers and Greenpeace officials.

Although founded ahead of official permission, Sonoma Mission forged the last link in a six-hundred-mile-long loop chaining up the natives and their land. Its final rusting lock clicked shut here, at the terminus of a long Cross and Sword campaign of colonial statewide bear-flagging reaching at long last to

THE END OF THE MISSION TRAIL
1523 – 1823

I squinted through the bright sunlight. A girl with big breasts hanging over a bare midriff handed a biker a bottle of beer. Behind her, an attractive Mexican lady somewhat older than I returned a smile from the shade of a café table, but when I had passed and turned around again, she was gone. The digital camera hung at my right hip. From over the mission courtyard wall I heard children's laughter.

As I walked by the plaque and set foot into this, the northern-most mission on El Camino Real, a classical piece sounded its few final notes from the ranger's desktop radio. My ear caught Beethoven's *Eroica* symphony. Was that the shade of Joseph Campbell chuckling just out of hearing?

The ticket was one dollar. I paid—in God we trust—and entered a small museum with the usual mission accoutrements. The bone-colored chapel was dim and quite spartan in its furnishings. Stations of the Cross to my right and my left, and a painting of Jesus lying below a busy workman just about to pound in the first nail. No incense. The disrespectful whir of my camera. The sun momentarily blinded me when I pushed open the door to the courtyard.

Orchards and croplands had hinted at "Who" was here miles before I encountered the earth mother icons and fertility images of Sebastopol, where an unwritten dress code requires sandals and wrap skirts even in chilly weather. Once a bastion of conservatism, Sebastopol became the only town in California with a Green Party majority on the city council. With the city officially nuclear- and wireless-free, the conservative shadow has withdrawn to the flagpoles of Cunningham, the ranches of Schaeffer, and Canfield, site of a bedraggled back yard flying the Stars and Bars over rusty automobiles. Throughout the area collectors of old junk—more politely, family heirlooms—have set up shop as antique dealers. By map Bodega Bay lies fifteen miles to the west but takes almost an hour to reach by car.

In Sebastopol I dreamed of a giant dark figure I recognized as Poseidon tearing apple trees right out of the ground. The dream brought to mind the angry storm god blowing Odysseus all over the ocean as well as the god's rape of fair Demeter, goddess of grains, crops, fertility, and growth. I could feel her maternal powers all around me in the largely undeveloped county rooting, waving, and blossoming fragrantly in her embrace. It extended from chickens hatching centuries of eggs in Petaluma, identified by Sarah Rankin as a place of phoenix-like rebirth, to vines drooping with grapes in Healdsburg and beyond. Had disruptive Poseidon cast his impatient, shape-changing shadow over the rushed opening of a mission without authorization, the harvesting of immature grapes, the rebels appearing on horseback at dawn? Would he throw another imaginal tsunami at me? Somehow I thought not.

I AM THE GUARDIAN OF THE GATE announced a plaque on the winged sculpture squatting on a dewy lawn at Sebastopol's southern entrance. A clock on the antique mall across the street stood frozen at half past six. An autumn visitor could stroll through these rural neighborhoods picking and eating ripe blackberries, oranges, persimmons, lemons, and Gravenstein apples. Admiring a long snake curled up around the rail of a wood-plank bridge over the lagoon, *All this Eden lacks*, I thought, *are the Tigris and Euphrates*, and then I remembered the endless flows whooshing along the unbroken 12 and 116 crossing in the center of town. According to an old story, the town got its name when a long fistfight prompted someone to compare the brawl to the Siege of Sevastopol, Russia, during the Crimean War. Cain and Abel get around. Before I left town a feminine figure named "Evie" would greet me in my dreams.

As elsewhere in California, builders and large businesses concentrated in the east county while liberals, Greens, and activists flocked westward. I heard much here about the Goddess, the Buddha, permaculture, shamanism, ecopsychology, and Starhawk. Wendell Berry and Paul Shepard were mentioned often and favorably, as were the Quakers and the Amish. I could see myself stopping right here and picking up a hoe. I would enter old age among the proud redwoods of the Russian River watershed, visiting the coast to listen to the sea and watching autumned maples drop red and yellow leaves. Glancing at the birthmark on my forearm, I wondered whether a gardener nicknamed "Cain" in another life could stay in a place like this forever.

As I spoke with local residents about increasingly ominous signs of the times—mass surveillance, mass extinctions, endless war, climate change—I began to sense a pattern in the responses I received. They had to do, not surprisingly, with the cultivation and growth of indigenous ritual, a spiritual practice, a plot of land. It dawned on me that people lived here who sincerely believed that burning incense and making masks could constitute an adequate answer to the problems of our day. When I mentioned this to an acquaintance involved with ecopsychology, a multidisciplinary exploration of our relationship with the environment, he asked, "What do you have against incense?" Obviously literal-mindedness did not confine itself to the monotheistic worldview.

Through all this ran an unspoken but discernible streak of unconscious conservatism, especially in talk of returning to "the feminine," as though the oppressive nature of essentialism had not been demonstrated by generations of feminists. The anti-technological bias, the idealization of Earth as bounteous mother, the drum beat of rhetoric about localization, the cheery assumption that tradition held our salvation, and other down-home, back-to-nature prescriptions required no renewed engagement with land and myth, politics and psyche, but instead a series of retreats into the grassy lap of Demeter. They were not written out wrongly, it seemed to me, who favored some of them, so much as tied too tightly to her apron strings.

Tilling the soil could not by itself resist five hundred years of colonial savagery, here or anywhere else. What we needed, I suspected as I drove for Sonoma, was nothing less than a new myth, a new vision of our place in the world sewn from fresh discoveries and bold experiments—scientific as well as animistic—interwoven with old lore that could dispense useful hints but no longer satisfy us with its archaic style of thought. We needed terrapsychologies to rechart the living planet, brave elders to show us how to keep alienated, ecocidal tyrants from the powerful positions they craved, and sophisticated homegrown approaches for relating to Terra as responsible adults, not as spoiled children alternating between worship and contempt. We needed to grow not only down, but up.

I walked outside among groups of fourth graders there to learn a sanitized history of the missions. Some weaved baskets in the red-brick fountain in the center of the courtyard. Glancing around, I saw a large iron pot and a great mound of cacti, a few busy birds, and little else. White walls, dark rafters, barred windows, bare dirt. Distracted dads in white aprons cooked up steaming piles of hot dogs. I reentered the museum, glanced at a map of Sonoma to get my bearings, and stepped forth from California's last mission.

And that was it, except for marauding cars jostling to park around the plaza, a sidewalk shopper to dodge as she talked on the phone, and the jarring June heat and shimmer. A camino most unreal. I was appalled at the banality of it. Centuries of genocide, cultures forced out of existence, vast landscapes destroyed, thousands of species driven from the earth—and at the end of it all, an oversized hotdog stand topped by a red tiled roof. What had I expected? The satanic sphincter at the bottom of some Dantean hell? A statue of Serra bursting spontaneously into flames?

Rounding the corner, however, I came at last to a lone memorial of stone and glass. Positioned near the sidewalk, it had been dedicated in 1999 to

> MEN, WOMEN, AND CHILDREN OF THE LOCAL COAST
> MIWOK, PATWIN, WAPPO, AND POMO TRIBES. THEY
> BUILT, LABORED, AND DIED AT MISSION SAN FRANCISCO
> SOLANO.

They certainly had. Some of the victims were listed, but only by their Spanish names bestowed by the padres. The Native names were gone forever.

Of an original five hundred tribal groups of three hundred and ten thousand people dwelling within distinct microclimates all over the statewide garden they had tended, most were gone. Even hardy northern and inland survivors never seduced into missions had suc-cumbed to diseases and murder dealt by incoming trappers and miners. Their elders struggle to pass on what remains of fifty native languages left from more than a hundred—and this in a state with twelve counties bearing Native Californian names.

After all this journeying, I was still waiting, I realized then, for an explanation, for a narrative that could cover it all, reassemble the broken pieces, reanimate the faces of the dead, bring their voices back to life, and answer the eternal post-colonial question always hiding in the umbra of empire:

What was it all for?

The Spanish Crown thought it was for state security, and the missionaries for the saving of souls. The tycoons and developers and industrialists who came after thought it was all for profit. But maybe it was all for nothing, and therein lies the meaning: meaning as meaninglessness, truth as nullity, substance as shadow cast by the disappearing land and its disappeared inhabitants converted soullessly away into the spent currencies of ethereal ideologies. Missionizing is entropic, for in the end these unfinished castles too shall pass away, rained down, shaken down, burned up, or weeded over, joined at last to all the silenced absences broken and buried under the ringing mission bell.

And still the injured land abides. The harbored protection of defended San Diego, the dolorous fogs of moody San Francisco, the perpetual youthfulness of lovely Santa Cruz, and all the other places upon which marching, preaching, buying, thieving, and selling opportunists spent their dreams and fears and struggles would still be here restoring themselves long, long after whatever fate we make for ourselves finally overtakes us.

In the meantime I would go on with the labor of opening my

heart to what had happened here and what was happening still, but I would do it deprived of the fantasy of some final accounting approved by survivors, blessed by the land, and authorized by the restless dead. Sometimes the presence to be tended manifests most urgently, California had taught me, as a ragged absence.

I bowed for a moment to the spirits behind all those transplant-ed names, then exited stage left, minding the bikes and bottles.

Down and over dappled dunes blows a sea-blue wind. Froth flags flap on crenellated outcroppings. Waves march shoreward, march shoreward, march shoreward below a purple promontory broken into boulders at sad Bodega Bay. Salt simultaneously damp-ens and dries the air.

Mist melts headland outlines; wild weeds wink. Gulls gyrate below the cobalt dome. Winding wooden steps drop down toward rasping sand. Zero precipitation.

It has been a long, wrenching journey, a trail of loss and heart-break, but also of wonder and anticipation. He stands there wearily among driftwood, eyes out on the ocean. Draws a deep breath. And catches from the very edge of perception a sound that is not a sound, a voice beyond hearing, alien and yet familiar, an imaginal, emotion-al, intuitive sound that unravels the length of the mystery so long on his mind in one breathy pulse of entirety:

That is what it is, the very air, water, fire, and soil of invaded California whisper straight through his ledger of losses, *to feel exiled, alienated, used, and orphaned.*

He sits down on the sand as the insight that brought him there finally unfolds—

For the uprootedness, alienation, fury, and sorrow he had con-sidered only his own were ultimately of the land beneath him. What we do to the land and on the land, he knows at last, reverberates back into us from the land, and from us back into the land, two charged poles of an inescapably interactive field as haunting as any ghastly midnight masque performed over and over and over. Lines out of Poe come back to him: *And Darkness and Decay and the Red Death held illimitable dominion over all...*

But it didn't have to be that way, for every symptom is also a sacred message. These replays of historical events and themes and sufferings, too persistent, too place-based ("My name is San Diego"), too psychic and mythic to be merely social diffusions, echoed down into the most intimate of sufferings like a warning buoy unheard, like flashings from a lighthouse unmanned set going by a coastline unlistened to: *I live! I live! I live! I live....* As without, so within, again and again and again, the face we turn to place throughout our careless history there reflected back to us in repeating, history-soaked, panpsychic bids for our attention brought forth in the earthly language we too once spoke and understood: that of symptom and symbol.

I live, said the land. *Listen to me. Listen...*

The sudden salty gust left it simple and solved, the cool, full wash of a clarity so long deferred.

That is what it is, said the land, said California, *to be unwanted.*

I hear you now from the very center of that knowing.

At last....

The cry of a circling bird.

I am the queen of a large seigniory....

Five hundred years after the cry of Cihuacoatl, a child of the Moon, having overheard a sorrowing goddess crying out in pain, and having pursued the missionary stigmata of divinized suffering to the top of the Royal Road walked over as dust, pavement, asphalt, and steel, descends a wooden stairway cut into the rocky hillside, the while lowering himself from parking lot to sea's edge, wave-washed, tide-churned, rock-worn, its elements goaded into motion by a ceaseless wind.

Watched by overhanging boughs waving in the wind, the Queen's Highwayman kneels before the inflowing foam, breaths in the salt air, bows his head, and thanks the gods, Calafía, and the bronzed Lady of Sorrows for seeing him safely to his destination despite his confusions, detours, and many wrong turns, so that he could reach out at last to the hidden source of a voice too long unheard. "Forgive me, Mother, for my noisy life..."

There at land's end, a land so very hungry for the empathy of outcasts and exiles, he rests on one knee, thinking back on it all; and as he does, a single tear curves leeward in the gust, sparkles as it falls, and, an instant later, loses itself to the all-absorbing Pacific.

When the ocean wind turns to parallel the shoreline at Sonoma State Beach, the eddies and currents of sand it sets in motion sizzle in an audible reminder of the awesome power of weathering. Not the highest barriers, either outer or inner, can stand forever against that relentless blast.

With one hand on my heart and the other on windblown sand, I savored the hard-won knowledge that my wandering lot over the years had been California's as well, as through it all the mother of my mothers, named after a dangerous queen taken captive by Christian knights, had been silently but emphatically addressing me in the only way she could by speaking to me right through my deepest sense of exile.

This is what it is to be displaced from your own ground. The wordless anguish crept up from below and passed through my heart for translation. Afterimages of it blew away on the cleansing wind.

After a while I rose to go, but instead I began picking up driftwood for my evening camp fire. I sniffed. Tonight it would be cold. The wind freshened as I wandered over the beach.

> I only went out for a walk and finally concluded to
> stay until sundown, for going out, I discovered, was
> actually going in.
>
> — John Muir

Climbing back up the rough-cut steps at sundown, I turned once more toward the sand, the waves, the blue-grey horizon. Was I dreaming, asked the native San Diegan? Had I really heard what I heard, felt what I was feeling now? Had my intuition served me, or had I lived in mystical Los Angeles too long? Could any of this be nailed down? wondered the compass-bearing Alamedan I now carried inside me.

Perhaps not. This new knowledge reflected larger and subtler interdependencies than single causal lines could ever encompass. Perhaps the storied, symptomatic voice of place that infects us all grows audible only in a heart leaning down to catch pulsations of story and myth and history echoing upward from below, present to presence and wound to wound, listening in for subterranean voices murmuring in their own way and on their own metaphoric terms. The right tool for the right job.

> Eureka. We have found it! It is no longer just gold, oil, money, grapes, orchards, an agribusiness that invents square tomatoes and never-spoil milk, tomatoless tomatoes and milkless milk... microchips, religious cults, the entertainment and aerospace industries, but also a complicated way of being human, a nationality without an army—per-haps an exaggerated mirror for the American dream, the universal dream of a sweeter elsewhere.
>
> — Herbert Gold

But for me that elsewhere was now *here*, in the pulsing ground I knelt again to touch. Its sands breathed cool and moist below my palm.

When Odysseus asked Minerva where the hell she had been dur-ing all his despairing wanderings and shipwrecks, she startled him with a mild answer:

I was never away from your side. I was looking out for you when your com-panions were lost and your vessels capsized, in triumph and in danger, sorrow and fury, through all your heartsick wanderings. And I'm looking out for you right now.

And watching me receive, perhaps, the long-postponed blessing of finally belonging, and of understanding at last that for all my sense of exile, this living coast, from San Diego to Sonoma, was my homeland, heartland, and soulland, nor was I ever really away from it. I knew my place, and it knew me. *Thank you,* I thought to every-thing around me, *for seeing me safely me to this moment of revelation.*

The foghorn mooed again, and again, while the rain fly over my tent flapped restlessly in the wind, but my sleep that night was peacefully dreamless.

When dawn had spread her fingertips of rose over the terminus of the King's Highway in Sonoma County, I drove southward, stopping at a strip mall for coffee. In the foyer stood a large statue of none other than Poseidon holding his mighty trident. Suddenly awake, I started and then walked slowly around him. A scaly limb curled up one of his muscular legs.

When you are finally home, the shade of Tiresias the seer had advised the lost Man of Wrath, *gather driftwood as a peace offering to Poseidon, that he might not send you across the angry seas again.*

I nodded toward the statue, remembering my driftwood fire.

And with that, as gently as foam meets the littoral and disperses, I felt the ancient odyssey I had relived come apart around me.

Odysseus had descended into the underworld because he needed sound advice before sailing any farther, before any more inadvertent adventures, losses, and deaths. Down he had headed into Pluto's dark kingdom as his men waited fearfully aboard the ship wondering if their captain would ever return.

He knew many of the ghosts who crowded around him, attracted by the smell of the ram he had sacrificed: Elpenor, dead in Circe's hall. There was Tyro, who had lost her mind near the river Enipeus, stern Agamemnon, mighty Heracles....and, to his sudden distress, his own weeping mother, dead and come to the underworld.

"Child," she asked him, "how could you cross alive into this gloom at the world's end?"

"Mother, I came here driven to the land of death in want of prophecy...."

Three times he tried to embrace her, and three times he failed as she sifted into shadows in his hands. Then he too wept, crying out in the darkness, "O my mother, will you not stay, be still, here in my arms, may we not, in this place of Death, as well, hold one another, touch with love, and taste salt tears' relief, the twinge of welling tears?"

"No flesh and bone are here," confirmed his mother sadly, "none bound by sinew, since the bright-hearted pyre consumed them down—the white bones long exanimate—to ash; dreamlike the soul flies, insubstantial."

What a strange hero, if such he really be. Unable to rescue anything from the kingdom of Hades, he asked instead to keep the spirits company.

Seeing his hesitation, the weeping woman said:

"You must crave sunlight soon. Note all things strange seen here, to tell your lady in after days."

At this precise moment, the moment of realizing that he can neither redeem her back to life nor stay with her below, the old campaigner, master of sea ways and land ways, weaver of stratagems and wrecker of nations, suffers his deepest pang of transformation yet by changing from a warrior into a storyteller. Bidden to bear along tales of woe from the world under the world, he has finally become responsibly daimonic by allowing ghostly voices live again—in him.

Thinking about this raised long-standing questions for me once again:

Beyond so vocally representing the oppressed woman who refuses to be tamed or silenced, who is lost Llorona? What is her relation to Our Lady of Guadalupe, whom Ana Castillo described as "the great dual force of life and death?" Why do variants of the two appear in so many of the same places?

The images of Guadalupe and Llorona make up the severed halves of a split archetype, the spiritual poles of an original goddess whose numinous face was torn in two when conquest separated her defeated children from her devastated lands. In Christian terms, Llorona—said to be named Maria in some tales—and Guadalupe reflect the dark and bright aspects of Mary, mother of Jesus and mediatrix of salvation. Mary had in turn been declared by the Council of 431 to be a virgin just like Sophia, a resident goddess of Ephesus, the ancient, ruined city where the Council was held. Mythologically speaking, virginal Sophia is a Greek version of the Aztec Cihuacoatl, an originally whole goddess of the sacred land

and its dwellers.

Llorona and her sad sisters around the troubled globe—Medea, Rachel, Lilith, Lamia, Siren, Banshee, Crying Wind—always haunt the footsteps of conquerors because these spectral pursuers weep with the voice of the demonized, colonized ground severed from human appreciation. They are its wailing earthly sufferings fallen down into folklore. While La Virgen brings comfort to the displaced, Llorona haunts the territories captured and fenced by the displacers. The more colonized the territory, the likelier that she will possess unfortunates who live there but never find their voice. Her victims include Kisha Bethel (Miami), Christine Wilhelm (Hoosick Falls), Susan Smith (Union), Leonora de Rodriguez (Premont), Betina Mixon (Southaven), Rebekah Amaya (Lamar), Andrea Yates (Houston), Lashuan Harris (San Francisco)...Lorna Legg (San Diego and Hawaii)....

Through the tears of Llorona weeps the land for its afflicted, lost, and dead indigenous children—and for its bewildered occupiers too, whether possessed by its tormented spirit or killed by its unthinking acts of Gaia. To paraphrase what Jung wrote about the unconscious, Earth cannot help but turn toward us the face that we turn toward it, benevolent and gentle when respected, but violent and deadly when mistreated. Tsunamis and pandemics slay millions, hurricanes head for oil refineries and flood out cities and counties, animals attack the tamers who treat them as objects and disregard their needs...and Llorona cries out from just behind us, ever in shadow but staring back through the darkness.

> You know, I thought she was talking about us Indians and how we are supposed to get along. I found out later by my older sister that mother wasn't just talking about Indians, but the plants, animals, birds—everything on this earth. They are our relatives and we better know how to act around them or they'll get after us.
>
> — Lucy Smith, Dry Creek Pomo

How, then, can we ever be reconciled with her? How shall she and we ever be redeemed?

In the end only one way lies open: to be reconciled with the lands on which we live and with the people who once lived here or try to even now while caught in the struggles of post-colonial survival at the edge. We must find ways to bring all the displaced voices, human and nonhuman, to our table and hear what they have to express to us.

It's not enough to tinker green gadgets or sage new houses or eat tamales on the Day of the Dead. As Dr. Martin Luther King observed about the oppressed, so with places and the life within: "A riot is the language of the unheard."

Here in my homeland we must welcome Queen Calafía and her subjects and Wisdom herself back from their long night of exile. To do that will require learning how to listen again, as our ancestors could, but with contemporary tools, starting from the ground up and hearing through the heart with love and concern and through the mind with intelligence and discernment.

To the extent that we succeed, our own alienation from the once-hallowed ground, from each other, and from ourselves finds the freedom to transmute itself into the lasting joy of coming deeply home.

At the end of my odyssey a series of dreams came to me. This was one of them:

> I stand before a white wall. Touching it with my finger brings it to life, a viewing screen displaying images of the lady in white. Knowing this procession is important to my research, I grope for my camera but can't seem to find it. I look up again in time to see a final image: not a fearsome ghost or a wailing woman, but a smiling mother gently holding a child from within a lush garden. She looks a bit like Mary, I realize, as a word I wrote with my finger reappears below her, a word that activated the images and glows forth now in the color of

dried blood coagulating around a healing injury: Llorona.

I choose to believe that Llorona's son survived his campaign because I played my wanderer's part instead of letting the part go on playing me, extracting from me what I had refused to give freely, until I chose to soulsee and participate actively. Although pursued at first up El Camino Real by the shade of lost Llorona, somewhere along the way my ship tacked about, the momentum shifted, and I began pursuing her. By driving before the wind until duty became inextricable from love, I reached a point where I could begin to rewrite the old story from the inside out.

I also believe that this dream opens onto an overlooked realm of my soul where demonic Llorona, whose voice I had struggled so long to comprehend, might finally find redemption in her original form, as a white-clad mother named Laura or Maria, or perhaps even Malintzin, forbear of an alchemically combined heritage born in strife but pregnant with hybrid possibilities.

As for me, I too had come home, not a drifter anymore but abiding in locales that spoke to me and heard me.

When I stood up to leave the beach at Bodega Bay, a strange sensation had passed through my chest, like a hand caressing me from the inside. It took me more than a month to realize what it was, and why, in the unexpected absence of a lifelong ache, I had finally ceased to feel like an orphan:

The orphan-sized hole torn in my heart forty years ago had been permanently healed.

Epilogue: The Other Coast

> Our bodies were made from the sacred earth, our beautifully colored skin given to us by the sacred fire. The breath of life came to us from the sacred sky. In our bodies flowed the unending sacred rivers. By all the sacredness blending together— earth, fire, air and water—our bodies and blood were created. Through these sacred elements, the people lived and were connected to everything.
>
> — Matt Vera, Yowlumni Yokuts

Having reached the center of the garden labyrinth, I stood there for a moment. A coast live oak shaded me from the late September heat. Someone who had gone before had arranged the small rocks at my feet to spell out LOVE.

The labyrinth had been laid out stone by stone with a concentrated intentionality the walker could actually feel, there in the Pleasant Hill garden at the university. Although I was a new core faculty member, my schedule had already picked up enough that I needed these lunch breaks to reconnect with the land. A few months ago this plot of ground had been bare claypan dominated by dry weeds. Now it overflowed with vegetables and flowers. An herb spiral curled near at hand, glistening with new moisture, and I saw thick yellow squash about ready to be picked.

Before coming here to Contra Costa ("Other Coast") County, I had spent a year in Sebastopol, where the former winged sculpture had been replaced by two trunk-like columns blossoming with hands and mirrors for leaves. Tree of Knowledge and Tree of Life? I had lived in peace on a small ranch with chickens for company and lowing cows for an alarm clock. It was a pleasant place to come home to after driving to five different Bay Area campuses to teach psychotherapy, mythology, dream work, ecopsychology, and Jung to graduate students and undergrads.

A few days after I sent in the last manuscript corrections for *Terrapsychology* I received word that the Alzheimer's that had taken my mother's memory had claimed her life as well. Death himself had finally released her from imprisonment in the myth of La Llorona. I had no tears left to grieve: so many had already been shed for this long ago. And what of my father? I had learned that he saw me in the hospital on the day I was born. After realizing this, I dreamed about putting on a large white tunic with the words MOURNING FOR THE FATHERS written on the front. The sorrow of their absence is still with me. Too many absent and unaccountable lovers of Llorona.

Along the way I had also found myself released into a wider story. Dreams had been hinting for a long while now that just as the tale of Llorona and her child lived inside my version of the Odyssey, so it was contained in an even larger tale, one that had always been with me forming a core myth around which the other tales had turned as they came to life and unfolded. Although I felt eager to see what the larger plot demanded, it sufficed me for the moment to teach and write...while worrying about California.

The outlook here is grim and getting grimmer, and not just because the ballooning state budget keeps coming out billions too short. Climate change has brought a two-year-long drought and increased melting of the Sierra snowpack, our primary source of water. Two hundred million acre-feet might sound like a lot of annual precipitation, but unsustainable agricultural factories in the fields drink up 80% of it, and our six major water systems cannot keep up with the demand. Having ravaged much of the coast, sprawl now dismantles entire watersheds across the smoggy Central Valley. Far too many people live in this state, and nothing is being done to manage the population—except by the Catholic Church, of course, which keeps telling people not to use birth control.

Wetlands continue to shrink to a fraction of their former size, nine-tenths of the once-lush riparian vegetation is gone, as are nine-tenths of the coastal salt marshes, and the Bay Delta serving two thirds of our population is collapsing. In the northwest, a mere 10% of salmon spawning sites remain viable. Similar figures stalk diminishing populations of too many land, sea, and air species to count even as seasonal temperatures rise while displacing native flora and fauna. Will Southern California end up with a climate like that of parched Baja? Will we inherit Southern California's? Will the redwoods die out? On a global scale, will we? No one knows, and the "leaders" at both the state and national levels are missing in action.

> Why do we so dread to think of our species as a species? Can it be that we are afraid of what we may find? That human self-love would suffer too much and that the image of God might prove to be a mask? This could be only partly true, for if we could cease to wear the image of a kindly, bearded, interstellar dictator, we might find ourselves true images of his kingdom, our eyes the nebulae, and universes in our cells.
>
> — John Steinbeck

We certainly don't lack solutions to ecological problems. All around the world permaculturalists are turning patches of desert into food-growing oases and teaching classes on how to trap and recycle water. Every day organic farmers using minimal irrigation and no harmful pesticides grow and harvest fruits and vegetables far tastier and more nourishing than anything trucked in by a grocery conglomerate. As bioregionalists and indigenous governments run successful experiments with direct democracy and nature-based community, biomimicry experts design low-power high-yield technologies patterned after how nature already does it right.

No, we do not lack the means to lead high-quality lives and build just and abundant communities to ensure our survival and that of our fellow species. The real question is whether we can muster the necessary psychological maturity to face our responsibilities and take back our authority from those who misuse it.

Given a choice between an honest candidate and a lying crook, a substantial number of people vote for the crook. Culturally advanced nations throw away hard-won freedoms and cheer in police states with exuberant displays of flagolatry. As millions of spiritual people allow medieval institutions to shame them, blame them, and tell them what to think, believe, and read, otherwise intelligent individuals invest in an economic system that robs undeveloped countries, lays waste to entire biomes, triggers ongoing wars, and leaves millions poor and thirsty. We then leave it all up to certificated experts to solve—the experts who have brought it all down on our heads to begin with.

In the end, whether we submit to further destruction and catastrophe or design pleasant communities respectful of Earth's needs depends squarely on the education of our consciousness, the lever of survival and sustainasanity. A mode of consciousness saddled with ignorance, exclusion, restriction, self-deception, passivity, projection, and paranoid fear stands no chance of weathering the multiple environmental, political, and spiritual crises that arise from its own rigid narrowness. It does not need "solutions" so much as retraining, some of it by initiated elders and mentors who teach by personal example and real expertise.

A truly holistic education—an ethical, ecological, and humanitarian education of the heart and intuition as well as of the body and the mind—might start by showing people just how intimately the world reaches into us. When a mind so educated shifts from a procedural orientation to a relational one, it recognizes the need to come deeply home, not like a child on its knees, but like an adult grown up enough to love the old homestead for what it is instead of despising it for what it isn't or idealizing what it might have been.

Before he died, Joseph Campbell intuited that a "new myth" offering a collective frame of orientation and meaning would center on our earthly home. As spontaneous emanations from deep within the collective psyche, true myths cannot be artificially constructed, and once dead cannot be resurrected by any amount of incense or ritual without regressions into vicious fundamentalism. But if a myth of the future is already upon us, calling out in the language of earthquakes and storms, perhaps we can tend its birth in our consciousness by coming home one location at a time, beginning with "heartsteading" the place where we dwell right now. That would at least dissolve the ancient dualism between self and world at its source. It could also ground new approaches to sustainability, ecoliteracy, and community in a more realistically connective mode of being. A crowd of lively subjectivities has always been easier to love and relate to than a cold congeries of categorized objects.

As a living place and everything in it—soil, rocks, plants, creatures, artifacts, elements, history, climate—become consciously respected facets of ourselves, fitting their deep roots along the interstices of personality, we find ourselves realizing how profoundly we partake of each place we come to, with everything—self, people, place, planet and beyond—nested in sentient webs. Perhaps the cosmic weavers imaged in mythic figures such as Indra, Neith, Ariadne, Athena, Hera, Brigid, Urdr, Clotho, and Spider Woman would be delighted by how human appreciation might enrich their intricate connective work.

Delighted we would be as well to see the last of anguishing reenactments. Not by persuading anyone that the work needs doing, but by doing it ourselves.

"I could use a vacation," I told the labyrinth.

When Spaniards entering this "other coast" along the San Francisco Bay saw local Native ceremonialists painted red, they named the ceremonial site Mount Diablo and pulled away in fear. However, places do seem to participate in their own namings. On the flanks of that uncanny mountain whose watershed extends through much of Contra Costa County crawl tarantulas and rattlesnakes just as summer gives way to fall. The summit provides a view no less sweeping than that offered Jesus by the Tempter.

Far below it glimmer the strangely Leggo-like office buildings of downtown Walnut Creek; overbuilt Concord, whose name sounds like "conquered," a recent victim of almost nightly armed robberies; Antioch, whose name means "stubborn, resistant"; exclusive Blackhawk, a gated Danville community literally overseen by its hilltop builder; a former military weapons depot; and, off in the arid distance, the oil refineries and smokestacks of Martinez, once the home of John Muir, and of Richmond, coastal hub of heavy industries like shipping, volatile fuels, and, formerly, whaling and high explosives.

With assistance from three female friends I moved from Sebastopol into a detached Walnut Creek rental unit right beside the creek. At first it felt like moving from Eden to Erebus, especially given a neighborhood of many cul-de-sacs, two funeral parlors, a nursery school named Pied Piper, and the Rossmoor Retirement Community and its guards and hedges. An ambulance sped there daily, presumably to restart yet another failing heart; after a time I thought of the noisy passage of flashing red lights as the Rossmoor Express. Amateur cyclists riding on the sidewalks and against the flow of traffic routinely forced pedestrians into the bike lanes. All in all, though, it was a pleasant green valley in which to mark an ending, and to write about one too. A street up the hill bore the name "Avalon," as did a massage school, a metaphysical school, and an assisted living establishment. Being here felt at times like dwelling in a vale of dream.

While walking one day I was startled to look over the creek and see a mission bell monument in a backyard. No mission had invaded this county (one of the reasons I had moved here), yet there the thing was, grey bell hanging from a metal shepherd's crook, but without the EL CAMINO REAL sign. Someone must have bought it as a keepsake. I thought it over. Had it been a dream image, I would have taken it for a softening, an echo, like a symbolization of a former tormentor but without the pain or fear involved. A good place to heal, this green East Bay vale, until I was ready to re-emerge.

From the center of the labyrinth I looked back on the mazes, streets, byways, freeways, alleyways, and shorelines I had known up and down the King's Highway. How far I had come from clutching the bars of a crib back in boxy El Cajon, a frustrated infant unaware of what destinations awaited him. Still awaited for that matter. As the continent's edge moves ever westward, it scrapes what was once sea floor into new hills and peaks along our coast as geological ruptures force what was hidden to the surface. To be wholly Californian is to balance and rebalance on ever-moving surfaces "west of the West" where no destination remains final for long.

I walked out of the labyrinth and drove home. To sleep, perchance, and dream...

> ....I am in a large room—a ballroom perhaps. A beautiful woman who resembles actress Alfre Woodard approaches and asks me to dance. As we come together I tell her I haven't danced for a long while and am probably very rusty. She responds by leading, and we go circling around the dance floor together.

Upon awakening I thought about Woodard playing Lily Sloan in *Star Trek: First Contact*, about Queen Calafía's many faces, and about how odd it was that we sought contact with extraterrestrial aliens when the alienated terrestrial below us wanted so badly with a mineral yearning to make itself known to us. Woodard had also starred in *Remember My Name* and *Follow Me Home*...

With a familiar mixture of anticipation and caution I wondered what would come of following Calafía's lead once again. I can't recall the tune to which we danced, but I am tempted to select Loreena McKennitt's "Never-Ending Road."

Every demon is a guide untrained. To me, Llorona stands by to monitor our perpetual responsibility to reconcile ourselves with the places we encounter and that encounter us. When she takes on her frightening aspect, we can be sure we have gone down the wrong path, away from the land and toward its subjugation and destruction, calamities that rebound and ricochet deep within. At that point we can only bend earthward and relearn how to listen. When we do this, she shows her other face, in which we glimpse a lost and yet living indigenous original.

After more than forty years of grappling with the dualism deposited in me by my manically restless culture, it still feels strange to walk the world without the old pain of exile. Fall is finally here on the Other Coast after a summer of intense heat waves. Looking out at what travel-worn Mary Austin called the "Earth Horizon" after the manner of indigenous custom, I pass familiar sights and sounds in review as twilight cools down the closing day: an Italian restaurant draped with green awnings, an animal hospital, gravel underfoot, ducks arrowing toward the creek, the house with the crooked brick chimney, the lady who grows pumpkins in her front yard, the two redwoods together like lovers, a lovers' bench beneath them, the ivy-covered yard with the mean black dog named Angel, squirrels crunching on newly dropped acorns; and all of it and more no longer alien or obscure, but as familiar as the beats of my wanderer's heart come definitively home to Queen Calafía's edgy realm.

> I have not been entirely happy in my adjustments. I have suffered in my life, in my means, in my reciprocal relations; but I have this pride and congratulation, that I have not missed the significance of the spectacle I have been privileged to witness....I have known, to some extent, what the Earth Horizon has been thinking about.

POSTSCRIPT:
Missions as Sites of Reconciliation

As global displacements on a scale never before seen continue to send billions to the edge of existence, an emerging body of social trauma theory and research* insists that when the history of a group or a people is blotted out, their legacy of psychic injuries unmourned and unmemorialized, that legacy returns to both silenced and silencers as symptoms that can persist down many generations: symptoms such as psychic numbing, shame, dissociation, uprootedness, bewilderment, addiction, and post-traumatic stress.

These symptoms run rampant as overwhelmed frameworks and narratives of meaning are silenced or destroyed by imposed ideologies and culturally sanctioned lies. The very sense of subjectivity fades with the disappearance of opportunities to connect honestly and realistically with other people. "Our lives begin to end," noted Martin Luther King Jr., "the day we become silent about things that matter."

Tending these injuries requires the creation of safe places for ongoing dialog about their impact, tools for stitching together the fragments of image and story that survive, and efforts at reconciliation that bridge social stratifications, differences of perspective, and artificial barriers of geography and politics.

To that end I would like to share a fantasy that the missions of California become centers of post-colonial healing in which Native Californians set up exhibits, presentations, and discussion groups to share their view of California's legacy of colonization, support each other in overcoming it, and encourage deep, sincere, transformative conversations across cultural, political, and religious lines, if necessary bypassing the official machinery of the Catholic Church to reach out directly to priests and parishioners.

As mutual understanding grows and the wounds of colonization begin to close, the missions could also work as centers of ecological healing by implementing sustainable landscaping practices while providing free education about them. The past cannot be undone, but it can be acknowledged and responded to with dialogs that open the mind and heart, and with carefully constructed memorials that remind us all of what can happen when one group of people attempts to improve another.

   * See Watkins and Shulman, *Toward Psychologies of Liberation* (Palgrave Macmillan, 2008), Singer and Kimbles, *The Cultural Complex* (Brunner-Routledge, 2004), and Homans, *Symbolic Loss* (U of Virginia Press, 2000).

APPENDIX 1:

Presence of Place or Projection?

Deep work with place is bound to stir the steaming cauldron of the human psyche. In fact, as explained in my book *Terrapsychology*, we depend on that sort of "ecotransference" to indicate that the work has really set into the researcher. But when we say that frowning San Diego is depressed, or that an egg-and-chicken theme hatches repeatedly in Petaluma, or that Sonoma County is home to a fertile generosity like that of bounteous Demeter, don't we just see patterns where we want to see them? Aren't we anthropomorphizing? Aren't we projecting our biases onto the land? Let's consider these three concerns in that order.

Behold a psychotherapist meeting a client for the very first time. As the client nervously explains why he chose to come, he snaps and claps his fingers together three times in a row. Is that behavior significant? Taken by itself, a single behavior can mean almost anything: a nervous mannerism, an old habit, a passing fancy, an attempt to distract, a test of the therapist. One behavior does not a diagnosis make. As the client does it again, however, the therapist notices the edge of a handkerchief hanging out of the client's pocket, his rather primped appearance, and his refusal to shake hands because of "germs."

None of those behaviors, individually, is much good for a diagnosis. Anyone can snap and clap their fingers, or carry a hanky, or hate germs. When considered together, however, as possible indications of a syndrome, these ritualistic acts of decontamination begin to take shape as a possible Obsessive-Compulsive Disorder. They do not "prove" anything; a therapy session is not a laboratory, and the therapist's assessments do not wait for convenient quantifications or charts of behavioral averages. They are preliminary indicators that to a trained eye suggest a potential disturbance requiring further exploration.

Similarly, if a vacationing terrapsychologist steps out of his car in Needles, California, for the first time ever, and a song on the local radio at the gas station is blaring "....can't you hear me, SOS" over and over, "That could happen anywhere," as those new to this kind of framework often point out. True enough. But then, not half a mile from the sluggish meanders of the heavily dammed Colorado River, we must add to the list the waterless concrete fountains in a nearby hotel, a hotel room coffee maker that squeezes out only a trickle, and an unoccupied swimming pool filled several inches too low. The place felt emptier and thirstier—dammed up drier and drier—from one incident to the next, including the less-than-half-full glass of water brought an hour later by a waitress complaining that her eyes were smarting and teary Comstock miners next door in Nevada had caught that symptom shortly before succumbing to mercury poisoning. My eyes smarted from her perfume. Bedtime in that thirsty town brought a night-long multi-episode nightmare of being shot by .45s, gambling and losing (bits of Nevadan history leaking through?), and choking with an unquenchable thirst. As with the wounded river drained of its former fullness, so with the place, the people, their town, its images, and my dreams, all pointing to ecopsychic vitality strangled to a trickle.

To insist on seeing these images separately, atomizing and compartmentalizing them, is to render them down into a puddle of coincidences, as though they were meaningless fusses and finger snaps. But to a mind focused on detail while open as well to broad influences and possible patterns, seemingly disconnected happenings feel less like random events and more like syndromes, signals, and bids for attention. The more they multiply, the more urgent they seem, up to and well over the line where the awestruck witness, caught tightly in the interactive field's building tension, feels able to dump them on the much-abused head of Coincidence. (Skeptical ancient Romans consigned what they could not explain to the realm of Fortuna, goddess of random acts.)

Thematically rich commonplaces spread their hidden narratives under our noses all the time. We miss their significance because we do not think of places as psychically active beings, of what they present to us as symbols, or of sequences of happenings as meaningful symptoms synchronized with our own. A local syndrome, which we might as well call an *ecological complex*, seems arbitrary mainly to those not educated about how such complexes work, where they come from, how they can be recognized, and how accurate deductions and even predictions (e.g., the GMO ban's failure in bear-flagged Sonoma County) can follow from recognizing them. (See Chapter 4 of *Terrapsychology* for a list of preliminary criteria for identifying such complexes or "placefield syndromes.") Early psychotherapists had a very tough time convincing skeptical colleagues in black coats and bow ties that the patterns of pathology they saw again and again were real. Times have not changed, at least in academia.

I've occasionally heard the suggestion that these ecological complexes—syndromes, patterns, and recurrences of place—be pinned down like butterflies with statistical analyses of their frequency. I doubt this would get us very far. Somebody with mild OCD might not clean or check windows more often than someone without it, yet might make titanic silent efforts to avoid those compulsive acts. A well-trained bear dangerously enraged by its trainer might obey orders for decades, then turn one day and rend its tormentor, whereas a bear that nips more frequently (and is deemed more aggressive by the numbers) might never kill anyone.

Evaluating whether a local event or fact belongs to a greater pattern of terrapsychological activity cannot yield much as a merely intellectual effort. Drawing as well on affect and memory, place-focused evaluation relies more on intuition, imagination, and field experience than on trying to isolate variables strung together like cold popcorn along simple causal chains. We could learn something about Shakespeare's *The Tempest* through a content analysis of the words it contains, but we'd learn more through a sympathetic and educated reading sensitive to dramatic spells and thematic twists. Numbers compiled toward a false search for certainty and control will never replace the inner burst of meaning when we learn something new fully and holistically by seeing it crest as part of a larger current.

Anthropomorphism refers to draping the nonhuman with human qualities. Until very recently, our best ethologists, who study the behavior of nonhuman animals, gave the objects of their research numbers instead of names out of a phobic horror of perceiving them as unduly human.

As ethologist Marc Bekoff points out, however, not only does objectifying animals pad the research with an unnecessary layer of psychological distance, it often provides less fruitful data than allowing a bit of playful anthropomorphizing. After all, we are not so fundamentally different from the beings who share our world with us. Shouldn't we use our natural empathies and inclinations to understand them and their habitats better so long as we remain aware of the risk of bias? Abraham Maslow argued convincingly that studying what you love made for clearer, deeper knowledge than studying what you felt indifferent toward.

Mountains of social science research have demonstrated over and over that the fantasy of objectivity is just that—a fantasy; and as Richard Tarnas has pointed out more than once, reducing our relations with nature to "anthropomorphizing" actually performs the sleight of hand known as *anthropocentrism*, which means believing that the aliveness and intelligence around us originates solely from us. The truth, of course, is that all we will ever know as truly human evolved from eons of mysterious alchemy cooked and decanted by the organic and mineral intelligence of the natural world.

We need not succumb any longer to a superstitious dread of rejoining our human qualities to the Earth from which they evolved. We won't fall off its watery edge into the uncharted abyss. But we can learn much by playing animistically along, as in the film Surfing LA when James Hillman refers to a squatting jailhouse squinting back at the camera as "paranoid."

As for *projection*, it's important to know why we project to begin with.

Projection is a form of unconscious identification that attempts to rid us of something we do not want to face. Psychoanalysts regard projection as a fairly high-level ego defense because to cast something out of the self assumes an adequately consolidated self.

Although some would argue that everything we do is colored by projection, this extreme position, known to philosophy as "solipsism," is untenable as well as narcissistic because it reduces the outer world to a series of subjective states, rather like when a frightened boy assures himself that he imagines the ominous midnight creaks he hears downstairs from the safety of his bed. For more about the dismaying consequences of regarding the world as a mere artifact of human consciousness, read the environmental news.

Nor will it help to dismiss our relations to our surroundings as that form of projection known as *participation mystique*, a diffusion of boundaries supposedly characteristic of those whom Lucien Levy-Bruhl thought of as primitives and savages. Levy-Bruhl was an amateur anthropologist who developed the concept in his patronizingly named book *How Natives Think*. So consistently was this racism attacked that he eventually retracted the concept and admitted it was packed with eurocentric bias. Jungians continued to use it without realizing that if anyone has a case of unconscious identification with the world, it is not those whose survival depends on differentiating its astonishingly complex cycles and features, but we children of industrialization who remain so psychologically severed from it. To repress and react against something is to be tied to it, as every rebel demonstrates.

Projection is best understood in its analytical sense, as an operation in which we attack or idealize in other people aspects of ourselves we cannot access consciously. When this happens, the person who is projecting perceives the projection carrier only in terms of what is projected—in other words, as a kind of billboard or stereotype, as an object instead of a person. So much has been adequately established about how this works over a productive century of analytical literature and research.

To believe this to be the normal state of affairs crosses the line into reductionism. When cynical therapists describe love as a projection, for example, what they mean (aside from what they reveal about their own relationships) is that the beloved is of no importance except for what they represent to the lover. Obviously this has nothing to do with love but everything to do with egotism, inner depletion, self-alienation, and loss of real contact. The same applies to love and care for the reality of a place as valuable and endearing in and of itself.

Reducing everything to projection not only falls into a tired old Cartesian splitting of people from places and self from world, it reinvokes the circular logic of Inquisition by taking its own false premise as proven. Do you admit to being in league with the devil? Then you are. Do you deny it? Even guiltier. Freud used this logic to "prove" that those who resisted his reductive interpretations were actually validating them. This sort of automatic disconfirmation—at bottom a form of projected paranoia plentifully mixed with cynicism—acted as a major factor in delaying psychotherapy's acceptance by people alert enough to know better.

Do we sometimes project onto a place? Certainly. Our complexes can distort our perceptions of anything reflected in their carnival mirrors. But just as human relationships offer more than a trading of projections under the big top of our failings, so do our relationships with objects, animals, and landscapes. To the degree we do project onto them, contact goes dead and they shrink to the status of objects. One of the reasons for having support when doing terrapsychological investigation is so people outside the placefield can watch for whether the investigator's complexes are interfering. It's not difficult to spot the deadening effect of projections onto place. Descriptions of it go dry, become trivial or bombastic, or sound rigidly absolutist, as when the place or Earth are described as all good and human beings as all bad (i.e., splitting). Outer busyness becomes an excuse for neglecting inner work.

This is not to say, however, that getting triggered by a place necessarily means seeing it only through the distorting lens of one's projections. Generations of psychoanalysts have demonstrated that constellation of an analyst's complex can open a door straight into the complexes of the client. In fact, some analysts have argued that the work lacks depth and spark unless the therapy pulls the countertransference trigger. As with analysis, successfully investigating a place demands a robust capacity for working on oneself. Those who conduct deep work with place need to have been in exhaustive and rigorous therapy or some other long-term relationship of sustained self-exploration. Constant contact with peers and supporters is indispensable while out in the field.

C. G. Jung observed that misinterpreting a dream image was often followed by attempts at correction administered by subsequent dreams. That is why he placed more emphasis on the dream series than on the interpretation of single dreams. Like the psyche, the placefield seems to be intolerant of too much projection. When I first investigated Orange County I spent too much time on what seemed to be a recurrent motif of monogamy, from swallows building mud homes at the mission to large families propagating themselves like the Irvines and the Karchers. While writing up the results I was visited by a dream in which a feminine figure resembling my Orange County lover handed me the results of a study. The crisp white pages were awash in red corrective ink. This dream confirmed my suspicion of missing something important and helped me understand that my fantasies of creating a family with my partner were interfering with my sense of the place. When I began to write about Orange County giantism, the writing went better and my sleep was undisturbed.

Because the possibility of subjective bias can never be ruled out completely, we must bear it in mind while taking all these steps to avoid it. Another corrective is to check our understanding of a place against that of locals who have lived there. Yet another is to ask for dreams at the end of the study. When I finished my work in San Diego County, I dreamed I stood on a college campus with a group of robed women before me. In the dream I recognized them as feminine personifications of all the places I had tried for so long to understand and listen to. A ceremony was in progress. When one of the women stepped up and handed me a graduation certificate, I recognized her as a softened version of the angry dream figure who had chastised me at the start of the work for failing to recognize her. "*You see* San Diego," she told me, emphasizing the words beyond the pun (UC San Diego) they contained. I accepted the sheepskin, thought for a moment about all I had learned on El Camino Real, and replied quietly, "I see...home."

APPENDIX 2:

The Great Ancestral Question Mark

As "Minutemen" heaped together junk to fence famished Mexicans out of Arizona, long-awaited lab results arrived in the mail to invite my imagination along on an ancient pilgrimage. Its footprints have penetrated every futile border and barricade raised since history's recorded beginnings.

National Geographic's unfolding Genographic Project tracks the human journey first embarked on by our globe-trotting ancestors. How do they track it? Through extensive fieldwork, travel around the world, interviews with people living in many countries and climes—and above all, genes. As geneticist Spencer Wells states it, "The greatest history book ever written is the one hidden in our DNA."

For about $100, someone like me with an interest in his "deep ancestry" can order a small kit from National Geographic. It contains instructions, a CD with a video narrated by Dr. Wells, plastic swabs, and two small containers. Rubbing the swabs inside a cheek collects the DNA, which is placed inside the sealable containers and mailed off to National Geographic. Their analysis takes about eight weeks if all goes well. A web site allows the participant to monitor their progress.

This detective work makes use of genetic markers, otherwise known as *mutations*. Every now and then a kink appears in one of the enormously complex sex chromosomes passed down through the generations. When and where these kinks first appeared allow researchers to determine who inherited them from whom, collectively. For example, the kink M168 first appeared about fifty thousand years ago in a male dwelling somewhere in eastern Africa. From him descend all males who departed from there to walk in other lands.

When tweaks and bends appear in conjunction with ancestral

sojourners going off on their own, tracing their descendants is even easier. A *haplogroup* is a collection of people sharing a common marker. Each haplogroup represents a subplot of the long ancestral story still telling itself restlessly into being from meridian to meridian and pole to pole.

My test results appeared a few days after the National Guard arrived at the Mexican border.

Of course, plenty of evidence places the origin of human beings in Africa, continental mother to us all. But actually holding in my hands a map of the travel route walked by my ancestors—from East Africa into India, southern Asia, the steppes of Russia, and westward into Europe—brought home to me, yet again but even more emphatically, the futility, absurdity, and paranoia of institutionalized, systematized intolerance. As though walling out the "aliens" could ever make one's own self-alienation whole!

In a flash I grasped what it must be like never to feel this sense of kinship, of solidarity with the ancestors and belonging to the well-walked world, or to delight in the ramifying complexity of the great human family. Those intent on raising fences around their "homelands" (also a word from the time of apartheid), slicing up a world in which they did not truly feel at home, were already isolated by still taller fences surrounding their hidden hearts. It saddened me to realize that they did not know, and perhaps would never understand, that there is no real "outside" except in themselves. *They* were the true exiles and outcasts, these fearful sentinels of divided consciousness inflicting their wounds of displacement on others.

What Cortés, Columbus, and Cabeza de Vaca lacked, what all conquerors, conquistadors, and empire-builders lack, is the steadying feeling of belonging-to-the-world at the very foundations of the tortured quest for Eden. To soothe themselves they might raise soaring palaces, skyscraping citadels, ideologies of "blood and soil," symbol systems of heavenly light, nations bulging to the weaponed borders with waving ribbons and flags, but doing these things would give them no psychological sense of home on the animated planet onto which they projected their hostility. Captain Ahab spoke for them all by judging himself damned in the midst of Paradise.

Our shared ancestral history carried other ironies too. I was grimly amused to discover myself a direct descendant of Cro-Magnons (marker M343) who had daubed fantastic animal images on the walls of caves in southern France. All those centuries of stereotyping people of color as primitives and apelike savages, only to find ourselves descended from the earliest examples of budding *Homo sapiens!*

So far the Genographic Project operates in its early stages, but the yield of information grows steadily as more of us participate by adding the biological pieces we bear to the puzzle of where we all came from. When personal results are displayed online and accessed by the code provided in the kit, the participant is given the option of submitting them to the Project or keeping them private.

Looking at the road map whose signposts my ancestors had carried in their flesh as I do in mine, I marveled at what a splendid symbol of earthly embodiment these genetic markers offered. We are what we are in part because of where we have been. The lonely routes taken, the dangers negotiated safely, the pilgrimages embarked upon in hunger, hope and fear form wrinkles upon the blue-green face of our living homeworld, ancient creator of our evolving human family, that never really leave us, nor we them. We don't just visit these places, camera in hand: in a very real sense we are them, and perhaps they are us as well.

Even from space the great globe peers benignly back at us from out of the measureless dark. Look closely at it and see the landscape of your being, its imprint stored faithfully away in every pulsating cell.

I was born on July 6, the day Cabrillo raised a telescope and spotted the Californias. From one point of view, this is when the invasion of my homeland began. At a deeper level, however, it marked the acceptance, however unknowing, of an invitation into the unrealized possibility of a new relationship with place. This relationship requires a doubling of the heart into indigene and wayfarer, ecologist and cosmologist, and dreamer and doer joined to each other by *querencia*, the ancient Spanish word for a profound love and yearning for home. That invitation into a dual citizenship of the terrestrial and celestial has yet to be more consciously, responsibly, and lovingly accepted by those who now live here on the edge of a continent trembling like magma over forms weathered down.

On the map in my hands the geographic pathway taken by the ancestors inscribed the shape of a giant question mark. Where do we go from here?

Bibliography

Abram, David. *The Spell of the Sensuous*. New York: Vintage Books, 1996.

Alley, Bowen, & Co., eds. *History of Santa Clara County, California*. San Francisco: Alley, Bowen & Co, 1881.

Alvarez, Jose. *Leyendas Mexicanas*. Spain: Editorial Everest, 1998.

Anderson, Lorraine, ed. *Sisters of the Earth: Women's Prose and Poetry About Nature*. New York: Vintage, 1991.

Angel, Myron. *A Reproduction of Thompson and West's History of San Luis Obispo County, California*. Berkeley: Howell-North, 1966.

Anzaldua, Gloria. *Borderlands*. San Francisco: Aunt Lute Books, 1999.

Asbury, Herbert. *The Barbary Coast: An Informal History of the San Francisco Underworld*. Garden City: Garden City, 1933.

Atherton, Gertude. *Golden Gate Country*. New York: Duell, Sloan & Pearce, 1945.

Austin, Mary. *Earth Horizon: Autobiography*. New York: The Literary Guild, 1932.

Baker, Joseph. *Past and Present of Alameda County, California*. Chicago: S.J. Clarke, 1914.

Bakker, Elna. An Island Called California: An Ecological Introduction to its Natural Communities. Berkeley: University of California Press, 1971.

Bancroft, Hubert. *History of California, Vol. 1: 1542-1800*. Santa Barbara: Wallace Hebberd, 1963.

Basso, Keith. *Wisdom Sits in Places: Landscape and Language among the Western Apache*. Albuquerque: University of New Mexico Press, 1996.

Baudrillard, Jean, and Poster, Mark, ed. *Selected Writings*. Stanford: Stanford University Press, 1988.

Beal, Richard. Highway 17: *The Road to Santa Cruz*. Aptos: The Pacific Group, 1991.

Bean, Lowell, ed. *California Indian Shamanism*. Santa Barbara: Ballena, 1992.

Bearchell, Charles, and Fried, Larry. *The San Fernando Valley: Then and Now.* Northridge: Windsor, 1988.

Bennett, Melba. *The Stone Mason of Tor House: The Life and Work of Robinson Jeffers.* Los Angeles: Ward Ritchie, 1966.

Benson, Jackson. *John Steinbeck, Writer.* New York: Penguin USA., 1990

Birmingham, Stephen. *California Rich: The Lives, the Times, the Scandals and the Fortunes of the Men and Women who made and kept California's Wealth.* New York: Simon and Schuster, 1980.

Bishop, Morris. *St. Francis of Assisi.* Boston and Toronto: Little, Brown, 1974.

Bouvier, Virginia. *Women and the Conquest of California, 1542-1840: Codes of Silence.* Tucson: University of Arizona, 2001.

Brechin, Gray. *Imperial San Francisco: Urban Power, Earthly Ruin.* Berkeley: University of California Press, 1999.

Brook, James, and Boal, Iain. *Resisting the Virtual Life: The Culture and Politics of Information.* San Francisco: City Lights, 1995.

Brook, James, Carlsson, Chris, and Peters, Nancy. *Reclaiming San Francisco: History, Politics, Culture.* San Francisco: City Lights Books, 1998.

Bronson, William. *How to Kill a Golden State.* New York: Doubleday, 1968.

Camarillo, Albert. *Chicanos in a Changing Society: From Mexican Pueblos to American Barrios in Santa Barbara and Southern California, 1848-1930.* Cambridge and London: Harvard University Press, 1979.

Camus, Albert. *The Plague.* New York: Vintage, 1991.

Camus, Albert. *The Myth of Sisyphus and Other Essays.* New York: Vintage, 1991.

Camus, Albert. *The Rebel: An Essay on Man in Revolt.* New York: Vintage, 1992.

Carrico, Richard. *Strangers in a Stolen Land: American Indians in San Diego 1850-1880.* San Diego: San Diego State University, 1986.

Castillo, Ana, ed. *The Goddess of the Americas: Writings on the Virgin of Guadalupe.* New York: Riverhead Books, 1996.

Cisneros, Sandra. *Woman Hollering Creek and Other Stories.* New York: Random House, 1991.

Clarke, Thurston. *California Fault: Searching for the Spirit of a State Along the San Andreas*. New York: Ballentine Books, 1996.

Cleland, Robert. *The Irvine Ranch*. San Marino: The Huntington Library, 1984.

Clendinnen, Inga. *Aztecs: An Interpretation*. Cambridge: Cambridge University Press, 1991.

Clough, Charles. *San Juan Bautista: The Town, the Mission & the Park*. Fresno: Word Dancer Press, 1996.

Colton, Walter. *Three Years in California*. New York: A. S. Barnes, 1850.

Columbus, Christopher, and Fuson, Robert, trans. *The Log of Christopher Columbus*. Camden: International Marine, 1992.

Costo, Rupert, & Costo, Jeanette, eds. *The Missions of California: A Legacy of Genocide*. San Francisco: Indian Historian Press, 1987.

Counting Crows. "The Rain King." *August and Everything After*, 1995.

Crespí, Juan, and Brown, Allen, trans. *A Description of Distant Roads: Original Journals of the First Expedition into California, 1769-1770*. San Diego: San Diego State Press, 2001

Cuero, Delfina, and Shipek, Florence. *Delfina Cuero: Her Autobiography, an Account of her Last Years, and her Ethnobotanic Contributions*. Menlo Park: Ballena Press, 1991.

Cunningham, Lawrence, ed. *Brother Francis: An Anthology of Writings by and about St. Francis of Assisi*. New York: Harper and Row, 1972.

Curtis, Mabel. *The Coachman was a Lady*. Watsonville: Pajaro Valley Historical Association, 1959.

Dallett, Janet. *Listening to the Rhino: Violence and Healing in a Scientific Age*. Aqeuitas Books, 2008.

Dana, Richard. *Two Years Before the Mast: A Personal Narrative of Life at Sea*. New York: Modern Library, 2001.

Darlington, David. *In Condor Country: A Portrait of a Landscape, its Denizens, and its Defenders*. Boston: Houghton Mifflin Company, 1987.

Dasmann, Raymond. *The Destruction of California*. New York: Macmillon, 1965.

Davies, Nigel. *The Aztecs*. New York: G. P. Putnam's Sons, 1974.

Davis, William. *Seventy-Five Years in California*. San Francisco: J. Howell, 1929.

Davis, Mike. *City of Quartz: Excavating the Future in Los Angeles*. London and New York: Verso, 1990.

Del Castillo, Ana, ed. *Between Borders: Essays on Mexicana/Chicana History*. Encino: Floricanto Press, 1990.

DeNevi, Don, and Moholy, Noel. *Junipero Serra*. San Francisco: Harper & Row Publishers, 1985.

Downing, Christine. *The Goddess: Mythical Images of the Feminine*. New York: Crossroad, 1981.

Eagle, Adam. *Alcatraz! Alcatraz!: The Indian Occupation of 1969-1971*. Berkeley: Heyday, 1992.

Eargle, Dolan. *California Indian Country: The Land and the People*. San Francisco: Trees Company Press, 1992.

Eisen, Jonathan, Fine, David, and Eisen, Kim, eds. *Unknown California*. New York: Collier Books, 1985.

Eliot, Marc. *Walt Disney: Hollywood's Dark Prince*. New York: HarperCollins, 1993.

Emerson, Ralph Waldo. *Essays and Lectures*. New York: Library of America, 1983.

Fages, Pedro, and Priestley, H., trans. *A Historical, Political, and Natural Description of California by Pedro Fages, Written for the Viceroy in 1775*. Ramona: Ballena Press, 1972.

Falzarano, Joanna. "The Development of the San Fernando Valley: A History of Natural Resource Issues and Prospects for the Future." Pepperdine University, February 15, 2003.

Findlay, John. *Magic Lands: Western Cityscapes and American Culture After 1940*. Berkeley, Los Angeles, Oxford: University of California Press, 1992.

Fisher, Andy. *Radical Ecopsychology: Psychology in the Service of Life*. New York: State University of New York Press, 2002.

Fisher, Anne. *The Salinas: Upside-Down River*. New York and Toronto: Farrar & Rinehart Incorporated, 1945.

Fink, Augusta. *Monterey, the Presence of the Past*. San Francisco: Chronicle Books, 1972.

Fogel, Daniel. *Junipero Serra, the Vatican, and Enslavement Theology*. San Francisco: Ism Press, 1988.

Forbes, Jack. *Native Americans of California and Nevada*. Happy Camp: Naturegraph Publishers, Inc, 1982.

Freeman, Leslie. *Alameda County: Past and Present*. San Leandro: Press of the San Leandro Reporter, 1946.

Freud, Sigmund, and Katz, S., ed. *Freud on War, Sex, and Neurosis*. New York: Arts and Science Press, 1947.

Freud, Sigmund, Einstein, Albert, and Strachey, James, trans. *Why War?* New York: W. W. Norton, 1933.

Fromm, Erich. *The Anatomy of Human Destructiveness*. New York: Henry Holt, 1992.

Futcher, Jane. *Marin: The Place, the People, Profile of a California County*. New York: Holt, Rinehart and Winston, 1981.

Gilliam, Harold, and Bry, Michael. *The Natural World of San Francisco*. Garden City: Doubleday, 1967.

Gillis, Mabel. *The WPA Guide to California*. New York: Pantheon Books, 1939.

George, Herbert. *Progress and Poverty: An Inquiry in the Cause of Industrial Depressions and of Increase of Want with Increase of Wealth*. New York: Robert Schalkenbach Foundation, 1996.

Green, Julien. *God's Fool: The Life and Times of Francis of Assisi*. San Francisco: Harper & Row, 1985.

Greenwood, Robert. *The California Outlaw Tiburcio Vasquez*. New York: Arno Press, 1974.

Gutiérrez, Ramón, and Orsi, Richard, eds. *Contested Eden: California Before the Gold Rush*. Berkeley, Los Angeles: University of California Press, 1998.

Hageman, Fred, and Ewing, Russell. *California's Mission La Purisima Conception: The Hageman and Ewing Reports*. Santa Barbara: Santa Barbara Trust for Historic Preservation, 1991.

Hale, Dennis, and Eisen, Jonathan, eds. *The California Dream*. New York: Collier Books, 1968.

Hamilton, Michael, ed. *This Little Planet*. New York: Charles Scribner's Sons, 1970.

Hawley, Walter. *The Early Days of Santa Barbara, California: From the First Discoveries by Eeuropeans to December, 1846*. Santa Barbara: Santa Barbara Heritage, 1987.

Hawthorne, Hildegard. *Romantic Cities of California*. New York and London: D. Appleton-Century Company Inc, 1939.

Heinberg, Richard. *Memories and Visions of Paradise: Exploring the Universal Myth of a Lost Golden Age*. Los Angeles: Jeremy P. Tarcher, 1989.

Heizer, Robert. *The Destruction of the California Indians*. Lincoln: University of Nebraska Press, 1974.

Herbert, Frank: *The Santaroga Barrier*. New York: Tor Books, 2002.

Herbert, Frank: *The White Plague*. New York: Putnam, 1982.

Hillman, James, ed. *The Puer Papers*. Dallas: Spring, 1979.

Hinton, Leanne. *Flutes of Fire: Essays on California Indian Languages*. Berkeley: Heyday, 1996.

Holliday, J. S. *The World Rushed In: The California Gold Rush Experience*. New York: Simon and Schuster, 1981.

Jackson, Robert, and Castillo, Edward. *Indians, Franciscans, and Spanish Colonization: The Impact of the Mission System on California Indians*. Albuquerque: University of New Mexico Press, 1995.

Jensen, Derrick, ed. *Listening to the Land*. New York: Context Books, 2002.

Jorgenson, Lawrence, and Siegele, Susan, eds. *The San Fernando Valley: Past and Present*. Los Angeles: Pacific Rim Research, 1982.

Johnson, Marilynn. *The Second Gold Rush: Oakland and the East Bay in World War II*. Berkeley, Los Angeles, London: University of California Press, 1993.

Jung, C. G. *Aion*. Princeton: Princeton University Press, 1979.

Jung, C. G. *Mysterium Coniunctionis*. Princeton: Princeton University Press, 1963.

Jung, C. G., and Sabini, Meredith, ed. *The Earth has a Soul: The Nature Writings of C. G. Jung*. Berkeley, CA: North Atlantic Books, 2002.

Keegan, Frank. *San Rafael: Marin's Mission City*. Northridge: Windsor Publications, 1987.

Kelley, Don. *Edge of a Continent: The Pacific Coast from Alaska to Baja*. Palo Alto: American West Publishing Company, 1971.

Kidner, David. *Nature and Psyche: Radical Environmentalism and the Politics of Subjectivity*. New York: State University of New York Press, 2001.

Klein, Norman. *The History of Forgetting: Los Angeles and the Erasure of Memory*. New York: Verso, 1998.

Kling, Rob, Olin, Spencer, and Poster, Mark, eds. *Postsuburban California: The Transformation of Orange County since World War II*. Berkeley: University of California Press, 1991.

Koch, Margaret. *Santa Cruz County: Parade of the Past*. Fresno: Valley Publishers, 1973.

Kowalewski, Michael, ed. *Gold Rush: A Literary Exploration*. Berkeley: Heyday Books and the California Council for the Humanities, 1997.

Kraul, Edward, and Beatty, Judith. *The Weeping Woman: Encounters with La Llorona*. Santa Fe: The Word Process, 1989.

La Perouse, Jean Francois. *Life in a California Mission*. Berkeley: Heydey Books, 1989.

Lee, W. Storrs, ed. *California: A Literary Chronicle*. New York: Funk and Wagnals, 1968.

Le Guin, Ursula. *Dancing at the Edge of the World: Thoughts on Words, Women, Places*. New York: Grove Press, 1997.

León-Portilla, Miguel. *Aztec Thought and Culture: A Study of the Ancient Nahuatl Mind*. Norman: University of Oklahoma Press, 1963.

Leon-Portilla, Miguel, ed. *The Broken Spears: The Aztec Account of the Conquest of Mexico*. Boston: Beacon Press, 1992.

Leopold, Aldo. *A Sand County Almanac*. London: Oxford University Press, 1969.

Lotchin, Roger. *Fortress California: 1910-1961: From Warfare to Welfare*. New York and Oxford: Oxford University Press, 1992.

Malone, Michael. *The Valley of Heart's Delight: A Silicon Valley Notebook 1963-2001*. New York: John Wiley & Sons, 2002.

Mander, Jerry. *In the Absence of the Sacred: The Failure of Technology & the Survival of the Indian Nations*. San Francisco: Sierra Club Books, 1991.

Margolin, Malcolm, ed. *The Way We Lived: California Indian Stories, Songs, & Reminiscences*. Berkeley: Heyday, 1993.

Mason, Jack. *The Making of Marin, 1850-1975*. Inverness: North Shore Books, 1975.

Mayers, Jackson. *The San Fernando Valley*. Walnut: John D. McIntyre, 1976.

McCaleb, Charles. *Surf, Sand and Streetcars: A Mobile History of Santa Cruz, California*. Glendale: Interurbans, 1977.

McCaleb, Sarah. "Rock n' Roll Berkeley: Giving Voice to a Trembling Earth." Unpublished paper, 2008.

McFee, John. *Assembling California*. New York: Noonday Press, 1993.

McKeever, Michael. *A Short History of San Diego*. San Francisco: Lexikos, 1985.

McWilliams, Carey. *Factories in the Field: The Story of Migratory Farm Labor in California*. Boston: Little, Brown and Company, 1939.

McWilliams, Carey. *Southern California: An Island on the Land*. Berkeley: University of California Press, 1979.

Merchant, Carolyn, ed. *Green versus Gold: Sources in California's Environmental History*. Washington, D.C.: Island Press, 1998.

Merritt, Frank. *History of Alameda County, Calilfornia*. Chicago: The S. J. Clarke Publishing Company, 1928.

Michaels, Leonard, Reid, David, and Scherr, Raquel, eds. *West of the West: Imagining California*. San Francisco: North Point Press, 1989.

Miller, Arthur. *After the Fall*. New York: Viking, 1980.

Miller, Bruce. *The Chumash: A Picture of Their World*. Los Osos: Sand River Press, 1988.

Miller, Bruce. *The Gabrielino*. Los Osos: Sand River Press, 1991.

Moore, Robert, and Gillette, Douglas. *King, Warrior, Magician, Lover: Rediscovering the Archetypes of the Mature Masculine*. New York: HarperOne, 1991.

Morris, Hernando, and F. Bayard, trans. *Five Letters of Cortes to the Emperor*. New York: W. W. Norton, 1962.

Muir, John. *Nature Writings*. New York: The Library of America, 1997.

Mumford, Lewis. *Technics and Civilization*. New York: Harvest, 1963.

Mumford, Lewis. *The City in History: Its Origins, Its Transformations, and Its Prospects*. Harvest, 1968.

Murphy, Arnold, ed. *A Comprehensive Story of Ventura County, California*. Oxnard: M & N Printing, 1979.

Murphy, Celeste. *The People of the Pueblo: or, the Story of Sonoma*. Portland: Binsfords & Mort, 1948.

Nadeau, Remi. *California: The New Society*. New York: David McKay, 1963.

Nash, Roderick. *Wilderness and the American Mind*. New Haven and London: Yale University Press, 1969.

Nietzsche, Friedrich, and Kaufmann, Walter, trans. *Basic Writings of Nietzsche*. New York: The Modern Library, 1992.

Palóu, Francisco. *Life of Junipero Serra*. Washington, D.C.: Academy of American Franciscan History, 1955.

Parmelee, Robert. *Pioneer Sonoma*. Sonoma: The Sonoma Index-Tribune, 1972.

Paynes, Stephen. *Santa Clara County: Harvest of Change*. Northridge: Windsor Publications, 1987.

Perez, Domino Renee. "Caminando con La Llorona." In *Chicana Traditions: Continuity and Change*, edited by Cantú, Norma, and Nájera-Ramírez, Olga. Urbana and Chicago: University of Illinois Press, 2002.

Perez, Domino Renee. "Revitalizing the Legend: Manifestations and Cultural Readings of La Llorona in Contemporary Literature and Film." Unpublished dissertation, University of Nebraska, 1999.

Petty, Tom, and the Heartbreakers. "King's Road." *Hard Promises*, 1981.

Pitt, Leonard. *California Controversies: Major Issues in the History of the State*. Arlington Heights: Harlan Davidson, Inc, 1987.

Pitt, Leonard. *The Decline of the Californios: A Social History of the Spanish-Speaking Californians, 1846-1890*. Berkeley and Los Angeles: University of California Press, 1970.

Pitti, Stephen. *The Devil in Silicon Valley: Northern California, Race, and Mexican Relations*. New Jersey: Princeton University Press, 2003.

Polk, Dora Beale. *The Island of California: A History of the Myth*. Lincoln: University of Nebraska Press, 1991.

Quinn, Arthur. *Broken Shore: The Marin Peninsula, a Perspective on History*. Salt Lake City: Peregrine Smith, Inc, 1981.

Rankin, Sarah. "A Terrapsychological Study of the Psyche of Petaluma as Found in the Stories of the Land and as Mirrored by My Own Psyche." Unpublished master's thesis. Rohnert Park, CA: Sonoma State University, 2007.

Rawls, James. *Indians of California: The Changing Image*. Norman: University of Oklahoma Press, 1984.

Rebolledo, Tey Diana. *Women Singing in the Snow: A Cultural Analysis of Chicana Literature*. Tucson/London: The University of Arizona Press, 1995.

Rebolledo, Tey Diana, and Rivero, Eliana, eds. *Infinite Divisions: An Anthology of Chicana Literature*. Phoenix: University of Arizona Press, 1993.

Reynolds, Malvina. "On the Rim of the World." *The Malvina Reynolds Songbook*, 1973.

Rieff, David. *Los Angeles: Capital of the Third World*. New York: Simon and Schuster, 1991.

Riesenberg, Felix Jr. *The Golden Road: The Story of California's Spanish Mission Trail*. New York: McGraw-Hill Book Company, Inc, 1962.

Rodriguez de Montalvo, Garcia, and Little, William, trans. *The Labors of the Very Brave Knight Esplandian*. Binghamton: Medieval & Renaissance Texts & Studies, 1992.

Rodriguez, Jeanette. *Our Lady of Guadalupe: Faith and Empowerment Among Mexican-American Women*. Austin: University of Texas Press, 1994.

Rogers, Everett, and Larsen, Judith. *Silicon Valley Fever: Growth of High-Technology Culture*. New York: Basic Books, 1984.

Rorabaugh, W. J. *Berkeley at War: The 1960s*. New York, Oxford: Oxford University Press, 1989.

Rosenthal, Rob. *Homeless in Paradise: A Map of the Terrain*. Philadelphia: Temple University Press, 1994.

Rosenus, Alan. *General Vallejo and the Advent of the Americans*. Berkeley: Heyday, 1999.

Roszak, Theodore, Gomes, Mary, and Kanner, Allen, eds. *Ecopsychology: Restoring the Earth, Healing the Mind*. Berkeley: University of California Press, 1995.

Royce, Josiah. *California: From the Conquest in 1846 to the Second Vigilance Committee in San Francisco*. New York: Alfred A. Knopf, 1948.

Ruscin, Terry. *Mission Memoirs*. San Diego: Sunbelt Publications, 1999.

Ryden, Kent. *Mapping the Invisible Landscape: Folklore, Writing, and the Sense of Place*. Iowa City: University of Iowa Press, 1993.

Sale, Kirkpatrick. *The Conquest of Paradise: Christopher Columbus and the Columbian Legacy*. New York: Alfred A. Knopf, 1990.

Sanchez, Cynthia. "'Blessed is the Fruit of thy Womb': The Politics of the Representation and Reproduction of the Mythical Mother in New Mexico Cultural Traditions." Unpublished dissertation, New York University, 1998.

Sawyer, Eugene. *History of Santa Clara County, California*. Los Angeles: Historic Record Company, 1922.

Schrag, Peter. *Paradise Lost: California's Experience, America's Future*. Berkeley, Los Angeles, London: University of California Press, 1999.

Schuman, Dovey, ed. *Headlines: A History of Santa Barbara from the Pages of its Newspapers, 1855-1982*. Santa Barbara: News-Press Publishing Company, 1982.

Shelley, Mary. *Frankenstein, or The Modern Prometheus*. New York: Bantam, 1984.

Shepard, Paul. *Nature and Madness*. Athens: University of Georgia Press, 1998.

Shipek, Florence. *Pushed into the Rocks: Southern California Indian Land Tenure, 1769-1986*. Lincoln and London: University of Nebraska Press, 1988.

Shiva, Vandana. *Staying Alive: Women, Ecology, and Survival in India*. New York: St. Martin's Press, 1989.

Singer, Thomas, and Kimbles, Samuel. *The Cultural Complex: Contemporary Jungian Perspectives on Psyche and Society*. New York: Brunner-Routledge, 2004.

Smith, Barbara. *Ghost Stories of California*. Renton: Lone Pine, 2000.

Spaulding, Edward. *A Brief Story of Santa Barbara*. Santa Barbara: Pacific Coast Publishing Company, 1964.

Springsteen, Bruce. "Fifty-Seven Channels (And Nothin' On)." *Human Touch*, 1992.

Starr, Kevin. *Americans and the California Dream, 1850-1915*. New York and Oxford: Oxford University Press, 1973.

Starr, Kevin. *Coast of Dreams: California on the Edge, 1999-2003*. New York: Alfred A. Knopf, 2004.

Starr, Kevin. *Embattled Dreams: California in War and Peace, 1940-1950*. New York and Oxford: Oxford University Press, 2002.

Starr, Kevin. *Endangered Dreams: The Great Depression in California*. New York and Oxford: Oxford University Press, 1997.

Starr, Kevin. *Inventing the Dream: California Through the Progressive Era*. New York and Oxford: Oxford University Press, 1985.

Starr, Kevin. *Material Dreams: Southern California Through the 1920s*. New York and Oxford: Oxford University Press, 1991.

Starr, Kevin. *The Dream Endures: California Enters the 1940s*. New York and Oxford: Oxford University Press, 2002.

Steinbeck, John. *The Grapes of Wrath*. New York: Penguin, 1992.

Steinbeck, John. *The Log from the Sea of Cortez*. New York: Penguin, 1997.

Stegner, Wallace. *Where the Bluebird Sings to the Lemonade Springs: Living and Writing in the West*. New York: Random House, 1992.

Stephanson, Anders. *Manifest Destiny: American Expansion and the Empire of Right*. New York: Hill and Wang, 1995.

Stuart, David. *Alan Watts*. Radnor: Chilton Book Company, 1976.

Tac, Pablo. *Indian Life and Customs at Mission San Luis Rey, Written About 1835*. Oceanside: San Luis Rey Mission Indian Foundation, 1998.

Tajnai, Carolyn. "From the Valley of Heart's Delight to the Silicon Valley: A Study of Stanford University's Role in the Transformation." Standford University, 1996.

Terrell, John. *The Arrow and the Cross: A History of the American Indian and the Missionaries*. Santa Barbara: Capra Press, 1979.

Thomas, Mark. *Wielding the Gavel: The Story of the Courts of San Benito County from 1874 through 1994*. San Jose: Alma Press, 1996.

Tompkins, Walter. *Santa Barbara Yesterdays*. Santa Barbara: McNally and Loftin, 1962.

Trautman, Baxter. *Spirit of the Valley: An Ecological Mythology of an Oak Savanna*. Santa Margarita: Black Mountain Press, 1998.

Triem, Judith. *Ventura County: Land of Good Fortune*. San Luis Obispo: EZ Nature Books, 1990.

Tuomey, Honoria, and Emparan, Luisa. "Mission, Presidio, and Pueblo of Sonoma." Unpublished manuscript, 1923.

Turner, Frederick. *Beyond Geography: The Western Spirit against the Wilderness*. New York: Viking Press, 1990.

Turner, Jack. *The Abstract Wild*. Tucson: The University of Arizona Press, 1996.

Verardo, Jennie, and Verardo, Denzil. *The Salinas Valley: An Illustrated History*. Northridge: Windsor Publications, 1989.

Villanueva, Alma. *Weeping Woman: La Llorona and Other Stories*. Tempe: Bilingual Press, 1994.

Von Franz, Marie-Louise. *The Problem of the Puer Aeternus*. Toronto: Inner City Books, 2000.

Vonnegut, Kurt. *Breakfast of Champions*. New York: Dell, 1991.

Walker, Dale. *Bear Flag Rising: The Conquest of California, 1846*. New York: Forge, 1999.

Walton, John. *Storied Land: Community and Memory in Monterey*. Berkeley: University of California Press, 2001.

Wayburn, Cynthia, and Scott, Peter, eds. *In the Ocean Wind: The Santa Cruz North Coast*. Felton: Glenwood, 1974.

Webb, Edith. *Indian Life at the Old Missions*. Los Angeles: Warren F. Lewis, 1952

Winslow, Ward, ed. *The Making of Silicon Valley: One Hundred Year Renaissance*. Palo Alto: Santa Clara Valley Historical Association, 1995.

Whitehead, Richard. *Citadel on the Channel: The Royal Presidio of Santa Barbara, its Founding and Construction, 1782-1798.* Santa Barbara and Spokane: Santa Barbara Trust for Historic Preservation and The Arthur H. Clark Company, 1996.

Wheelwright, Jane. *The Ranch Papers.* Santa Monica and San Francisco: The Lapis Press, 1988.

Wouk, Herman. *The Caine Mutiny: A Novel.* New York: Back Bay Books, 1992.

Wyatt, David. *Five Fires: Race, Catastrophe, and the Shaping of California.* New York: Addison-Wesley, 1997.

Wyatt, David. *The Fall into Eden: Landscape and Imagination in California.* Cambridge: Cambridge University Press, 1986.

Young, Stanley, and Levick, Melba. *The Missions of California.* San Francisco: Chronicle Books, 1998.

CPSIA information can be obtained at www.ICGtesting.com
Printed in the USA
LVOW050120200712

290778LV00001B/19/P